BEST RADIO
PLAYS OF 1991

C000182583

Previous Giles Cooper Award volumes

BEST RADIO PLAYS OF 1991

with an Introduction
by Alan Drury

The Giles Cooper Award Winners

Robin Glendinning: The Words are Strange
John Purser: Carver
Tom Stoppard: In the Native State
Steve Walker: Micky Mookey
Craig Warner: Figure with Meat

METHUEN/BBC PUBLICATIONS

First published in Great Britain in 1992
by Methuen Drama
an imprint of Reed Consumer Books Ltd
Michelin House, 81 Fulham Road, London SW3 6RB
and Auckland, Melbourne, Singapore and Toronto
and BBC Publications
35 Marylebone High Street, London W1M 4AA
and distributed in the United States of America
by HEB Inc.,
361 Hanover Street, Portsmouth, New Hampshire, NH 03801 3959

ISBN 0–413–67170–4

A CIP catalogue record for this book
is available at the British Library

Typeset in 10/11 pt Garamond by Centracet, Cambridge
Printed in Great Britain by Cox & Wyman, Cardiff Road, Reading

CONTENTS

THE GILES COOPER AWARDS: a note on the selection

Giles Cooper

As one of the most original and inventive radio playwrights of the post-war years, Giles Cooper was the author who came most clearly to mind when the BBC and Methuen were in search of a name when first setting up their jointly sponsored radio drama awards in 1978. Particularly so, as the aim of the awards is precisely to encourage original radio writing by both new and established authors – encouragement in the form of both public acclaim and of publication of their work in book form.

Eligibility

Eligible for the awards was every original radio play first broadcast by the BBC domestic service from December 1990 to December 1991 (almost 500 plays in total). Excluded from consideration were translations, adaptations and dramatised 'features'. In order to ensure that the broad range of radio playwriting was represented, the judges aimed to select plays which offered a variety of length, subject matter and technique by authors with differing experience of writing for radio.

Selection

The editors-in-charge and producers of the various drama 'slots' were each asked to put forward about five or six plays for the judges' consideration. This resulted in a 'short-list' of some 30 plays from which the final selection was made. The judges were entitled to nominate further plays for consideration provided they were eligible . Selection was made on the strength of the script rather than of the production, since it was felt that the awards were primarily for writing and that production could unduly enhance or detract from the merits of the original script.

Judges

The judges for the 1991 awards were:
    Pamela Edwardes, Editorial Director, Methuen Drama
    Alan Drury, Literary Manager, BBC Radio Drama
    Peter Davalle, radio critic for *The Times*
    Gilly Fraser, playwright

INTRODUCTION

The jeremiads for the single play as a form continue. As I
write, the West End is in one of its worst periods ever, and
although television soap opera may be about to strike
Spanish gold, the pressure is still on the one-off drama.
Radio also is beginning to change its shape as the first of the
national commercial networks, Classic FM, runs up to come
on air. Classic FM will not be broadcasting drama, but it has
already had a knock-on effect. Radio 3 is cutting its speech
programmes by 50 per cent, responding to the current
wisdom that channels should have an easily identifiable
profile. These cuts inevitably affect drama, but happily not as
swingeingly as in some other fields. Initially the 104 Radio 3
drama slots a year were to be cut to 52. A reprise has been
won on a further 13, thanks in part to a magnificent
campaign of protest led by the dramatists themselves. The
cut represents less than 10 per cent of the Drama
Department's output, but it is a significant proportion.
Specially written drama on Radio 3 has been traditionally
quirky and challenging, covering subject matters and forms
that would not suit other channels. It has been criticised for
being elitist and obscure, and at times, as with anything
experimental, it has been. It has also allowed generations of
writers to establish their own voice, to the benefit not just of
radio but the culture as a whole. The historical examples are
well known: Robert Bolt's *A Man For All Seasons* and Bill
Naughton's *Alfie* were originally Third Programme plays. In
March this year the Royal Court, Hampstead and Almeida
theatres in London, all of them national centres for new
work, were running plays that had either originally been
radio plays or commissioned in association with BBC Radio
Drama. Two of these three, by James Saunders and Howard
Barker, were Radio 3 commissions. (The third, by Ron
Hutchinson, was a Radio Theatre co-commission with the

Lyric Theatre, Belfast). Of the five 1991 Giles Cooper Awards (the scripts in this volume), three were originated on Radio 3.

The cut, however, should not be seen as a statement that the BBC is beginning to become inimical to radio drama. Although it will make the nurturing and development of certain types of drama a little more difficult, the commitment is still very much there. There is a growing flexibility and diversity of plays on Radio 4; indeed the range of work it presents has widened considerably over the last five or six years and we anticipate further initiatives to continue the process from two-hour blockbusters, to a late night erotic season, to the new range of daytime half-hour serials. Radio 5, working separately from the Drama Department, has formed its own very distinctive presence, as its award-winning play in this collection shows. The World Service continues its global mission, some of its programmes also being broadcast on the UK channels, and also co-commissioning with the Drama Department the annual Globe Theatre season. The most tangible proof of the BBC's continuing commitment to the form was the opening in July of a new drama studio in our studio complex at Maida Vale, London. This scale of major capital investment is not made in a dying art form. The general public also seems to agree. The number of scripts submitted to BBC Radio Drama this year so far has gone up by an eighth.

I mentioned Bill Naughton's *Alfie*. The film started out as a Third Programme play, *Alfie Elkins and his Little Life*, which was re-broadcast earlier this year as a tribute to the author, who had recently died. Also re-broadcast were *The Mystery* and his last play, *Derby Day*, which was premièred in 1991 on Radio 4. *Derby Day* is an epic portrayal of the early twentieth-century working class North West where he was brought up, and as it came in two ninety-minute chunks was ineligible for this volume. It showed his characteristic delight in common humanity; its strengths and failings and its foibles. It is full of sentiment but very little sentimentality, and brings his work round full circle; a return to the roots and the basic themes of the man who, as he points out in one of the asides to the reader in the script, almost invented *Coronation Street*.

The 1991 winners are also characterised, in the main, by their strong emotional content, although there is also a confirmation of the previous year's mythopoeic tendencies.

It's also recidivists' year. Three out of the five winners have won a Giles Cooper before.

Robin Glendinning's *The Words are Strange* sounds on paper to be a bit worthy. It's a teacher play, with the usual clash between liberal and illiberal outlooks. The central battle focuses on the school play. This is about par for the genre. In addition, it takes on board the recent reforms in educational administration which make schools far more openly competitive. Furthermore it's set in Northern Ireland. However, the real focus of the piece slowly reveals itself to be the teacher's domestic life, particularly his relationship with his dyslexic son. We also slowly realise that the play is really about the need to be receptive and open to communication, and the setting Mr Glendinning has chosen enables him to explore this on a personal, institutional and political level. The play doesn't preach and is warmly funny. It ends in the personal with a profoundly moving father-son sequence Mr Naughton would have been proud of and which by implication illuminates the other areas of the script; proof of the power of sentiment.

A handicapped son is also central to *Carver* by John Purser; in this case Davie, the fictional illegitimate son of Robert Carver, the sixteenth-century Scottish liturgical composer. In a time of theological and political upheaval music composed to the glory of God is not the neutral disengaged activity it may seem and questions of commitment, vocation and survival become paramount. The final image of the play is the retarded Davie reacting to the emotional certainty of the music, rescuing a score with no thought to the consequence. Mr Purser is an authority on the history of Scottish music, which again makes the project sound worthy. It is not, and again shows us the ease with which radio can take us into an historical period compared to the enormous effort needed with visual costume drama. *Carver* has also won a Gold Medal Award at the New York International Radio Festival.

The first recidivist is Tom Stoppard, who previously won in 1982 with *The Dog It Was That Died*, which was subsequently picked up by television. The 1991 winner is *In The Native State*, which has already received a Sony Award. The action takes place in two time scales: in 1930's India where 35-year-old Flora Crewe is having her portrait painted by Nirad Das; and in present day Shepperton where Flora's sister, 83-year-old Mrs Swan, is talking to the painter's son,

Anish Das. The unconventional nature of the 1930's encounter catalyses both peoples' views of their cultures, undermining assumptions and roles on both sides. Similarly in Shepperton attitudes are questioned in the aftermath of the Empire. The tone is oblique and ironic, and knowledge comes more from personal reaction than any overt political agenda. It is a rich, full play, rather Chekhovian in feel and clearly a major work.

Steve Walker is the first person to have won two years running; last year with *The Pope's Brother*, this year with *Mickey Mookey* a self-contained play from his Radio 5 series *Whoppers*. The series, as its title implies, has a Baron Munchausen central character telling a series of tall and shaggy-dog stories. The baroque imagination revealed last year is now allowed to roam untrammelled and the result is, according to one critic, 'the most inventive use of radio since *The Goons*'. Although intended for a younger audience, it taps the childhood fears in all of us, being both funny and the stuff of nightmares, but on a rational, non-Jungian level, I'm not sure it means anything at all.

A similar shaggy-dog feel is evident in *Figure With Meat*. (Craig Warner also won in 1989 with *By Where the Old Shed Used to Be*.) Its central proposition is that the afterlife is what you believe it to be, from which it traces intersecting arabesques involving a fly, singing cats, a talking Francis Bacon painting, a Mary Whitehouse figure, Madonna, Noah and much more. Underneath it is questioning what informs our moral sense, particularly in a relativist world. It is flashy, unfair and has something in it to offend virtually everybody.

Alan Drury
Literary Manager
BBC Radio Drama
June 1992

A leaflet, 'Writing Plays for Radio', outlining the sorts of work the BBC is looking for and other basic information, can be obtained free from The Literary Manager, BBC Radio Drama, Broadcasting House, London W1A 1AA.

THE WORDS ARE STRANGE

by Robin Glendinning

Robin Glendinning was born in Belfast in 1938 and educated at Campbell College, Belfast and Trinity College, Dublin. After teaching for eleven years, he became a full-time Party Organiser for the Alliance Party of Northern Ireland. He stood twice for Parliament, losing his deposit both times. He returned to teaching in 1976 and taught for sixteen years in RBAI, a grammar school in Belfast city centre. He left teaching in 1992 to become a full-time writer. His work for BBC Radio and Television includes: *The Artist, Condemning Violence, Culture Vultures* and *Faith. Stuffing It* was broadcast on Radio 3 and staged at the Dublin Festival and at the Tricycle Theatre, London; *A Night of the Campaign* was shown on BBC1 in 1985; *Mumbo Jumbo* was joint winner of the 1985 Mobil Playwriting competition and performed at the Manchester Royal Exchange and The Lyric, Hammersmith and *Donny Boy* was premièred at the Royal Exchange and won the Best New Play Award in the Martini-Rossi Regional Theatre Awards and the Manchester Evening News Theatre Award.

The Words are Strange was first broadcast on BBC Radio 4 as a 'Monday Play' on 6 May 1991. The cast was as follows:

TOM FAIRFAX	John Hewitt
HEADMASTER	T P McKenna
SALLY FAIRFAX	Eleanor Methven
ALISON	Heather McIlwaine
JONATHAN	Damian O'Hare
GARY	Mark Lamb
DEPUTY HEAD	John Keyes
JIM	Wesley Murphy
ARTHUR	Anthony Finigan
STUART	B J Hogg
SIR RICHARD	Patrick Duncan
BLACK	Robert Taylor
URSULA	Galina Tanney
SCHOOLBOY	Mark Phelan
SCHOOLGIRL	Helen Nelson

Director: Eoin O'Callaghan
Running time, as broadcast: 75 mins

The playwright thanks Michael Longley and Nick Stanage for permission to use their poems *The Civil Servant* and *Belfast Shops* in the play. Michael Longley's poems are published by Secker & Warburg. Nick Stanage is a former pupil of the playwright.

Interior Acoustic.

DEPUTY HEAD. Each department and subject area must agree and publish a policy or assessment to take account of the purposes and modes of assessment and objects of each department in relation to guidelines laid down in the National Curriculum.

TOM (*to himself*). I have recently discovered a way of listening to the Deputy Head without having to think about what he is actually saying. I just sit here trying to turn the language he's using into verse . . . The *National Curriculum* . . . ha, ha, an iambic trimetre. Just put the stress in the right place and even this stuff is convertible . . . *Assessment modes* and *purposes* . . . done it again! The concentration required makes me look alert, but I avoid the real pain of having to try and understand what he's actually saying . . .

DEPUTY HEAD. Assessment serves several purposes; formative, diagnostic, summative, evaluative; and assessment tasks can be analysed in terms of three assessment modes, viz: the presentation mode, the operation mode and the response mode . . .

TOM (*self*). Is *it* diagnostic or summative /this *mode* that now sits *heavy on* my *soul*. Two pentameters! A vintage meeting of the Curriculum Review Committee or the triumph of style over content, beauty over the beast. . . . Ha, ha, ha, you're a genius, Tom Fairfax, a maker of silk purses out of sows ears by appoint . . .

DEPUTY HEAD. Yes, Mr Fairfax?

TOM. Wha . . . ?

DEPUTY HEAD. I thought you had something to say.

TOM. Oh . . . no . . . nothing to say . . . nothing to be done
. . .

DEPUTY HEAD. What?

TOM. Nothing. . . . Sorry . . .

DEPUTY HEAD. You have applied for the job, Mr Fairfax.

TOM. Job?

DEPUTY HEAD. The Extra Staff Representative in the
School Management Team . . . or ESRSMT . . .

TOM. Oh, yes . . .

DEPUTY HEAD. Well, I would have thought that further
assessment policies would have been of interest to you.

TOM. Oh yes. Yes.

DEPUTY HEAD. Right. The basis of topics – subjects to be
assessed – should be the attainment targets and profile
components detailed in the National Assessment
programmes . . .

Acoustic for classroom, twenty or so pupils.

TOM. 'To plump the hazel shells with a sweet kernel.'
Plump? Plump? What about the word plump?

FIRST BOY. Fat.

TOM. More than fat. Come on, come on . . .

SECOND BOY. Round . . .

TOM. More than round, come on!

BLACK. Full-bodied.

Laughter.

TOM. What is the joke? (*Laughter.*) What is it, Morrison? It
was you, Morrison, wasn't it? Come on, Morrison, don't
be shy. Let us all in on the joke . . .

MORRISON. Like breasts, sir.

Laughter.

TOM. *Shut up!*

Silence. Pause.

Yes, Morrison, like breasts, fat, round, full-bodied, plump
. . . young breasts, Morrison, breasts so beautiful they
make you gasp, Morrison, breasts to take your breath
away. (*Pause.*) Plump . . . plump . . . listen to it . . . plump
. . . Anything else?

BLACK. He's using it as a verb sir . . . well, usually it's an
adjective . . .

TOM. Yes, Black, Yes . . . 'To plump the hazel shells with a
sweet kernel.' What does he do to the vines?

Increasing excitement

BLACK. Load and bless, sir.

FIRST BOY. Bend, sir.

TOM. Bend, bend, bend is right; words have muscles boys,
not just meaning, bend . . . bend . . . bend . . . hear them
flex their muscles . . . The gourd?

SECOND BOY. Swell!

TOM. Fruit?

FIRST BOY. Fill!

TOM. Fill, Fill, Fill!

BLACK. And 'to set budding more, And still more later
flowers for the bees . . .'

TOM. Yes, Black, yes . . . 'For summer has o'er-brimmed
their clammy cells.'

Fade to exterior acoustic: the school quad at break.

TOM (*self*). Boys mill about. Big boys push small boys who
are chasing tennis balls and bump into smaller boys who
are jumping up and down in puddles . . . *Quad One* . . . A
play by Tom Fairfax . . .

BLACK (*approaching*). Sir? Sir? Sir?

TOM. Had I three ears I'd hear thee Black . . .

BLACK. Can I join the play, sir?

TOM. Well, it isn't exactly a play this year, you see . . .

BLACK. I know, I know it's an evocation of twenty years of the Troubles in words and music, sir.

TOM. Ah, you've read my notice I . . .

BLACK. Radical, sir . . .

TOM. No, I think after twenty years we should make some response, since . . .

BLACK. In this place, sir?

TOM. Why not this place Black?

BLACK. King George the Sixth Royal School Belfast, sir?

TOM. So?

BLACK. This is *the* establishment, sir.

TOM. I'm afraid all schools in Ulster are some sort of establishment, Black.

BLACK. This place is for the sons of businessmen, sir, accountants, civil servants, doctors, lawyers, judges and the members of rugby clubs, sir.

TOM. And who are you the son of, Black?

BLACK. An accountant, sir *and* a member of a rugby club. Sir, he thinks the Troubles are an invention of the television.

TOM. Time he thought differently then?

BLACK. Exactly sir, radical.

TOM. Glad of your support.

BLACK. You've got it, sir.

TOM (*self*). Tom Fairfax's play . . . Tom Fairfax's admirable play *Quad One* is in the radical tradition of . . . of . . .

Fade up sound of quad and fade to staff room.

TOM (*self*). My colleagues assembled, slumped in chairs, slurping coffee, the odd, furtive guilty cigarette or just staring at the wall in the vain hope that the bell will never ring again . . .

STUART. A scrum half? A scrum half? For God's sake the child is handless, footless and witless, how could he make a scrum half?

TOM. He can pass Stuart, I've seen him . . .

STUART. Pass? He couldn't pass water!

TOM (*self*). Ah, to shape one's mind, sharpen one's wits in the intellectual rigours of the average Ulster staffroom.

JIM. You still here?

TOM. Yes, Jim.

JIM. I thought I told you to get out of teaching.

TOM. Twenty years ago, Jim.

JIM. And you haven't?

TOM. And once a week since.

JIM. I can do nothing for you.

TOM. *Flies in Amber* – a novel by Tom Fairfax . . . Tom and his colleagues . . . The fall of numbers on school rolls . . . Situation exacerbated by School's City Centre site, etc., etc. . . . Flies to a corpse.

ARTHUR. Have you applied? For the ESRSMT?

TOM. Yes, Arthur.

ARTHUR. Wouldn't have thought it was your cup of tea, old man.

TOM. No?

ARTHUR. Management structures? Reacting creatively to the changes in the school curriculum?

TOM. Well . . .

ARTHUR. But you could do with the money?

TOM. Yes.

ARTHUR. Look, old man, I don't mean to belittle your . . . aspirations . . . but what this place needs is someone with experience in business.

TOM. You?

ARTHUR. I did five years on a tea plantation in the White Highlands of Kenya.

Fade to acoustic for study.

HEADMASTER. *Which troubles?*

TOM. Our Troubles.

HEADMASTER. You mean the Northern Ireland Troubles?

TOM. Yes.

HEADMASTER. You can't be serious.

TOM. An evocation in words and music.

HEADMASTER. What words?

TOM. Poetry, prose, drama.

HEADMASTER. But which poems? Which plays?

TOM. I was going to start with some that are on the new GCSE course.

HEADMASTER. About the Troubles?

TOM. Yes.

HEADMASTER. My god, I'd no idea they put that sort of thing on the course!

TOM. Oh, yes.

HEADMASTER. I shall have to clear it with my Board.

TOM. Oh?

HEADMASTER. Could be controversial, Mr Fairfax. Dangerous. Shrinking rolls, Mr Fairfax. Free for all. Redundancies, Mr Fairfax.

Open air acoustic. Rugby practice.

TOM (*self*). The school drive. Rugby goal posts to right and left. Perspectives of white, uprights receding into the distance. *Moving the Goalposts*: a novel by Tom Fairfax. Boys run, converge, congeal, collapse and slowly rise from the mud to run again and again . . .

STUART (*shouting*). OUT OUT OUT, you moron.

TOM (*self*). The Coach is a balding, disappointed forty-year-old, named Stuart . . .

STUART. RUN, RUN, RUN. CUT HIM OFF, CUT HIM OFF, HIT HIM LOW, LOW, LOW . . . BALL, BALL,

BALL! GET HIS HANDS OFF IT, BEND HIS
FINGERS BACK AND HE'LL LET GO!

TOM (*self*). Stuart believes in the ultimate triumph of
technique . . .

STUART. BEND HIS FINGERS, FINGERS, FINGERS,
BREAK HIS BLOODY FINGERS!

TOM (*self*). He delights in skill, applied skill . . .

Loud whistle blast.

STUART. That was woeful, pathetic, hopeless. Right,
punitive lap.

Groans.

Until I blow the whistle . . . GO! (*To* TOM.) Hi Tom.
Have you ever seen such a bunch of cretins?

TOM. They lack technique.

STUART. Moonmen, stumers, spacers. (*Shouting.*) RUN
YOU LEGLESS LOONIES, RUN! (*To* TOM.) Had a
quiet word with the Deputy Head.

TOM. Oh.

STUART. After this morning's meeting of the Curriculum
Review Committee. He's backing me. For the ESRSMT.
Well, he didn't exactly say it outright, but . . . a nod's as
good as a wink to a horse in harness . . . (*Shouts.*)
McAuley, if you don't shift that heap of flesh you call a
body I'll come and shift it for you with the toe of my boot
. . . By the way, he thinks you are bored by the whole
thing . . . 'Not Mr Fairfax's cup of tea, I'm afraid . . .' His
very words . . . (*Moving off.*) McAuley, the toe of my boot
is on its way.

BLACK. He employs a special sort of language, doesn't he
sir?

TOM. Oh . . . Black? Yes, I suppose he does . . .

STUART (*from a distance*). IF IT HURTS YOU, BOY, IT'S
DOING YOU GOOD!

BLACK. Sir, I've been thinking.

TOM. Yes, Black?

BLACK. Why not invite another school to join us, in our
evocation of twenty years of the Troubles?

TOM. Why?

BLACK. Another point of view, sir. I was thinking of a Catholic school.

TOM. Ah . . .

BLACK. That would widen the viewpoint, wouldn't it sir?

TOM. Yes, Black, it would.

BLACK. Are you catching a number 17 sir?

TOM. Yes, I suppose I am.

BLACK. Then, we can discuss it on the way, sir.

Fade up bus and traffic. Interior of bus.

TOM. A bus through the heart of Protestant East Belfast . . . Red bricks. Loyalist graffiti. FTP. God Save the Queen. A crudely painted Union Jack. *Wall Pictures*: a novel by Tom Fairfax. Mr Fairfax's savage realism pulls no punches, there are no soft landings, easy options, the reader is impaled on the ruthless skewer of his vivid prose.

BLACK. Sir?

TOM. Yes, Black.

BLACK. I've been thinking, sir.

TOM. Yes, Black.

BLACK. If we teamed up with a school from a really Republican area sir, I mean produced a clash of cultures and ideology . . .

TOM. Yes?

BLACK. Well, that would really liven things up, wouldn't it, sir?

Fade bus to interior of house.

ALISON. Hi Dad, I got seventy-five per cent in my physics test.

TOM. Well done, Alison.

ALISON. My biology's tomorrow.

TOM. Where's Mum?

ALISON. She had to leave the plumber home.

TOM. Leave the plumber home? Why did she have to leave the plumber home?

GARY (*arriving*). Hello, Daddy.

TOM. Gary . . . how did the spellings go, son?

GARY. F . . . F . . . F . . . Five.

TOM. Five? Only five wrong out of thirty? That's splendid! I told you you could do it . . . Gary? Gary? Cry baby.

JONATHAN (*arriving*). . . . Hi Dad.

TOM. Jonathan . . .

JONATHAN. I read two books.

TOM. Great.

JONATHAN. One of them was about trolls.

TOM. Trolls?

ALISON. Digestion.

TOM. Digestion?

ALISON. My biology test.

TOM. Oh . . .

SALLY (*entering*). Oh, you're home . . .

TOM. Yes.

SALLY (*bustling*). What kept you?

TOM. What do you mean, what kept me?

JONATHAN. The other book was about giants.

SALLY (*crashing about with cutlery*). Why is Gary crying in the hall . . . ?

TOM. Crying . . . ?

SALLY. Did you shout at him again?

TOM. No! On the contrary . . .

ALISON. In the buccal cavity salivary anylase changes anylase to maltose . . .

SALLY (*appropriate business*). You might have set the table at least.

TOM. On the contrary, I . . .

ALISON. In the gastric juices pepsin changes protein to peptides . . .

TOM. I congratul . . .

SALLY. I had to drive the plumber all over the bloody town . . .

TOM. Why did you have to drive the plumber all over town?

SALLY (*business*). Because he's changing his car. (*Crash*.) Because the new model is not available until tomorrow. (*Crash*.) Because the only way he would agree to come and look at our leak today was if I lifted and laid him. (*Crash*.)

ALISON. And maltose changes maltose to glucose . . .

JONATHAN. On the whole, I think I like trolls better . . .

TOM. What did the plumber say?

SALLY. It's not a big job . . .

TOM. I told you . . .

SALLY. But the leak has been going on for so long that the ceiling in the two front rooms may have to come down . . .

TOM. What?

SALLY. He recommended a builder.

TOM. A builder, but we've only just . . .

ALISON. And trypsin changes protein to peptides . . .

JONATHAN. Trolls are better than giants any day.

SALLY. That estate agent took you for a ride.

TOM. Me?

SALLY. He was your friend, not mine . . .

TOM. I was at school with him. I wasn't . . .

SALLY. Well, go and make it up to Gary. It's nearly tea time.

TOM. All I did was congratulate him on only getting five spellings wrong!

ALISON. Right.

TOM. What?

ALISON. He only got five spellings right.

TOM. Only five out of thirty???

ALISON. Yes.

JONATHAN. He's got dyslexia.

TOM. He doesn't try, I tell you he doesn't bloody well try.

SALLY. Don't shout.

JONATHAN. He is dyslexic.

TOM. I wasn't.

SALLY. It does no good shouting. . . . Will you turn that radio off.

(Business still.)

TOM. But I wasn't shouting at him, I was . . .

ALISON. And chrymntrypsin changes hypotrypsinage to hymtrypin . . .

TOM. Alison, not now!

ALISON. But my biology test is tomorrow.

TOM. Later, dear, later . . .

ALISON *(going)*. That's what you always say . . .

TOM. Alison?

ALISON. Later, later, later. *(Door.)*

TOM. What did I say?

SALLY. If you came home earlier in the afternoon you would have more time for your children!

TOM. I came home as soon as I could.

SALLY. Another play starting!

TOM. I can't help that. I . . .

SALLY. I can't think what you're doing on that Curriculum wotsit . . .

TOM. Review Committee.

SALLY. You hate it, you are always moaning . . .

TOM. I joined it to work against it.

SALLY. Oh, very subtle.

TOM. It's threatening changes I don't like . . . changes to the study of literature . . .

SALLY. Well, there are changes happening here, Tom. The children need you. (*Still business.*) Gary especially. Dammit, I need you. For God's sake, what are we to do if this leak has done serious damage and we have to employ a builder . . .

TOM. I don't know, I just . . . I just don't know.

SALLY (*final business*). Well, neither do I!

TOM. I mean, the new mortgage is . . .

SALLY (*strident shout*). TEA TIME!

JONATHAN. Where does dyslexia come from, Dad?

TOM. What?

JONATHAN (*impatiently*). How do you get dyslexia?

TOM (*absently*). I don't know.

JONATHAN (*resignedly*). You don't know very much, do you?

Fade acoustic from working kitchen to Headmaster's study.

HEADMASTER. *Which* school, Mr Fairfax?

TOM. St Brigid's.

HEADMASTER. From West Belfast?

TOM. Yes, you see . . .

HEADMASTER. And girls?

TOM. Well yes, I think that will add to . . .

HEADMASTER. Nuns.

TOM. Well, not at this stage . . .

HEADMASTER. In the audience, Mr Fairfax. To be received and entertained . . . You have very little appreciation of what this puts *me* through you know . . .

TOM. Well, of course I . . .

HEADMASTER. *And* I've got to live with the potential for disaster.

TOM. Disaster?

HEADMASTER. And not just an average disaster either . . . not just a shambles in front of my own parents; this would be a very public affair . . . My Board, nuns, bishops, God knows what . . . the Press?

TOM. But there's such potential for good publicity.

HEADMASTER. Of course, and I need hardly say in these days of falling rolls . . . It's all very well for you, you know, you can bury yourself in rehearsals; I've got to sit here alone and worry. Talking about worry, there's this afternoon's lecture. As you know, the Honourable Sir Richard Rawlinson, Minister of Development and Manpower Services, is to talk to the Sixth Form on 'The Entrepreneurial Spirit'. Now I know it's a feather in my cap that Sir Richard has chosen to address my Sixth Form on such an important subject, but there has to be an audience, there have to be intelligent questions, there has to be good behaviour . . . The Press will be there and in these days of parental choice and open competition we all know how important good publicity is; you will be there, Mr Fairfax?

TOM. Well actually, I could use the time to organise the school play . . .

HEADMASTER. Ah, voluntary time . . .

TOM. What?

HEADMASTER. Time devoted to the play is voluntary time.

TOM. Is it?

HEADMASTER. Oh yes.

TOM. And what is the lecture?

HEADMASTER. Directed time, Mr Fairfax. Directed time. I'm sure you will enjoy the lecture, Tom. A very entertaining and lively man, Sir Richard . . .

Bell rings.

Quad.

BLACK. Sir?

TOM. Yes, Black?

BLACK. What about some extremist verse? For the entertainment, sir? I mean, if we really want to evoke twenty years of the Troubles. What do you think, sir?

TOM. Well . . .

BLACK. I wonder where you could get some extremist verse . . . ?

TOM. Is there any?

BLACK. Must be, sir.

TOM. Look, Black, I think one of the rules we should apply is that the poetry, the prose, must be good, not just representative of various points of view.

BLACK. Oh, I agree sir, but if we really want to show what a hunger striker or UVF man really feels, maybe we should read what *he* has to say . . .

TOM. Well yes, but if we use the criteria of . . .

BLACK. I mean as a contrast, sir, to the good stuff. Just a few selected pieces, genuine populism, sir, the authentic touch.

TOM. Well . . .

BLACK. I'll try in the public library, shall I sir? For some extremist verse?

TOM. Yes, I suppose . . . we can always . . .

BLACK. I'm really looking forward to our joint meeting, sir . . . with St Brigid's.

TOM. Oh, good . . .

BLACK. 'Bye, sir . . .

TOM. Oh, Black?

BLACK. What sir?

TOM. Keep the . . . the, ah, extremist verse . . . back for a . . . for a . . .

BLACK. Later meetings. Good idea, sir. I wouldn't want to

ruin the whole show by being too radical at the start.
Softly, softly catchee monkey, sir? Trust me, sir. (*Goes.*)

TOM (*to self*). Yes . . . Well . . .

Fade quad to common room.

JIM. Have I warned you today, Tom?

TOM. Not today, Jim.

JIM. Consider yourself warned.

TOM. Oh, come on, teaching's not that bad a life . . .

JIM. . . . And an extra warning.

TOM. What?

JIM. Watch out for that boy Black.

TOM. Why?

JIM. Dangerous enthusiast.

TOM. Actually, I find him most refresh . . .

JIM. By the way, I've applied for the ESRSMT.

TOM. You?

JIM. I know, I know. I'm earning more than the scale
offered, but if he appoints me he won't have to give me the
money and he can use his little bit of leverage somewhere
else.

TOM. But what on earth has that job got to offer you?

JIM. A reduced timetable. There is no true status without a
reduced timetable. Those with the highest status have the
biggest white spaces in their timetables. That's what we all
want, after all . . . less time in front of those massed faces,
with their silly questions and yawning mouths and
babbling voices and into a nice, private little office with an
in-tray and out-tray and a door with Mr named on it, that
shuts! Let the rest of the youngsters know they have me to
beat . . .

TOM (*self*). Youngsters? I'm forty . . . *A Door With My
Name On It* – A novel by Tom Fairfax. Oh, the hunger
for the niche, the little world, the safe space, the calmness

of tasks completed in order, the uninterrupted production
of pieces of paper . . .

Fade to auditorium for lecture.

Burst of cheering and laughter from the audience.

MINISTER. Well now boys how did this particular
publisher get away with it?

Salacious laughter.

A magazine full of

Whoops of glee.

topless ladies . . .

Whistles.

and a centre page spread of

TOM (*whisper*). Excuse me please. Sorry Jim.

MINISTER (*continues over* TOM's *entrance*). two colossal

Pandemonium, banging of feet, shouts, whistles, cheers.

JIM (*whisper*). Tom, what are you doing here?

MINISTER. What made it all possible?

TOM. Directed time.

JIM. Same here, old man.

MINISTER. Come on, you're all young and your
Headmaster tells me you are intelligent, what's the key?

FIRST BOY. Sex?

Laughter.

MINISTER. No, I think you can do better than that.

SECOND BOY. Money?

MINISTER. Send that boy to the top of the class.

TOM. Is this serious?

JIM. I think so. The Head seems to be enjoying it anyway.

Cheers.

MINISTER. But it's no good just throwing money around.
Look at the product.

Whistles

I mean the paper.

Laughter.

It's very good paper, it's very well printed, it has classy advertising, it has articles by fashionable and reputable writers; it looks great, feels great and sounds intelligent, like one of these excellent young ladies with a double first.

Cheers.

It appeals openly and frankly to sex, but it is not tawdry. It appeals to men's acquisitive instincts, their macho image of themselves and it flatters their intellect. It is also expensive. In the market-place, it's a winner!

Cheers.

TOM. Is this really the Secretary of State for Development and Manpower Services?

JIM. I'm afraid so, old boy.

MINISTER. Now, boys, the money he made from his first club he put into his magazine and the money he made from the magazine he put into more clubs until he had built an empire employing thousands and became a multi-millionaire . . .

TOM (*to self*). 'In Xanadu did Kublai Khan a stately pleasure dome decree . . .'

MINISTER. . . . First he identified his market. He was after the hard-working, high-achieving, heterosexual male, who liked whiskey and steak and fantasized about compliant bimbo women. Let's face it, the world is full of them. So you could only eat steak and drink whiskey in his restaurants and you were served by nubile young ladies dressed as bunny rabbits, at which they could look but must not touch. He recognised his market, kept down his overheads and went after it with single-minded ruthlessness. That's the entrepreneurial spirit, boys, and it's the same if you're selling machine tools or linen or the tourist industry . . .

TOM (*self*). In Xanadu, did Kublai Khan
A stately pleasure dome decree
Where high achieving macho man

Is chomping steak and swilling scotch
But dare not touch the bobbing tails
Of bunny girls within his reach
But fantasize of sex in sheets
Of Kublai's glossy magazine . . .

Outburst of applause, boys leaving hall, etc.

HEADMASTER. Well now Sir Richard, that was quite an education.

MINISTER. Well, I know it was naughty of me, headmaster – actually makes them sit up and take notice.

HEADMASTER. Oh of course, Minister . . . now let me introduce . . . (*shouts.*) Mr Fairfax, would you come and meet the Minister . . .

MINISTER. Hello.

TOM. Hello.

HEADMASTER. Mr Fairfax teaches English and produces our plays, marvellous production of *The Tempest* last year . . .

MINISTER. Did you make a profit, Mr Fairfax?

TOM. A profit?

MINISTER. On your production.

TOM. I . . . I don't know . . .

MINISTER. You don't know?

TOM. Well, I didn't really think that was the object of the . . .

MINISTER. But surely here is a perfect chance to demonstrate to boys the skills and excitements of the market-place? Estimates, costs, advertising, selling, balance sheets? (*Pause.*) Let me show you something, Mr Fairfax. Here. Page 53. Just after Miss December, starkers in front of Ye Olde Yule fire . . . The Legend of Stratford. Four page article by professor somebody on Shakespeare, popular but scholarly, lovely pics of Anne Hathaway's cottage, swans on the Avon, Dame Judi Dench in period costume. Now that paid for itself, that made a profit, no one had to go cap in hand, whining for a subsidy to produce that . . .

TOM. No, they were able to sell it.

MINISTER. Of course.

TOM. And themselves . . .

MINISTER. Sorry?

TOM. They sold themselves. For money. It's called prostitution. It's been a sure-fire winner for centuries.

Pause.

HEADMASTER. Mr Fairfax, I don't think that's what Sir Richard means . . .

TOM. Well, it's what I mean!

HEADMASTER. Mr Fairfax . . . ?

TOM. Sorry, got to go.

HEADMASTER. Afternoon tea with Sir Richard . . . ?

TOM. Urgent phone call . . .

HEADMASTER. Directed time!

TOM. Sorry, I'm expecting

(*Going.*)

a Person from Porlock!

Acoustic for Kitchen.

TOM. Is that the plumber's new car outside?

SALLY. Yes.

TOM. Thought so. (*Self.*) *The Plumber's New Car:* a short story by Tom Fairfax. It had always struck Tom as comic that the plumber, someone whom he considered a mere tradesman, could afford a brand new car while for Tom the MOT test was an annual mechanical and financial crisis . . .

SALLY (*tea making ritual*). I thought you were going to be home early.

TOM. I had to go to a meeting.

SALLY. Humph!

TOM. Is the van the plumber's too?

SALLY. Builder.

TOM. Oh, my God, I'd forgotten.

SALLY. Lucky you.

TOM. I'll go and see him in a minute. It can't be too serious.

SALLY. Humph! (*Business.*)

TOM. How were Gary's spellings?

SALLY. He wrote that.

TOM. This?

SALLY. It's a poem.

TOM (*reads*). 'he . . . was . . . edes . . . y . . . s . . . looks like Strumjoy . . . bo . . . u . . . of . . . no . . . ty . . . em . . .' It's gibberish.

SALLY. He had to write a poem for homework.

TOM. My God, what are they doing at the prep. school? Teaching him to write poetry when he can't even spell his own name! . . . Strumjoy . . . Sally, we've got to do something about this.

SALLY. You're the teacher, you come home in the afternoon and teach him!

TOM. Right . . . Tomorrow . . . No – I can't, the play . . . first meeting with St Brigid's.

ALISON (*entering*). There's a man in the living room.

SALLY. He's the builder.

TOM. How was the biology exam?

ALISON. Wee buns. Are we going to have an extension? My friend Julie's just had an extension to her house, are we going to have one?

SALLY. Just repairs dear.

ALISON. Repairs? We've just moved in.

TOM. We didn't know we needed repairs when we moved in.

ALISON. Why not?

JONATHAN (*entering*). That man upstairs has put his foot through the ceiling.

TOM. Oh, my God.

ALISON. Why didn't we know the repairs were needed before we moved in?

SALLY. Because the estate agent was a friend of your father's.

TOM. He was at school with me, he was not my . . . What in the name!?

Rending crashing sound in adjacent room.

GARY (*entering*). The ceiling's given way!

Fade to Staff Common Room.

Acoustic for Staff Common Room.

STUART. And what do you think happens?

TOM. What, Stuart?

STUART. The bloody ball lands on its bloody point. I mean, it is practically impossible for a rugby ball to land directly on its point, but not only does it land on its point but happens to land on the only hard square foot of turf on that bloody muck heap they insist on calling a rugby pitch and bounces not only upwards but bloody backwards as well . . .

JIM. Oh, bad luck, Stuart.

STUART. Bad luck, bad luck! I was just explaining to Tom here . . .

JIM. How you lost in the last minute, yes . . .

STUART. OF EXTRA TIME!

ARTHUR. I hear you covered yourself in glory at yesterday's lecture, Tom . . .

JIM. Accused Sir Richard of prostitution.

ARTHUR. Good God.

JIM. I have warned him against this before, haven't I?

ARTHUR. Saying what he thinks?

JIM. I think we can rule him out of the race for the ESRSMT . . .

TOM. Maybe they could do with someone who's going to call a spade a spade . . .

JIM. This is education, Tom, not agriculture . . .

STUART. And one of their three quarters, following up merely as a matter of form, catches the bouncing ball and races over between the bloody posts, they convert the bloody try, the bloody whistle blows and we're out of the bloody cup for another bloody year. I mean to bloody say . . .

JIM *and* TOM. Oh, bloody bad luck, Stuart.

Rehearsal. Echoing hall.

URSULA (*reading*). *The Civil Servant* by Michael Longley
He was preparing an Ulster fry for breakfast
When someone walked into the kitchen and shot him
A bullet entered his mouth and pierced his skull
The books he had read, the music he could play.

He lay in his dressing-gown and pyjamas
While they dusted the dresser for fingerprints
And then shuffled backwards across the garden
With notebooks, cameras and measuring tapes.

They rolled him up like a red carpet and left
Only a bullet hole in the cutlery drawer:
Later his widow took a hammer and chisel
And removed the black keys from his piano.

TOM. Thank you . . . ah . . . Ursula, is it? Well, we must get you to read that particular poem in the performance Ursula. Now . . . Any ideas? How might we present this in performance?

Nervous laughter.

TOM. Well, let's start with the poems. What are they about?

FIRST GIRL. Assassinations.

FIRST BOY. Innocent victims.

TOM. Well, what do we do with them?

SECOND GIRL. Act them out.

SECOND BOY. Too difficult.

FIRST GIRL. Why?

SECOND BOY. Too many poems, too many characters, incidents . . .

TOM. Actually, I think he's right. Besides, I think we want the words of the poet to do the work. After all, he didn't write a play, did he?

FIRST BOY. We could use bits of plays.

TOM. Of course . . . And that reminds me, I've started off our first get-together with my own selection of poems, but you've got to bring me the rest of the material, it's your show, it's your response to twenty years of the Troubles, for boys, for girls, two different schools.

BLACK. A symbolic representation.

TOM. What?

BLACK. Sorry, sir. I was thinking how we might present these poems . . . when you broke in with the commercial . . .

Laughter.

TOM. Well go on, explain . . .

BLACK. I think we should use things that go with assassinations, things that we associate with them . . .

TOM. What?

SECOND BOY. Funerals.

Laughter.

BLACK. Great, but let's think of the more immediate aftermath . . .

URSULA. White tape.

SECOND BOY. What?

URSULA. The police put white tape all round the scene to keep people away.

FIRST BOY. Dusting for fingerprints . . .

SECOND GIRL. Searching for evidence . . .

SECOND BOY. Going over the ground in lines . . .

SECOND GIRL. The whirr of helicopters . . .

BLACK. Bright lights . . .

URSULA. White chalk round the corpse . . .

FIRST BOY. Blanket over it . . .

FIRST GIRL. Measuring tape . . .

URSULA. White chalk round the bullet holes . . .

SECOND BOY. Police photographer . . .

SECOND GIRL. Flash bulbs . . .

BLACK. Reporters with notebooks . . .

FIRST GIRL. TV cameras . . .

FIRST BOY. Bystanders . . .

FIRST GIRL. Children with schoolbags standing . . .

FIRST BOY. Watching . . . And eating crisps . . .

Laughter.

Kitchen. Business as before.

TOM. Thought Gary . . . thought . . . th . . . th . . . ought . . .

SALLY. Is there a pay rise with this ES wotsit?

TOM. Oh, yes.

SALLY. Do you stand a chance?

TOM. Oh, yes.

GARY. Th . . . th . . . th . . . th . . .

SALLY. With all these repairs, we're going to need it.

TOM. I've spoken to the bank manager.

SALLY. And?

TOM. Sympathetic – come on, Gary.

GARY. Th . . . th . . . th . . . th . . .

ALISON. Why hasn't our builder got his name on his van?

TOM. Gary!

GARY. Th . . . th . . . th . . .

TOM. Stop saying th . . . and spell it . . .

SALLY. Now Tom, don't shout . . .

ALISON. When Julie's parents had their extension built, their builder had his name on all his vans and lorries in big red letters.

TOM. He was an orthodox builder.

JONATHAN. And what is ours?

TOM. Unorthodox.

ALISON. Why can't we have an orthodox builder?

SALLY. Because an unorthodox one is cheaper. Now shut up, the two of you, and help me set the table . . .

Table setting.

GARY. T . . . H.

TOM. Good, Gary, good . . . now come on . . . ought!

JONATHAN. But what is unorthodox?

ALISON. Not proper.

GARY. T . . . H . . .

JONATHAN. How not proper?

TOM. He's on the double.

SALLY. Shhhhh TOM!

GARY. T . . . H . . .

TOM. You've said that . . . Ought, ought . . . ought.

JONATHAN. What does 'on the double' mean?

ALISON. Illegal

JONATHAN. Illegal?

SALLY. Now shut up, you two, and set the table!

JONATHAN. But if he's fixing our house . . .

SALLY *and* TOM. Shut up, Jonathan!

GARY. T . . . H . . . A . . . U . . . T

Fade kitchen to Headmaster's study.

HEADMASTER. Well, let's just say you were overwrought, Mr Fairfax. I have, of course, apologised to Sir Richard on your behalf.

TOM. Thank you.

HEADMASTER. I told him you were overwrought, under pressure. I think he understood. He is a very understanding man, though I am bound to say it *did not* create a good impression.

TOM. Sorry.

HEADMASTER. Luckily the Press had all gone, so there is no lasting damage. Nothing that a suitable letter of apology from you to Sir Richard can't fix, that is.

TOM. Of course.

HEADMASTER. I will consider the matter closed then, shall I?

TOM. Please.

HEADMASTER. Very well, I shall say no more about it. I am bound to point out, however, that it will not look very good on your record, Mr Fairfax. (*Pause.*) Now, what's this I hear about funerals?

TOM. What funerals?

HEADMASTER. In the play.

TOM. Oh, yes. Well, as you know it's about twenty years of the Troubles, so the cast felt that funerals were an important source of imagery.

HEADMASTER. Sounds a bit gloomy to me.

TOM. Well, there have been a lot of funerals, of different kinds . . . civilians, RUC men, soldiers, IRA men, hunger strikers . . .

HEADMASTER. HUNGER STRIKERS?

TOM. The idea is that we will have slides projected onto screens while the cast are reciting poems . . .

HEADMASTER. More poems?

TOM. Well, of course.

HEADMASTER. I haven't seen these poems . . .

TOM. I didn't realise you wanted to see them.

HEADMASTER. My Board has insisted that I see them. My

Board feels that this school should not be involved in politics . . .

TOM. But how can I present . . . ?

HEADMASTER. Mr Fairfax, I sold my Board your idea by persuading them that this was an exercise in community relations in line with the government's new directive in 'Education for Mutual Understanding' and they were very happy with that, but I'm sure they won't understand what photographs of Republican funerals have to do with it!

TOM. But this is an approach to twenty years of the Troubles.

HEADMASTER. Well, keep Republican funerals out of it, Mr Fairfax.

Classroom.

TOM (*reading poem to class*).
To see a World in a Grain of Sand
And a Heaven in a Wild Flower
Hold Infinity in the palm of your hand
And Eternity in an hour

A Robin Red Breast in a Cage
Puts all Heaven in a Rage
A dove-house fill'd with Doves and Pigeons
Shudders Hell thro' all its regions
A Dog starv'd at his master's gate
Predicts the ruin of the State.

Pause.

TOM. What does he mean?

FIRST BOY. We look at small things . . .

SECOND BOY. And see big things . . .

TOM. What small things? Come on . . . come on . . .

THIRD BOY. A grain of sand . . .

BLACK. A Robin Red Breast . . .

FIRST BOY. A starving dog . . .

TOM. And what big things?

SECOND BOY. The State . . .

FIRST BOY. Heaven . . .

THIRD BOY. Hell . . .

BLACK. The world . . .

SECOND BOY. Infinity . . .

TOM. Well, how's it done? How are we to see the big in the small?

THIRD BOY. You just look.

TOM. Is that all?

SECOND BOY. Yes.

TOM. Just use your eyes?

FIRST BOY. And your imagination.

TOM. Go on.

FIRST BOY. To see the world in a grain of sand or predict the ruin of the state in a starving dog, you've got to use the power of the imagination . . .

TOM. Yes . . . Yes! How does the imagination express itself?

SECOND BOY. Words.

THIRD BOY. Poetry.

TOM. 'We are led to believe a lie
When we see not through the eye
Which was born in a night to perish in a night!'

Quad.

BLACK (*running up*). Sir!

TOM. Yes, Black?

BLACK. I've got it, sir.

TOM. What?

BLACK. The collected poems of Barney Quinn.

TOM. The hunger striker?

BLACK. Yes sir . . . here we are . . . *Freedom's Flame* . . . *Ireland's Hope* . . . Smuggled out of the Maze on pieces of toilet paper . . .

TOM. Look, Black, I wonder is this wise?

BLACK. Wise, sir?

TOM. To include this . . . this . . . verse . . . in our entertainment?

BLACK. But sir, it's representative of a point of view, an important point of view . . .

TOM. No, don't get me wrong. I admire your enthusiasm. But if we were to use one of these . . . rhymes, might we not be misunderstood?

BLACK. Might we not be misunderstood if we don't include one?

TOM. Black, Barney Quinn was a fanatic.

BLACK. And are there not fanatics?

TOM. Well yes, of course, but we might, might . . .

BLACK. Annoy somebody, sir?

TOM. Well, yes.

BLACK. That's not you, sir.

TOM. Not me?

BLACK. To be afraid of annoying people . . . look, sir, look here, a photograph of one of his poems written on a piece of toilet paper . . . look at the tiny writing, you'd have to use a magnifying glass . . . I can just make out the title with the naked eye . . . Then I . . . know . . . I'm right . . . Can we use this one, sir? Can I say it? Can I, sir? Please.

Acoustic for kitchen. SALLY setting table.

SALLY. Move those things, Jonathan.

JONATHAN. It's my project!

SALLY. I don't care what it is. I have to set the table . . . take it to your room . . .

JONATHAN. My room's all sand and cement . . .

SALLY. Well, just push it to one end of the table then!

TOM (*to self*). *The House Tom Bought* . . . a novel . . . The estate agent was an old school friend or contemporary, as Tom preferred to call him. This friend, or . . . contemporary, had been several classes below Tom, and

Tom had casually and cheerfully regarded him as thick. Now the . . . contemporary's equally thick son was Tom's pupil and the contemporary roared up to parent evenings in a new BMW and was casually and cheerfully condescending to Tom. In an odd moment in between more lucrative deals, he had casually and cheerfully sold Tom a house and casually and cheerfully pocketed his commission. (*To* SALLY.) To whom do I write this cheque, Sally?

SALLY. To the Craigantlet Pigeon Club.

ALISON. Why?

TOM. Why what, Alison?

AlISON. Why are you writing a cheque to a pigeon club?

TOM. It's to our builder.

SALLY. Alison, move those books.

ALISON. That's my homework.

SALLY. Does anyone in this house want a meal tonight?

ALISON. The rest of the house is a mess.

SALLY. Try and use less room!

JONATHAN. Don't squeeze into me.

ALISON. Why a pigeon club, Daddy?

TOM. Because the builder wishes to escape income tax . . . and other things . . .

ALISON. Is that illegal too?

TOM. Yes.

ALISON. They're going to lock us up.

JONATHAN. You're crumpling my project.

ALISON. Well, don't take up so much room.

SALLY. Shut up, you two!

ALISON. Is the cheque a big one?

TOM. No . . . it's a part payment . . . end of the week . . .

ALISON. Won't break the bank?

TOM. What do you know about breaking banks?

ALISON. That's what Julie's Mum says when she buys something expensive . . . Well never mind, it won't break the bank!

SALLY. Must everything be done at this table . . . here, Tom, this is for you.

TOM. What?

SALLY. More of Gary's poems.

TOM. For me?

SALLY. I think he leaves it there for you.

TOM. Why?

ALISON. Julie's Dad said the same thing about their extension . . . A bit of an extravaganza, but it won't break the bank!

TOM (*reading*). Win . . . win . . . I say . . . Hedjo . . . HEDJO? What the hell is hedjo supposed to mean? . . . Thee finish . . . Win . . . I cum . . . Cl . . . o . . . as . . . Thee hid . . . It's total gibberish.

SALLY. Do you think the prep. school is the right place for him?

TOM. If he's going to get in to the Senior School, Sally, the prep. is the only place. He's not going to qualify from anywhere else.

SALLY. Oh, I see.

TOM. What do you see?

SALLY. It's the old school tie after all.

TOM. What's that supposed to mean?

SALLY. And I thought poetry was what mattered.

TOM. I don't get the connection.

SALLY. Tom, the King George the Sixth Royal School is too academic for him.

TOM. No, it isn't – not if he tries. The trouble is he doesn't try.

SALLY. Don't shout.

TOM. I'm not shouting.

ALISON. Julie's Mum and Dad are always saying 'it won't break the bank, it won't break the bank . . .'

TOM *and* SALLY. Alison, shut up!

Fade to acoustic for committee meeting.

DEPUTY HEAD. I have attempted to produce a pro forma for the production of units of work so that they can all be produced in a uniform way. As you can see –

TOM. Sorry I'm late, I'd to get out of a rehearsal of the school entertainment for this.

DEPUTY HEAD. Yes well. As you can see this is, of necessity, very bulky indeed. The problem now facing us is how we can follow a proper curriculum review without generating an overwhelming amount of paper. We are, I am afraid, in insufficient control of the management of the process so that our work has lagged behind the production of material. We must now decide whether the process itself is more important than the detailed consideration of the paperwork produced . . .

TOM. Why don't you weigh it?

DEPUTY HEAD. Sorry?

TOM. Weigh it.

DEPUTY HEAD. Weigh it, Mr Fairfax?

TOM. Or measure it.

DEPUTY HEAD. The paperwork?

TOM. Well, if we decide that the process itself is more important than the detailed consideration of the paperwork it produces, then we will churn out the unconsidered paperwork in order to keep the all important process going.

DEPUTY HEAD *and* OTHERS. Yes?

TOM. So – weigh it.

Pause.

DEPUTY HEAD. We do have rather a lot of work to get through here.

TOM. I was only trying to help.

Pause.

DEPUTY HEAD. Now, if we all turn to page 42 of our Information Technology booklets . . . yes, here we are . . . 'By the age of fourteen, the pupils should have learned to investigate contexts in a systematic way, demonstrating that they vary their methods as appropriate until essential information has been required.

TOM (*self*). *Survived*: a pamphlet by Tom Fairfax. What was the only form of free human communication which survived the Stalinist terror in Russia? The novel was dead, the theatre was dead, history was dead, radio was dead, the cinema was dead. Even the paper on which ideas or stories might be written was rationed and only those in official State positions possessed the necessary ration cards . . .

DEPUTY HEAD. . . . Apply a broad range of knowledge about the consumer/user and business and industrial considerations, such as prices, costs and benefits, competition and consumer appeal . . .

TOM (*self*). The only form of free human communication which survived the terror was the lyric poem. It did not need paper or even ink. It could be short enough to be remembered, to be passed from mouth to ear, and yet it was expressive enough to encompass the fears and hopes and longings and loves and losses of the living and intense enough to commemorate the struggles and sufferings of the recent dead and disappeared. Mandelstam ran up to people in the street and told them his poems . . .

DEPUTY HEAD. If we could just look at the section combining English and English literature in the curriculum . . .

TOM. What?

DEPUTY HEAD. Remove English literature as a separate subject in the curriculum . . .

TOM. Why?

DEPUTY HEAD. Well, if we are to make room for new subjects such as Design and Technology, DT and IT, and taking into account recent reports from SHA, HMC, TGAT, SEAC . . .

TOM. You're mad!

DEPUTY HEAD. I'm sorry, Mr Fairfax?

TOM. I said 'you're mad'.

DEPUTY HEAD. Well, I thought you did . . .

TOM. Well . . . Well, not *you're* mad . . . per se . . . But I do think the view that we should combine English and English literature into only one subject on the curriculum . . .

DEPUTY HEAD. But Mr Fairfax, Tom, it's already been done.

TOM. Done?

DEPUTY HEAD. Tom, there is no separate report for English literature in the Curriculum Review. We must conclude from that that there will be no separate exam and, if there is no separate exam, there is no need for . . .

TOM. But the Curriculum Review lays very high stress on drama, poetry and prose . . .

DEPUTY HEAD. Well, Tom, you know all these things will be included in the course you teach and very good it will be too . . .

TOM. Just the course I teach?

DEPUTY HEAD. And all the others who think like you, Tom . . .

TOM. But it won't be essential?

DEPUTY HEAD. There will always be room in any curriculum for the real enthusiast.

TOM. But it won't be essential?

DEPUTY HEAD. Well . . . as I see it . . . a pupil will be able to pass GCSE English with only a minimum of literary content, but there is nothing to stop you . . .

TOM. Do you know the only form of free human communication which survived the Stalinist terror in Russia? Well, do you? Do any of you?

Pause.

DEPUTY HEAD. No, Tom. What was it?

TOM. The lyric poem.

DEPUTY HEAD. Well, I'm sure it will survive the Curriculum Review then. Now, gentlemen, if you will all turn to page 58 of your Information Technology booklets and have a look at the section on Desk Top Publishing . . .

TOM. There you are!

DEPUTY HEAD. What?

TOM. Desk Top Publishing!

DEPUTY HEAD. Well, what about it? I think it's a very exciting concept and one which we as a school should embrace whole . . .

TOM. What happens if they don't know enough words to publish anything worthwhile . . . on top of a desk . . . or anywhere else . . . what happens if the process becomes more important than the content . . .

DEPUTY HEAD. Tom – we haven't got all day.

TOM. If we drive English literature into some backwater of the curriculum . . .

DEPUTY HEAD. We've got to get through this stuff.

TOM. Oh God, I know . . .

DEPUTY HEAD. If this school is to survive, at its present size and staffing, in the present educational climate, we must, must be able to understand and react to all of this – ALL OF IT.

COMMITTEE MEMBER. Deputy Head, it's five-past-five . . .

DEPUTY HEAD. Oh, is it? I suppose we all want to go?

MEMBERS. Yes!

DEPUTY HEAD. Perhaps if a quorum . . . No . . . Well . . .

MEMBERS. It's awfully late Deputy Head.

Noises of departure.

DEPUTY HEAD. Look, everybody, read the next twenty pages yourselves and everyone, for God's sake, make yourselves au fait with the jargon!

Acoustic for quad.

BLACK (*approaching*). Sir?

TOM. Black?

BLACK. We're missing something, sir.

TOM. Missing?

BLACK. From the entertainment.

TOM. Now look, Black, don't get me wrong, but I've gone as far as I possibly can, further, to tell the truth, I'm right out on a limb as it is . . .

BLACK. A sense of alienation, sir . . .

TOM. What?

BLACK. That's what's missing. From our entertainment. We Protestants, sir, have a sense of alienation . . . from Ireland, from things Irish, from this place . . .

TOM. But our forefathers built this place . . .

BLACK. They built on a bog, sir . . .

TOM. Yes, yes, they built on a bog, but they built homes, public buildings, factories, ships, they . . .

BLACK. The city floods, sir . . .

TOM. They dreamed of noble institutions . . .

BLACK. Illusions, sir.

TOM. Yes . . . yes. I suppose they were . . . are . . .

BLACK. We need a sense of alienation, in the entertainment, sir, if we're to be truthful . . .

TOM. Well . . . How do we . . . ?

BLACK. I've written a poem, sir.

TOM. Have you?

BLACK. Yes sir. I have a sense of alienation. (*Pause.*) You did say, sir, that if any of us had work of our own, you would consider it . . .

TOM. Yes, yes I did, didn't I?

BLACK. Yes sir.

Staff room.

ARTHUR. Here he is!

JIM. The man of the moment . . .

STUART. No messing about with Tom . . .

ARTHUR. Gives it to him with both barrels . . .

JIM. Point blank range . . .

STUART. You're mad!

They laugh.

JIM. Oh my God, his face . . .

ARTHUR. When he realised you were serious . . .

STUART. You're mad!

They laugh.

JIM. And you start raving about Stalin and poetry . . .

STUART. YOU'RE MAD!

TOM. Ach, come off it, boys, I just said what I thought.

ARTHUR. That's dangerous for a start . . .

JIM. Radical . . .

STUART. Suicidal, ha, ha, ha, ha, ha.

ARTHUR. As for the ENTERTAINMENT?

JIM. Twenty years of the Troubles?

STUART. Now that *is* mad.

ARTHUR. The Head's terrified . . .

TOM. No he's not . . .

JIM. I blame it on that boy Black.

TOM. Black?

ARTHUR. He's dangerous, Tom, dangerous.

TOM. He thinks . . .

JIM. He poses, you mean . . .

STUART. Exocet . . .

ALL. Exocet?

STUART. I call him Exocet. You know, he's coming for you but you can do damn all about it.

JIM. Do you know what I found him reading in private study yesterday?

STUART. The Communist Manifesto?

JIM. The Collected Poems of Barney Quinn.

ARTHUR. The hunger striker?

JIM. He told me he was going to recite them in Tom's ENTERTAINMENT.

STUART. Barney Quinn?

JIM. In the school hall?

ARTHUR. In front of the parents . . .

TOM. Just one of them . . . just one poem . . . No one will even know it's by Barney Quinn . . .

JIM. The Head will know.

TOM. He won't . . .

JIM. When Black reads out the poem . . .

TOM. The Head has read the poem, he has read all the poems, he just doesn't know this poem is by Barney Quinn . . . It's a point of view that must be represented . . . somehow . . . It's a bad poem . . . It's about being right . . . No matter what . . . It's the way extremists think . . . Do none of you realise that?

Pause.

JIM. You've finally taken my advice then?

TOM. What's that, Jim?

JIM. To get out of teaching. You're provoking your own dismissal, aren't you?

TOM. No!

JIM. The only explanation that makes sense . . .

ARTHUR. Well, one thing's certain . . .

JIM. Go out in a blaze of glory . . .

ARTHUR. You can kiss goodbye to the ESRSMT . . .

STUART. What about your sons?

TOM. What about my sons?

STUART. You want them educated here, don't you?

Headmaster's study

HEADMASTER. Something positive, Mr Fairfax.

TOM. Well, yes . . .

HEADMASTER. My Board want a positive statement in the entertainment. My chairman, Sir Geoffrey Henderson, was quite specific. It's up to you, principally, that a positive statement is made. Something about this great city of ours. Its resilience in the face of a murderous onslaught. Its civic pride. Its life. Its bustle . . .

TOM. Yes, but don't you . . .

HEADMASTER. Sir Geoffrey is chairman of the Brighter Belfast Campaign . . .

TOM. Some of the boys have . . .

HEADMASTER. Belfast is buzzing, that kind of thing . . .

TOM. Well, of course we won't neglect . . .

HEADMASTER. I think that was Sir Geoffrey's own idea, actually . . . Belfast is buzzing . . . And of course it is. . . . New shops. New office blocks. New restaurants. Do you know, Mr Fairfax, my wife and I had a meal last night in a *Greek* restaurant, just think of that . . . *Greek* . . . Belfast is buzzing . . . Not just a story of murder and bombs, is it?

TOM. No, of course not, but . . .

HEADMASTER. And remember, the Press will be there, and maybe the TV cameras. It is vital in these days of falling rolls and freedom of choice that we present a positive image of ourselves . . . My chairman, Sir Geoffrey, said 'Headmaster, we now have to sell ourselves in the market-place . . . and we must not alienate potential customers . . . consumers . . . parents of prospective pupils . . .'. I'm relying on you, Mr Fairfax, as always . . . By the way, the Deputy Head tells me that you have been behaving rather oddly in the Curriculum Review Committee . . .

TOM. Oddly?

HEADMASTER. He thinks you may be under some sort of strain . . . having periods of silence. Sudden outbursts . . . You aren't under strain, are you?

TOM. No.

HEADMASTER. You are prone to the overwrought outburst, aren't you?

TOM. I thought that matter was closed.

HEADMASTER. So it is. I just mention it in passing. You're not worried about your boy at the Prep. school – are you? I'm told he has his difficulties, hasn't he?

TOM. Yes.

HEADMASTER. You do want him to come here, don't you?

TOM. Yes.

HEADMASTER. Yes . . . well, we must be positive mustn't we?

TOM. Yes.

HEADMASTER. So if you have any ideas for the Curriculum Review Committee, you had better put them, Mr Fairfax.

Acoustic for kitchen. Established bangs and thumps of evening meal preparation.

TOM (*harassed. He is in charge*). What did Mummy say was for pudding?

JONATHAN. Farola.

TOM. Where is it?

ALISON. Here.

TOM. Thanks, Alison . . .

GARY. Will I turn this off?

TOM. Yes, Gary . . . no, wait . . . not yet . . .

ALISON. I don't think these potatoes are done.

TOM. Milk? . . . milk? . . . Where's the bloody milk?

JONATHAN. In the fridge.

Fridge door, etc.

TOM. Did Mummy say where she was going?

GARY. No.

TOM. Oh, come on, children, she must have given some . . .
GARY, THAT'S BOILING OVER!

GARY. You told me not to turn it off . . .

TOM. You were watching it!

GARY. And you said yes, no, not yet.

TOM. Jesus, what a mess!

JONATHAN. There is no need to bring Jesus into it.

TOM. Stop crying, Gary.

GARY (*tearful*). I'm not crying.

JONATHAN. Jesus had absolutely nothing to do with it.

ALISON. Cloth?

TOM. No . . . no . . . later . . .

JONATHAN. Jesus died two thousand years ago and . . .

TOM. EVERYBODY SIT DOWN!

Pause . . . scraping of chairs.

TOM. Did Mummy say *anything* when she was going?

ALISON. Just that you were to make the dinner.

JONATHAN. For once . . .

ALISON. In a blue moon . . .

TOM. Come on, she must have said more than that.

GARY. No.

ALISON. I told you these potatoes weren't done.

TOM. EAT THEM!

ALISON. How can I eat them if they're hard . . . ?

JONATHAN. You'll get salmonella poisoning.

ALISON. You don't get salmonella poisoning from
potatoes, silly . . .

JONATHAN. Mad potato disease then . . .

ALISON. You just can't eat them, ugghhh . . .

JONATHAN. I think you've got it.

TOM. SHUT UP YOU TWO!

GARY. She was breaking the chair, of course.

TOM. What?

GARY. Smashing the chair. Mum. Banging it on the floor.
    That one over there.

JONATHAN. It's all loose.

ALISON. Falling to bits, actually.

TOM. You said Mummy was . . .

GARY. Banging it on the floor . . .

TOM. Why?

GARY. I don't know . . .

TOM. Tell me what happened.

GARY. I was doing my spellings and I heard this bang,
    bang, bang and I looked up and she was smashing the chair
    on the floor.

TOM. Jesus . . .

JONATHAN. Jesus had nothing to . . .

TOM. Why did she do it?

GARY. I don't know. I was doing my spellings and bang,
    bang, bang . . .

JONATHAN. Jesus . . .

ALISON. It would have smashed to smithereens if the
    builder hadn't walked in.

TOM. WHAT?

ALISON. The builder.

JONATHAN. With his bill . . .

TOM. And mummy was . . . ?

GARY. Smashing the chair . . .

JONATHAN. That's good 'the builder with his bill', isn't
    that good, 'the builder with his . . .'?

ALISON. Oh shut up, Jonathan, it isn't good at all . . .

JONATHAN. Yes it is, 'the builder . . .'

GARY. She had the chair right up in the air . . .

ALISON. Ready to smash it down.

GARY. And the builder was standing there with his mouth open.

ALISON. And she said, 'If you're going to hand me a bill, think again mister.'

TOM. And what did he say?

GARY. 'Jesus, Missus, take it easy . . .'

JONATHAN. I told him that Jesus . . .

ALISON. I bet it was a big one.

TOM. What happened next?

GARY. She threw the chair over there.

ALISON. Where it is now.

GARY. And marched out.

JONATHAN. Said you were to make the dinner.

GARY. And marched out.

JONATHAN. Once in a blue moon . . .

ALISON. Oh, I bet that bill was a whopper . . .

TOM. What did the builder do?

GARY. Said 'Jesus' again and put the bill on the shelf.

ALISON. Here it is.

TOM. Thanks . . .

JONATHAN. I can't understand why everybody says Jesus all . . .

ALISON. Is it big? I bet it's big.

TOM. It's none of your business. Get on with your dinner.

JONATHAN. Can we pay it?

ALISON. We've got an overdraft, silly.

JONATHAN. What's an overdraft?

ALISON. It's when you borrow money from the bank.

JONATHAN. Do you have to pay it back?

ALISON. Of course you have to pay it back, silly . . . plus interest. I can't eat any more of this.

TOM. Try the farola.

JONATHAN. What's interest?

ALISON. More money.

JONATHAN. Even more money.

ALISON. Lots more money. Interest rates are very high at the moment. Aren't interest rates very high, Daddy?

TOM. Eat your farola.

ALISON. It has lumps in it.

GARY. Daddy's farola always has lumps in it.

JONATHAN. Daddy, why does your farola always have lumps in it?

TOM. Now look, I've got to go.

GARY. But Mummy's not back.

TOM. I'm half an hour late already.

JONATHAN. Late for what?

TOM. It's the first night of the school play . . . entertainment.

GARY. Can we go?

TOM. On the last night, it's all arranged. Now eat up, wash up and get your homework done. Alison, you're in charge.

GARY. Oh no . . .

JONATHAN. She's horrible . . .

ALISON. Daddy, they don't do what I say.

JONATHAN. She's a tyrant.

TOM. STOP! Now please. I've got to go. Mummy will be home soon. Very soon. I've got to go.

Empty hall.

TOM (*self*). *The Empty Hall* . . . A poem by Tom Fairfax. This space awaits us/patient, passive/silent/It's darkness eager/For light and sound and laughter . . .

DEPUTY HEAD (*approaching*). Ah, Tom?

TOM. Deputy Head?

DEPUTY HEAD. Everything ready?

TOM. Hope so.

DEPUTY HEAD. I'm sure it will be very good.

TOM. I't been fun to do.

DEPUTY HEAD. Fun?

TOM. Interesting. You see the pupils themselves begin to discover . . .

DEPUTY HEAD. That was a spirited defence of English literature you put up this afternoon.

TOM. Thank you.

DEPUTY HEAD (*chuckling*). You know, you almost persuaded me that poetry is central to the curriculum.

TOM. It is.

DEPUTY HEAD. Now, Tom, I appreciate your . . . your passion, but be reasonable . . .

TOM. I am being reasonable.

DEPUTY HEAD. Do you know who you sound like?

TOM. Who?

DEPUTY HEAD. The head of classics. Thirty years ago. Ah, good news for you. The school has just invested in a computerised thesaurus.

TOM. 'We are led to believe a *lie*
    When we see not through the eye
    Which was born in a night to perish in a night.'

Pause.

DEPUTY HEAD. Tom, you're a hopeless romantic.

TOM. So was Blake.

DEPUTY HEAD. Who?

TOM. Sorry, Deputy Head, I have to go . . . The Entertainment . . . People are arriving . . .

Voices in an auditorium, orchestra tuning up.

TOM (*urgent*). Black? Where's Black?

BOY. I don't know, sir.

TOM. Has no one seen him?

BOY. He hasn't come past here, sir. Will I use the spot on its own in the prison poem, sir?

TOM. Is that what we decided?

BOY. No, but I thought it might be more effective, sir . . .

TOM. Well, all right then . . .

BOY. And we've found a lovely slide of a tricolour-draped coffin, sir . . .

TOM. Oh good . . . (*Calling out to boys passing.*) Have any of you seen Black?

VOICES. No, sir . . .

BOY. Oh, you'll love it when you see it sir.

TOM. What?

BOY. The coffin, sir. It has everything.

TOM. Someone should ring Black.

BOY. The tricolour, the black gloves, the black beret, an honour guard of girls in black skirts and black tights, very sexy, sir.

TOM. Does anyone know Black's number?

BOY. And of course, sir, the firing party in masks!

TOM. Good.

BOY. I'm going to project it during the funeral poem, sir.

TOM. Yes, good.

HEADMASTER (*approaching*). Mr Fairfax?

TOM. Yes, Headmaster?

HEADMASTER. What's this I hear about Barney Quinn?

TOM. What about him?

HEADMASTER. I've just been told there's a poem by Barney Quinn in the programme.

TOM. But I showed you the poem, Headmaster, I showed you all the poems . . .

HEADMASTER. But you didn't tell me it was by a hunger striker.

TOM. Headmaster, you read it! You didn't object!

HEADMASTER. I didn't know it was by a notorious Republican.

TOM. It's just a poem, three verses of a poem, about being right . . .

HEADMASTER. I don't give a damn what it's about!

TOM. We felt, the cast and I felt, that if the entertainment was to mean anything . . .

HEADMASTER. God, if the Press get hold of this . . .

TOM. . . . the extremist point of view . . .

HEADMASTER (*in horror*). Leading Belfast school features the poems of dead hunger striker Barney Quinn in Christmas Entertainment.

TOM. It's not featured.

HEADMASTER. You do realise what you've done . . . These are the days of falling rolls and open competition, you know . . .

TOM. It's merely a small . . .

HEADMASTER. Our main rivals are packing the parents in with *Joseph and his Technicoloured Dream Coat*.

TOM. It's only twelve lines.

HEADMASTER. Barney Quinn? In my school? With my boys? My God!

TOM. No one will notice, it's just one short poem.

HEADMASTER. CUT IT!

TOM. It's too late.

HEADMASTER. TAKE IT OUT, NOW!

TOM. There isn't time even if I wanted to.

HEADMASTER. YOU ARE A MEMBER OF MY STAFF.
  YOU WILL DO EXACTLY AS YOU ARE TOLD!

DEPUTY HEAD (*approaching*). Headmaster?

TOM. No!

HEADMASTER. I'LL CANCEL THE SHOW. I'LL DO
  IT NOW.

TOM. No you won't.

HEADMASTER. Yes I bloody well . . .

DEPUTY HEAD. Headmaster, please . . . ?

HEADMASTER. WHAT?

DEPUTY HEAD. The Mother Superior and her party . . .

HEADMASTER. WHERE?

DEPUTY HEAD. In the foyer, Head . . .

HEADMASTER. Mr Fairfax, either you . . .

TOM. No one is going to know!

HEADMASTER. Know? Know? Not know?

TOM. The poem could express a loyalist viewpoint, a
  loyalist paramilitary could have said exactly . . .

HEADMASTER. You haven't got them in it too?

TOM. Loyalists?

HEADMASTER. YES!

BOY. Here's Black now, sir.

DEPUTY HEAD. Headmaster, the Mother Superior and
  twenty nuns are on their way through the foyer now . . .

HEADMASTER. ARE THERE LOYALISTS IN IT?

TOM. I gave you the poems, you read them!

BOY. Bleeding, sir.

HEADMASTER. YOU DIDN'T TELL ME THEY WERE
  WRITTEN BY THUGS!

TOM. Black?

BLACK. Yes, sir?

TOM. What happened?

BLACK. I was beaten up, sir.

HEADMASTER. Beaten up? Beaten up? How? Where?

BLACK. Up the Falls Road, sir.

HEADMASTER. What were you doing up the Falls Road?

BLACK. Research, sir.

HEADMASTER. RESEARCH? RESEARCH?

DEPUTY HEAD. Headmaster, Sir Geoffrey and the rest of the board are arrived and the Mother . . .

TOM. What were you doing?

BLACK. I wanted a ride in a black taxi, sir. I wanted to see the deprivation and alienation at first hand. Before the performance, sir.

HEADMASTER. Mr Fairfax, is this more of your . . . ?

DEPUTY HEAD (*desperate*). Headmaster, please.

HEADMASTER (*immediate transformation to impressive unctuousness*). Ah . . . Reverend Mother, Reverend Sisters, welcome to *my* school . . . *this* way please, *this* way . . .

TOM. Are you all right?

BLACK. Oh yes, sir. I can manage . . .

TOM. Come and we'll get you cleaned up . . .

BLACK. I think it was the crown on my blazer pocket sir, and the word Royal . . .

TOM. It was an extremely silly thing to do.

BLACK. But you can understand how they feel about the symbols, sir, when you see the army in action . . .

TOM. Come on, we've got to get you on the stage. Look at the state of you.

Performance of entertainment. Music. Applause.

TOM (*self*). *Faces . . . Faces in an Audience*: a short story by Tom Fairfax. The Headmaster stares at the lit stage. He is

in the centre of the front row and on either side and at his
back sit his invited guests. Beyond that, the audience of
parents, friends, the Press, the merely curious, pack the
school hall. Although part of this audience, the
Headmaster is also on stage. He, too, must now carry off
his part, no matter what. He, too, cannot hide in the
comfortable dark. Though ramrod still, he, too performs.
On his lips, a smile. Of confidence? Of fear? Of delight?
Of embarrassment? Slowly, his tongue licks and moistens
those smiling lips.

Go on Black – give it to them.

BLACK (*performing*).
Today
Belfast's a spoilt brat who hasn't stopped
Grabbing at pre-planned units, well situated
Called 'boutiques', 'storehouses', 'concepts', rarely shops.
These, concrete-floored and faceless and fumigated,
Show sterile squared metres of spotlit range
Each 'Mirage' is floating on the Stock Exchange.

Applause.

TOM (*self*). We're winning. We are winning. Even Sir
Geoffrey Belfast Buzzing Henderson is applauding and
glancing round to see who sees him giving a lead, setting
the tone, the audience is buzzing Sir Geoffrey. The
Headmaster looks almost happy. The smile is almost
genuine. No disasters so far, it says . . . He's forgotten
Barney Quinn.

BLACK (*performing*).
Locked in my cell at night alone
I'm forced to question all I've done
There's no danger that I faced
No risks I took, no fears I taste
No sentence long and lingering
That's hard as this self-questioning.

But when I think that I was wrong
And almost count my cause a crime
I hear the voices of the past
Saying it was always thus
Then in the dark of this foul gaol
There glows a phantom Inisfael.

And then I know that I am right
That I must not give up the fight
But stand where others stood before
And try my courage to its core
And toss my doubts of night away
And wait the dawning of bright day!

Applause.

TOM (*self*). They bought it! They bought it! That boy Black fixed them with his swelling eye and they bought it!

HEADMASTER (*addressing whole audience and cast*). Reverend Mother, Sisters, ladies and gentlemen . . . We have witnessed tonight a group of young people coming together from different backgrounds and traditions to respond to the challenges of their times. I know I speak for everyone here when I say that we of the older generation have been entertained and profoundly moved by the vigour and sincerity of that response. They teach us all a lesson, ladies and gentlemen, and I for one am both humble and proud that this courageous and imaginative venture has taken place in my school and delighted also that it has been such a successfully co-operative venture with St Brigid's, who are our very welcome guests here tonight . . .

Applause.

Bedroom – door – TOM getting into bed, etc.

TOM. You awake? Sally?

SALLY (*sleepily*). Yes?

TOM. Thank God you're here.

SALLY (*sleepy*). What?

TOM. You came back.

SALLY. Oh . . . Yes . . . Sorry . . .

TOM. What happened?

SALLY. What?

TOM. Earlier?

SALLY. Oh, how did it go?

TOM. What?

SALLY. The Entertainment?

TOM. Oh, fine . . . great . . . The Headmaster made a speech
. . .

SALLY (*sleepily*). Oh, good . . .

TOM. Sally, why were you breaking the furniture?

SALLY. What?

TOM. When I came home you weren't there. The children
said you'd been smashing chairs. Sally love, what was
happening?

SALLY. It was Gary.

TOM. Gary?

SALLY. He kept getting his spellings wrong.

TOM. But smashing chairs, love?

SALLY. All the ones he'd got right before! Thought and
bought and ought. He'd got them all right yesterday and
here he was . . .

TOM. Shhhhhhhh

SALLY (*spelling*). CAWT . . . CAWT! Suddenly I wanted to
shout!

TOM. Love, it's twelve-thirty.

SALLY. He'd got them right yesterday and he's been so
proud and I was so happy . . . I was just checking . . .
confirming . . . Starting positively . . . caught – CAWT! I
wanted to scream caught, caught, caught!

TOM. And you blame me for shouting at him?

SALLY. I blame you for not being there.

TOM. I had a curriculum review meeting . . .

SALLY. And on he went – TAWT . . . FOWT . . .

TOM. Literature is to be removed as a separate subject on
the curric . . .

SALLY. Not just one or two here and there Tom, the whole
lot, all yesterday's, all the spellings for tomorrow's test, all
fifty of them!

TOM. Don't cry, love . . .

SALLY. SOWT . . . NAWT . . . and to stop myself shouting I
began crumpling up pieces of paper and on and on he went,
OWT . . . BAWT . . . THAWT and suddenly I was banging
the chair on the floor. Tom, I was trying to break the chair,
smashing it up and down and he was looking at me, those
big innocent eyes full of wonder at what they were seeing
. . . Mummy was going mad! . . . And I paused, the chair in
the air, up above my head, ready to split it finally in
smithereens and in waltzed the bloody builder, looking for
his no tax deductible cheque made out to the Craigantlet
Racing Pigeon Club and I . . . Oh, Tom, I ran, I ran . . . I
swore at the builder and ran and ran and . . .

TOM. It's all right, love, it's all right . . .

SALLY. I'm sorry.

TOM. No, I'm sorry . . .

SALLY. When I came back they said you'd gone and I
remembered that this was the night of the Entertainment
and I felt doubly guilty . . .

TOM. I'm going to spend more time here, love . . . I promise
. . . More time with Gary . . .

SALLY. What about plays?

TOM. I've just done the last one.

SALLY. The Curriculum Review Committee?

TOM. I'm resigning.

SALLY. Promotion?

TOM. The ESRSMT?

SALLY. Yes.

TOM. I've blown that. They think I'm a hopeless romantic.
I've no chance. Tomorrow I shall tell them to stuff it
before they tell me I'm not wanted . . .

SALLY. Gary wrote more of his poem.

TOM. Why? Why does he do it? It's gibberish.

SALLY. He does it for you.

TOM. I just find it embarrassing.

SALLY. He knows poetry impresses you, Tom.

TOM. If he would only learn to spell!

SALLY. I think I've worked out some of it. The words are strange . . . there, look.

TOM. Could be . . .

SALLY. Oh look at it, Tom.

TOM. I said you could be right.

SALLY. I think this word is know . . .

TOM. Sally, supposing the boys and I were to do some of the labouring . . . for the builder . . . evenings, weekends . . . We could reduce costs, speed things up. Good for them. And I would enjoy it.

SALLY (*dubious*). Would you?

TOM. Oh God, yes. I would love to work with my hands for a while.

SALLY. Tom, it's you they need – not some bloody role-player.

TOM. This isn't role-playing.

SALLY. They don't need a play producer, they don't need a committee member, they don't need a poetry teacher – they need you!

TOM. And they shall get me Sally – I shall muck in. Get my hands dirty. Do something that's going to last, that you can see. Abandon school for a while, mentally erase it, abandon it to its fate and use my body.

SALLY. It is 'know'. The words are strange/I do not know them . . . Tom, this makes sense . . .

TOM (*self*). *Integrity*, a short story by Tom Fairfax. . . . Tom's books were roped in boxes. He did not untie the knots, not yet. He had his integrity and it seemed to him that this labouring was a metaphor for his dogged refusal to compromise. Others might be promoted, he told himself as he levered the shovel against his knee, but he had his integrity . . .

Headmaster's study.

HEADMASTER. Just look at the morning press. 'Top schools join in courageous new venture.' Big photograph.

Look, you can just see the top of your head. Not a bad pic of me with the Mother Superior. My speech in full. Marvellous stuff, Mr Fairfax. I need hardly tell you what this sort of publicity does for the school. I gave the chairman a piece of my mind afterwards, I can tell you. Told him straight that all his doubts were misplaced. He was very pleased and asked me to pass on his warmest congratulations. How's that boy, by the way?

TOM. Black? Oh, he's fine.

HEADMASTER. Bit too enthusiastic for his own good.

TOM. Yes.

HEADMASTER. But Sir Geoffrey felt he was so sincere.

TOM. Yes.

HEADMASTER. Thought the make-up clever too (*Laughs.*)

TOM *laughs*.

Perhaps we shouldn't laugh.

TOM. No.

HEADMASTER. It might have been serious.

TOM. Yes.

HEADMASTER. Make sure it doesn't happen again. Oh, the Minister's secretary was on the phone. Wants you to address a Conference on Education for Mutual Understanding . . . Now business. The Ministry have set up a series of in-service courses on the management of schools. Implications of the latest legislation, you understand. Each secretary is to send one member of staff to the first course. I'm sending you.

TOM. Why?

HEADMASTER. Why?

TOM. Yes . . . why?

HEADMASTER. Because I'm appointing you as our new ESRSMT.

TOM. But the Deputy Head?

HEADMASTER. I make the appointments in my school, Mr Fairfax. You've made an astute move, you know. Management is going to expand. Management is a growth

industry in education and you are in on the ground floor
. . . There's no telling where you will end . . . No telling,
Mr Fairfax . . .

Staff room.

JIM. Congratulations, Tom.

TOM. Thank you, Jim.

STUART. Knew you would do it, Tom.

TOM. Did you, Stuart?

ARTHUR. Well done, Tom.

TOM. Thanks, Arthur.

JIM. You know why, of course.

TOM. Why?

JIM. I should have thought it was obvious.

TOM. No.

ARTHUR. Drawn your teeth, old man.

STUART. We've just been discussing it, Tom.

JIM. Only explanation that makes sense . . . wants to stifle
your objections to the reduction of English literature in
the curriculum . . .

TOM. But I still object.

STUART. But you're on the committee . . .

TOM. I'm in a stronger position . . .

ARTHUR. You're management, now . . .

JIM. Dangerous radical joins establishment . . .

TOM. No I haven't . . .

JIM. Wants you inside the tent pissing out . . .

STUART. Reduced timetable means less subversion in the
classroom . . .

JIM. Rather than on the outside of the tent pissing in . . .

TOM. Rubbish, I'm . . .

ARTHUR. Nullified you in a stroke . . .

TOM. No!

STUART. Well, congratulations.

JIM. You deserved it . . .

ARTHUR. An office of your own . . .

STUART. With an in-tray and an out-tray . . .

JIM. Silence . . .

ARTHUR. Bliss . . .

STUART. You can write that novel.

TOM. What novel?

JIM. The one you were always going to write . . .

STUART. In between committee meetings . . .

ARTHUR. Between the in-tray and the out-tray . . .

JIM. On your reduced timetable . . .

Quad. Boys.

TOM (*self*). Tom looked the committee straight in the eye
and said 'I . . .' And said 'I . . .' And said 'I want to make
my position absolutely clear . . . at the outset . . . so there
shall be no misunderstanding . . . none . . . absolutely . . .'

BLACK (*approaching*). Hello, sir.

TOM. Black?

BLACK. We shook them, sir.

TOM. We did. How are your injuries?

BLACK. Fine, sir. Nothing, sir.

TOM. Oh good.

BLACK. I was thinking, sir . . .

TOM. What, Black?

BLACK. There's a special Irish option in the literary course
. . . The Poetry of the Dispossessed . . . Any chance of us
dipping into it, sir?

TOM. I don't know.

BLACK. Personally I think it would be fascinating . . .

TOM. I won't be teaching you next term.

BLACK. Why not, sir?

TOM. Reduced timetable. I've been promoted.
  Administration.

BLACK. You, sir?

TOM. Yes me, Black.

BLACK. But you couldn't administer anything, sir.

  Pause.

TOM. Thank you for that vote of confidence.

BLACK. You're a teacher, sir.

TOM. I know.

BLACK. You should be teaching.

TOM. If I am on the inside I may be able to minimise the
  worst effects of these reforms. I mean to do that.

BLACK. Of course, sir.

TOM. I mean to carry the fight straight into the enemy
  camp, Black. All guns blazing.

BLACK. But are you not in the enemy camp sir?

TOM. What?

BLACK. Well, have you not joined the other side?

TOM. No.

BLACK. Establishment man, sir?

TOM. No, Black, no.

  Kitchen.

JONATHAN. Hello Dad?

TOM. Jonathan.

ALISON. Hello, Dad. Gary got thirty-five out of fifty for
  his spellings.

TOM. Oh, that's good.

ALISON. Well, good for him.

TOM. It's just good, Alison.

JONATHAN. Did you get the job, Dad?

TOM. Yes, I did.

ALISON. Did you?

TOM. Yes.

JONATHAN. Well, that *is* just good.

TOM. Thank you, Jonathan.

ALISON. Is there more money with it?

TOM. Yes, there is.

SALLY (*entering*). Tom?

TOM. Sally love . . .

JONATHAN. Mummy, Dad got the job.

SALLY. Did you?

TOM. Yes.

SALLY. But I thought . . .

TOM. So did I.

SALLY. But, Tom, that's marvellous.

TOM. The irony of it is that it was the Entertainment that clinched it.

SALLY. But I thought . . .

TOM. So did I . . .

ALISON. Well, all I can say is that I will now be able to look Julie straight in the eye.

TOM *and* SALLY. WHAT?

ALISON. We can now afford our builders and I shall be able to say 'It won't break the bank'.

SALLY. Have you no homework to do, Madame?

ALISON. I have always homework to do.

SALLY. Well, go and do it!

ALISON (*exiting*). Charming . . .

JONATHAN. I've a new book out of the library, Dad.

TOM. Good.

JONATHAN. It's about dinosaurs. I'll go and get it, shall I?

TOM. You do that . . .

SALLY. Tom, Gary has . . .

TOM. I know, thirty-five out of fifty, that's very good. He's definitely improving, he's going to make it.

SALLY. Forget about the bloody spellings, read this . . .

TOM. What?

SALLY. His poem. Gary's poem.

TOM. Not more of it?

SALLY. I translated it.

TOM. Translated?

SALLY. Well, I began to guess the meanings, see through the mis-spellings, the misplaced letters, some of them were upside down, you know, back to front and when I began to make sense of it, I got him to read it to me. Why didn't we do that, Tom? We just assumed it was nonsense because it looked like nonsense and we were no longer interested. I copied it out. Here . . .

TOM (*reads*).
The words are strange
I do not know them
They are not friends with me . . .

SALLY. Read on.

TOM (*reads*).
When I say hello
They vanish
When I come close
They hide
Why do they chat
To other people
And never, never speak to me?

I long to know
What 'tis they're saying
If only they would wait
Then I'd have time
To catch a meaning
Before it is too late

But the words are strange
I do not know them
They are not friends with me

SALLY. Well.

Pause.

GARY (*entering*). Hello, Dad. I got thirty-five out of fifty in
my . . .

TOM. It's a wonderful poem, Gary. A wonderful poem. Oh
God, Gary son, I've been blind . . . and DEAF. Deaf to
my own son. Oh Gary . . . Gary . . . Sally, don't you see
that poetry . . . that poetry is . . . is the most (*Pause.*) . . . I
am going to fight them . . . I am. I *am*.

GARY. What's wrong, Dad?

TOM. Oh nothing, nothing . . . Read me your poem son,
read me your poem.

CARVER

by John Purser

to Stuart Conn

John Purser is a Scottish composer, writer and broadcaster, born in Glasgow in 1942. He has published three books of poetry – *The Counting Stick*, *A Share Of The Wind* and *Amoretti*. Other publications include a study of *The Literary Works Of Jack B. Yeats*, and his recent radio series and book, *Scotland's Music*, have been widely acclaimed. *Carver* is his fourth radio play to be commissioned by BBC Radio Scotland, winning the gold medal in the Best Drama Special category at the 1991 New York International Radio Festival.

Robert Carver, from whom the play *Carver* takes its name, was a Scottish composer born in the 1480s, who died sometime after 1565. His music survives in one manuscript, much of which was written in his own hand. All the music heard in the play is by Carver.

The action takes place at Stirling castle and Dunkeld, between the years 1541 and 1559, during the reign of James V and the regency of his widow, Marie de Guise; but Carver's active life had also covered the reign of James IV, who was killed at the Battle of Flodden – a disastrous defeat for the Scots at the hands of the English which placed James V on the throne when he was still a baby. Carver's ten-part mass was performed at the hastily organised coronation.

James V himself died of melancholia. His two sons had died in infancy and the birth of a daughter, following his ignoble defeat by the English at Solway Moss, did nothing to relieve his depression. The daughter was the future Mary Queen of Scots.

Despite these reverses, the Scottish court was one of the great Renaissance Courts of Europe, excelling in poetry, enjoying the magnificent architectural achievements of James IV and V, and employing up to sixty-nine musicians. It was served by the Chapel Royal choir which, on the evidence of Carver's music, must have been among the most accomplished in Europe, for his music is technically very demanding but clearly confident of the effects that could be achieved.

Through most of Carver's life the forces that led to the reformation in Scotland were increasingly felt. His main antagonist in the play, Alan Richardson, was an historical figure and a reformer. Like Carver, he was an Augustinian canon, but he disapproved of elaborate church music, and his criticisms of it are quoted in the play.

Of Carver's own life very little is known. He may have been a baillie for the town of Stirling; he may have had three sons. In the play he is closely involved with three fictitious characters – his concubine Margaret; her son Davie who sings in the Chapel Royal Choir which Carver conducts; and Carver's own sister, Isobel.

Carver, commissioned by BBC Radio Scotland, was first
broadcast simultaneously on BBC Radio Scotland and on
BBC Radio 3 as the 'Sunday Play' on 31 March 1991. The
cast was as follows:

ROBERT CARVER	Tom Fleming
MARGARET	Anne Kristen
ARMOURER/ANDREW	Iain Agnew
ISOBEL	Hilary MacLean
ALAN RICHARDSON	Benny Young
MARIE DE GUISE	Anne Lacey
JAMES V	James Bryce
DAVIE	Kenneth Glenaan
ALEX KYD	Paul Hickey
STEVIE	Gary Bakewell
PETER	Stevie Hannan
JAMES	Stuart Bowman

Director: Stewart Conn
Running time, as broadcast: 100 mins

The music sung by The Taverner Consort, directed by
Andrew Parrott

The time is summer and then autumn of 1542, winter 1543
and summer 1559. The action takes place at Stirling Castle
and Dunkeld.

Note:
The following play reinstates cuts made for broadcast.
Therefore, neither the choirboy Graham nor the man
Duncan, appear in the cast list above.

Author's note:
I would like to acknowledge the generous and scholarly
assistance of Dr Isobel Woods, whose knowledge of Robert
Carver and his music is unrivalled. However, I have
knowingly ignored some information and have invented a
great deal. The play is a mixture of fiction and fact, but I
believe all of it to be historically plausible. Both Carver and
Richardson are historical figures. All the music used is
Carver's. The quotations from Richardson's *Commentary* are
genuine – as is his employment by Henry VIII, though I
have pushed it forward by a year so as to bring him and
James V into contact. With the notable exception of Marie de
Guise, the female parts are fictitious. So too is Davie. But
Carver was possibly the natural son of a bishop, and he had
three sons of his own whom he legitimised, so he must have
had somebody close to him to bear his children. His five-part
Mass may have been written in memory of one of his sons
who may have died in a plague epidemic. I have replaced this
possibility with related ideas of my own, but otherwise all
references to the occasions which may have prompted his
music, or details within it, are based on scholarship rather
than fancy.

Stirling. August 1542

Opening of 'O Bone Jesu'. Then music fades to scratching quill on vellum. Small room acoustic. CARVER *yawns, turns vellum pages.*

CARVER (*hums a phrase from 'O Bone Jesu'. Spoken*). 'O bone Jesu . . .' (*With surprise.*) I wrote that. (*Slowly with veneration.*) 'O dulcissime Jesu.' It's good. Huh, we had some larks in the trebles then – none of your pet spent sparrows. (*Scratching quill.*) What's the date? (*Scrabbles among papers. Announcing it.*) August the 7th, 1542, Stirling Castle. The feast of the name of Jesus. Is that what drew me back to it? (*Hums. More scratching of quill.*)

Armourer outside, hammering metal.

(*To self.*) That time already? The morning hymn of the world . . . an armourer turning ploughshares into swords. How can I compose a Dona Nobis Pacem with that vile trade hammering in my ears?

ARMOURER (*singing, bringing hammering into rhythm with it*). L'homme, l'homme, l'homme arme. L'homme arme. L'homme arme doit on douter . . .

CARVER. This is too much. (*He gets off chair and opens window rapidly.*) War-monger! Tin-smith!

ARMOURER (*shouting from a distance*). Did I wake ye from your devotional slumbers?

CARVER (*still shouting*). Blasphemer! (*To himself.*) No. That's not fair. (*Triumphantly.*) Bastard son of a diseased charcoal-burner and a tinker whore!

ARMOURER (*also triumphantly*). Look to your own

parentage – a sot of a bag-bellied bishop and a woman wi'
her arse in the air and the birds fallin' oot o' it for the
stench!

CARVER. Pax! Pax! Ah . . . Margaret. Thirty years I have
had to work next to an armourer's yard and I still can't
thole it.

MARGARET. Be fair Robert. He works in the day-time and
you mostly work at night.

CARVER. That's not true . . .

MARGARET. And that song he sings . . . you told me you
used it in a mass once, so you owe him . . .

CARVER. I didn't need *him* to sing it to me. We used to
howl it out in the streets of Louvain in my student days.
That song's hundreds of years old – besides it's filth . . .
pure filth . . . l'homme arme . . . ah Maggie, your man is
still well armed, am I not?

MARGARET. Get your hands off me, you're covered in
ink. Filth on your fingers, filth on your mind – even filth
in your music. How can you put a song like that in a work
for the glory of God?

CARVER. It was long ago. Everyone on the continent used
to do it – Dufay, all the best ones.

MARGARET. Well you don't all have to relieve yourselves
in the same nettle patch.

CARVER. It was dedicated to the Pope, no less. 'Cum
armorum insigniis.' All for war. Ha-ha. We lost. So much
for that crusade.

MARGARET. It's just such things that give that crabbit
Richardson his sense of virtue. What good is a dedication
to the Pope when Richardson's here to preach against him
. . . he'll corner you in the end.

CARVER. It's my sister Isobel he fancies cornering – if he
can get in there before our dear King.

MARGARET. It's not nice to speak of your sister like that.

More singing. CARVER *goes to window.*

CARVER. Stop your braying you flop-eared jackass!

ARMOURER. For a goose-feathered gut-bag – scrabblin' at

good vellum like an old rat? Your times are past! Give way
to the music o' war! (*Hammering*.)

CARVER (*shuts window*). That was good. He's on form
today!

MARGARET. I can't understand you, Robert. You're a
laughing-stock. And what bothers me is the world doesn't
know what a fine person you can be: what's your music to
them if all they hear is obscene shoutings at a coarse
tradesman?

CARVER. That man is the artist of war. There's nothing he
can't make from a dirk to a coat of mail fit for a bishop.
He's my counterpart – my other half . . .

MARGARET. I'm your other half and if you want your
breakfast you'd better eat it now.

CARVER. It smells of piss.

MARGARET. That's the kidneys. They're good for you.

CARVER. They're tasty bits . . . where did you get them?

MARGARET. Davie netted them this morning at sun-up –
and you needn't look at me like that, I know he was meant
to be with the choir but it was so lovely out.

CARVER. His voice has broken anyway . . .

MARGARET. I took a turn on the walls after he'd gone and
watched him far below . . . him and the dog, away away
below on the green, and all the rabbits casting such long
shadows from their wee brown sunlit bodies . . . that's
where Davie's happiest – not trilling in your precious choir.

CARVER. He shows promise to be a fine tenor.

MARGARET. Promise? What promise is there for a poor
daft boy? 'God has blessed him with innocence.' That's
what your father the bishop used to say of his like . . . If
that's God's blessing Davie would've done better with His
curse. You don't care do you?

CARVER. What can I say that I haven't said before? He's
blessed with a beautiful voice for singing – though you
wouldn't think it from the way he speaks – am I supposed
to ignore it?

MARGARET. You gave John and Thomas your name a year

past November, why not give Davie your name too? Your
uncle that had the twist in him, he was daft too.

CARVER. You remember him? He had his arm hanging
down from him like a broken wing and he used to chitter
away like a pet sparrow. I was fond of him.

MARGARET. Then why not our Davie?

CARVER. You know well I love Davie. It's not that.

MARGARET. You love him for his singing voice, that's all
you ever loved him for. And the boy's so loyal to you.
Have you any idea what it would mean to him? It isn't
fair. I sometimes think it'd be better for him if he'd never
been born.

CARVER. It would be a lie. You know well enough that my
blood never went into the making of him – you got him
off Matthew when I was away at Falkland. You blush
because it's true. Well, what do I care, it was long ago –
fourteen years – and the boy's a treasure to me. My father
was right. God has blessed his kind with innocence and he
has a right to peck at the same corn as his half-brothers:
but I can't legitimise him when he didn't come of my
crowing.

*Fade in several distant male voices in a church. Scraping of
chairs, footsteps on stone, receding.*

ISOBEL. Alan Richardson! You should not be holding my
hand in the kirk!

RICHARDSON. True, I forgot myself. I wish they'd get on
with this. The music's far too elaborate – self-indulgent. It
takes an hour to sing a mass. Ridiculous. They should give
their time to more serious studies.

ISOBEL. Like holding hands? And why must you take
against my brother's music? The King and Queen think
well of it . . .

RICHARDSON. I serve King Henry the Eighth – not some
provincial monarchy.

ISOBEL. You're a Scot. You shouldn't speak of your own
country like that.

RICHARDSON. One day, when we're married, Isobel, I'll

take you to England and to France. Then you'll
understand.

ISOBEL. I'd love that. But I don't suppose it'll ever happen.

RICHARDSON. And why not?

ISOBEL (*suddenly despressed*). Robert . . . other things.
Robert's music is beginning. Look, the Queen has come in
to hear it too . . .

We hear a passage from 'O Bone Jesu'.

MARIE DE GUISE. What do you think of this music?

Music repeated, but this time in background.

RICHARDSON. Madam, I think better of the music in
Notre Dame where they have simplified the service. Even
here we can learn from our greater neighbours.

MARIE DE GUISE (*slowly and deliberately, educating him.
Accent still French*). That is not how it used to be, nor how
I wish to think of it. But I have lived in France longer than
you, I think, and I can tell you that, small as this place is,
it can achieve great things – and this music is one of them.

ISOBEL. I think it is beautiful.

RICHARDSON. You have no experience of other places.
Nothing to compare it with.

MARIE DE GUISE. Ah, Richardson, you are a theorist
only, are you not? One day you will learn how to visit
your own country and you will be astonished then by
what you find. Think of who I am . . . there are plenty in
France and Europe who would happily have married a De
Guise – but I accepted Scotland, even by proxy, and I will
show you where honour and devotion is due . . . I see
your love is already . . . how shall I say . . . engaged?

Music ends. Footsteps, one set approaches.

Graham! come and speak with us . . . this cannot be easy
music to sing?

GRAHAM. Oh, yer majesty, we've bin workin' at it fur
weeks; ah'm fair buggert wi' praisin' the Lord . . .

MARIE DE GUISE *hoots with laughter.*

RICHARDSON. Such language is a disgrace.

MARIE DE GUISE. Excuse us. It is so comical . . . and no doubt very true . . .

Fade out on her laughing.
Fade in general talk of choir: men and boys.

CARVER. I'm proud of you all. You are the rocks I chisel!

GRAHAM. Ye've cut us mighty fine, Sir Robert. Ye'll no' get much more off o' us – we missed ye Davie on the Treble.

CARVER. You sing it well enough – after all there's few of us left now from the old days. Hands up who remembers. Three? Ah well: thirty years ago. No. It's fine, fine . . . now you must learn to sing it with feeling. James the Fourth offered this music to the memory of his father. A penance. You boys are too young to know. He wore a chain round his waist and added a link to it every year. It was quite heavy when he died. Remorse. Ah! remorse is terrible. But we should all feel it. Remorse for the suffering of Christ. (*He speaks the Latin pointedly to remind them of what they have been singing.*) O Bone Jesu. O Dulcissime Jesu!

A boy snickers.

CARVER. Who was that? Who snickered at the Holy Name? Alexander! You'll get a whipping for this! Don't you dare run away! (*As we hear Alex run off.*) Davie, let go of me.

DAVIE. He's feart.

CARVER. Let go of me!

DAVIE. He and me. We're friends. He's nice tae me. Naebuddy else is nice tae me. Dinnae whip him.

CARVER (*with sudden anxiety*). Am I not kind to you? (*Pause.*) Is everyone here terrifed of me?

Fade. Pause.

Into small room acoustic. 'L'Homme Arme' whistled heard from outside. Scratch of quill which stops suddenly.

CARVER. Damnation take it! That's my last quill! Davie!

DAVIE (*coming forward*). Ay. Whit do ye want?

CARVER. Go to the yard and pull me some goose feathers.

DAVIE. An dinnae like tae pull them. No' unless they're deid. It hurts them ye ken.

CARVER. They'll grow others Davie, and it only hurts them for a second. One good quill will write a lot of music. Mind and just pull them from the left wings. Which is your left, Davie?

DAVIE. This yin. Ah ken left and right fine.

CARVER. Which is it on a goose?

DAVIE. Thon's easy. Left o' it goin' forward an' me chasin' it.

CARVER. Good lad.

DAVIE. See thae geese that flies over and gaes wheep wheep wheep wi' their wings. One o' thae would be better. Thae feathers would be right tough and strong.

CARVER. Well, Davie, you grow wings and catch one.

DAVIE. Ah'm no sae stupid. You'd tak the feathers aff ae me. So ye would. 'Sides. Ah can catch thae geese oot on the flats below nae bother.

CARVER. I need a quill *now*, Davie. I can't wait for a migration.

DAVIE. Ah'll go, but ah dinnae like.

CARVER. Shake a little sand here where the ink has spread and put the rest on the fire to heat. (*Pause.*) That's good. Now, on you go. (*Pause.*) I suppose I could take a look at Richardson's damned book.

Gaggle of geese protesting from outside.

(*Quietly to himself.*) 'Hoc plane est contra istos, qui novas introducunt missas peculiares iuxta phantasias factas.' (*Exploding.*) Phantasias! I'll give him fancies! This is dog-shit Latin. He misreads Augustine. Tells me my masses are fancies . . . frivolities . . . vain delights. (*Sudden giggle to himself.*) I know why . . . because his own dog-shit mind is so close to the ground, when he looks up all he can see is arse-holes! (*Sniffs and exhales, then continues reading.*) 'Cantus *alius* commendabilis etiam . . . et illius venerabilis viri est domini Alexandri Patersonen sacrarii Regalis

collegii Stirlingen.' – He praises Paterson? . . . hmm . . .
hm . . . no mention of me . . . just as well . . . but
Paterson? That wrinkle-pricked prune? The man
practically sterilised the Chapel Royal. I suppose that's
Richardson's style.

*Sudden explosion of geese outside. Pause. 'L'Homme Arme'
whistled.*

(*Wearily.*) Why bother. Why do I bother my heart?
(*Listing them off.*) I glorify God, I love Christ, I honour
the Holy Virgin. I do these things in truth . . . well . . .
maybe not always in my life . . . but in my music, I do . . .
and what's my reward? It's to see the road in front of me
covered by these shapeless bits of excrement, gathering
praise round themselves like clegs. (*Pause.*) I wonder does
God really listen? (*Calls.*) God? Ah Davie, you've the
quills? Bring the sand over here. It should be hot enough,
and my pen knife . . . where is it?

DAVIE. Ouch!

CARVER. Did you burn yourself?

DAVIE. Aye! That was hot!

CARVER. Here, hold it with a rag. (*Pause.*) Davie, what do
   you think it'll be like when you reach heaven?

DAVIE (*firmly, a little defensive*). There a door.

CARVER. And what do you do? Do you knock on it?

DAVIE. Naw.

CARVER. You just wait?

DAVIE. Ay. Ah wait. An' ah catch rabbits. Lots o' rabbits
   there.

CARVER. D'you think the door'll open for you if you don't
   knock?

DAVIE. Naw. But ah'll slip in wi' some other body and
   they'll no see me. I hope there willna be geese there.
   There'll be nae gettin' in if there's geese . . . They're that
   watchful.

Intimate curtained acoustic: MARIE DE GUISE's
bedchamber.

MARIE DE GUISE (*waking*). James? . . . il est tard . . . I am half asleep.

JAMES V. You keep your room too warm. I am in a bad mood.

MARIE DE GUISE. Was your father so 'moody' as you say.

JAMES V (*irritable*). My father, my father! . . . God rot all Roberts!

MARIE DE GUISE (*yawning*). Robert who? Your father was James the Fourth King of Scots, not a Robert. Are you all right? . . . is it necessary that you put your boots on my bed?

JAMES V. I told you. I'm in a bad mood.

MARIE DE GUISE. Ah! Let me guess. Our friend back from France . . . that odious Richardson, is to marry your Isobel and you are jealous? But he is called Alan . . .

JAMES V. I don't know who you are speaking of . . . but it's nonsense.

MARIE DE GUISE. I do not distress myself with your amours . . . your kingly duties . . . your droits de seigneur . . . If I had to yield to all your desiring I'd be as dry as a stockfish for you! But this girl has made you jealous: perhaps I should be jealous too?

JAMES V. It's that man Carver, Robert Carver – your confessor – your not-very-ghostly confessor. I told him that I did not want and I do not need a new sung mass. The Chapel Royal must yield to the Parish Church. It is the way things are going. So then he asked me for more money for more voices. They cannot sing *O Bone Jesu* without nineteen voices. Nineteen! Where is the money to come from for nineteen voices? Want want want. My father is dead. There should be nothing left – even that crawls. But here is your confessor and he crawls in the old carcass looking for honey in my father's entrails, I am not my father's keeper. How can I be expected to keep the remnants of his household on top of mine. I have built palaces, tennis courts . . .

MARIE DE GUISE. They are to sing *O Bone Jesu* at my request. I am paying for it personally. I thought you would be pleased. It was written for your father, was it not? It was his prayer. We must keep his memory as he kept the memory of his own father with that chain he wore.

JAMES V. You dare to remind me of that? Have I not chains enough that you must add more links? He was guilty. Guilty. Does that satisfy you? My own father whom I never knew. I was a baby when he died, fighting fights for the French against the English. Am I to do penance for that, or should it not be YOU? Get me sons you useless Frenchwoman. Get me sons. They can do penance for ME.

MARIE DE GUISE (*very quietly*). I have got you sons.

JAMES V (*cruelly*). Get me sons that live!

MARIE DE GUISE. Have I not suffered enough that you must reproach me with this? You are hurting me . . . my first husband gave me healthy sons – and what joy have I had of them? All I have is a piece of string sent to me to show me how tall they'd grown. For you I have given all. Look at me! What do you think that I have done with my grief? I have had no one. No one to comfort me but my confessor. I did not dare ask YOU. You have too many worries.

JAMES V. Why do our sons not live?

MARIE DE GUISE. All I know is a great emptiness.

JAMES V. My love. Forgive me! I have twisted your hair in my hand. Your sweet scented hair. Forgive me. It's not easy for me either. Love me Marie. Love me.

MARIE DE GUISE. God help me. I do. And I will.

JAMES V. I have hurt you!

MARIE DE GUISE. Only a little. It is good to feel your hands in my hair.

November 1542

Autumn woods. Sound of distant axe on tree. Occasional bird calls – robin, wren, blackbird. CARVER *and* ISOBEL *walking.*

CARVER. They're beautiful, these Dunkeld woods; I am glad you and Richardson persuaded me to come with you.

I will try to like him. He's an upright man . . . more than that . . . truthful. That is worth much.

ISOBEL. Worth more than me . . . the rowans have held the berries late this year . . . I don't think I've ever seen them so plentiful.

CARVER. It means a hard winter ahead.

ISOBEL. Let's go back.

CARVER. Wait awhile. It's only when the sun goes that you can see the real colours of the trees in the dusk . . . that fine mesh of purple is the twigs of the birch: and those arthritic old fingers are the ash trees: and then there's the grey smoke branches of the rowan and the hazels. Isobel . . . what is it you are longing to share with me but cannot?

ISOBEL. It's nothing . . .

CARVER. A sister should be able to speak to her own brother. You don't usually care for walking, but you chose to come with me . . .

ISOBEL. It is the King. He has stolen me from Alan . . . he has slept with me . . .

CARVER. Aaah. I thought as much.

ISOBEL. And now he's had his taste of me, he's spat me out . . . but he still wants to parade me as Eve in some play or court foolery, and the hell is that I still want to do it for him.

CARVER. So you are his creature – at his beck and call?

ISOBEL. I'm more than that. I'm carrying his creature.

CARVER. What do you mean?

ISOBEL. I'm carrying his bairn . . . he has no heirs . . . maybe the son of the King . . . Robert, I'm terrified . . . and then sometimes I feel so important . . .

CARVER. How can you be proud of such a thing? He has bastards everywhere.

ISOBEL (*in tears of desperation*). What else can I be? What else if not proud?

CARVER. D'you think you're the first he has tinkered with? You were not favoured. You were abused.

ISOBEL. Must you be so cruel? (*Pause.*) What am I to say to him?

CARVER. To the King? Tell him of course. He'll pay.

ISOBEL. To Alan, I mean. What am I to say? You'll tell him, won't you Robert?

CARVER. Tell Richardson? I'm the last person to do it . . . you must tell him yourself, and unless I'm mistaken in him he'll have no more to do with you . . . but if you were able to betray him so easily you can't have cared for him that much.

ISOBEL. That's not true. I love him. He is a good man . . . too good . . . I . . . I needed love, Robert . . . not just words and holding hands. Alan is . . . well . . .

CARVER. When is the child expected?

ISOBEL. I don't know. Maybe in March.

CARVER. A bitter time of year to come into the world. Make it April or May if you can.

ISOBEL. Don't tease me Robert, not now.

CARVER. Not even a wisp of a smile out of you?

Sound of stream comes into foreground.

I used to take Davie here to guddle trout.

ISOBEL. I know. He showed me once. He was so quick: and as quiet as a cat. You and Maggie have been wonderful to him – you've done so much for him.

CARVER. No: no. I never have enough time.

ISOBEL. Look! I see one! That shadow there, just where the water's still.

CARVER. That's his home. In under the bank and his holidays behind a stone waiting to catch flies.

ISOBEL. If only our own lives were so simple.

CARVER. Yes. Better than being eaten by remorse.

More sound of stream.

ISOBEL. D'you think if I could find someone to take my child, then Alan would marry me?

CARVER. Marry? Marry? I never married Maggie. I just loved her. But I suppose Richardson would want a marriage. He puts chastity before charity . . . a pity that. But if Christ could say 'Go and sin no more' maybe Richardson could too.

ISOBEL. I don't want him to say 'go'. I want him to take me, not to send me away. He's not as you see him. He'll pity me. Surely he'll forgive me . . .

The stream is still just audible, but the axe on the tree is heard again, this time closer.
Cross fade. Tolling of a light bell which continues through the first few exchanges.

RICHARDSON. You should come to France! You'd think nothing of Dunkeld if you saw the cathedrals at Rheims and Notre Dame.

CARVER. I don't want to think nothing of Dunkeld.

RICHARDSON. Misplaced pride, Robert.

CARVER. You forget I've been to Louvain, Bruges, many such places.

RICHARDSON. But the world knows of Louvain . . . Paris . . . Rheims. Who has heard of little dull Dunblane? As for Dunkeld, what is it but a coarse pile of stones in a place that's no more than a gutter for the rain from the mountains.

CARVER. You're saying this to anger me.

RICHARDSON. I'm saying it because it's true.

CARVER. No it's not true. That 'coarse pile of stones' is a greater act of worship than Rheims and Notre Dame put together. Where were the fertile fields, the dripping udders, the fat ducks – huh – or the licentious lords to fund this great edifice? Little we had. Much we gave.

RICHARDSON. It's a poor thing nonetheless.

CARVER. There's poverty only in the spirit that says so. A gutter for the mountains? It's a chalice for the tears of heaven. Saint Kevin said the mountains were creatures too. Then great must be their patience; bearing their sorrows and discomforts with simplicity. Dunkeld is built with that same simplicity. I have been a builder – I know *why* it was done. Yes, it's gaunt. And full of nobility.

RICHARDSON. You're eloquent in its defence . . . but the hills oppress me. It is as though there were always the threat of a suffocating snow. I'm glad to be free of them. When I hear the heather sigh in a gust, or the mewing of a buzzard, I feel fear. Give me the sun; the sun.

CARVER. Oh-ho. Sun-worship! That is an old idolatry.

RICHARDSON. I do not worship . . . I rejoice merely in God's beneficence.

CARVER. Well God has been known to smile on Scotland too – and if He's manifest in nature then we here know more of his moods than any soul in France. I prefer the cold North. I do not fancy nature leading me by the hand to a rotten plum tree.

RICHARDSON. This is foolish talk. Let us speak of music.

CARVER. Happily – your own uncle was a faithful member of the choir here – and a fine choir it was too. D'you remember old Patrick Gardner?

RICHARDSON. Dimly . . . yes . . .

CARVER. He had good Gaelic . . . and what a voice . . . the voice of the hills. They have nothing like that in the South. But you've had your say on music in your book . . . I've read it, and I'm not so old-fashioned that I can't see when I'm being criticised.

RICHARDSON. Oh, it's fine music, Robert, of course. No one would deny your great skill – but it won't do for the people.

CARVER. It's what the people need. Something to raise them above themselves. Something that gives them a sense of awe and grandeur and mystery.

RICHARDSON. There should be no mysteries. There you are very much at fault. That mass of yours in six parts – you have set the *deprecationem nostram* as though it were some old Erse incantation.

CARVER. Of course, that's how people used to pray – how some still do. The old King; he spoke Gaelic. He

appreciated that passage at once, and he was a good
musician too.

RICHARDSON. It is superstition and you cannot hear the
words.

CARVER. Everyone knows the words of the mass. They
hear them week after week, year after year. I give the
words the space that alone can find the meaning in them.
Was it too much to use ten parts for the Feast of Saint
Michael?

RICHARDSON. Two is too many, what excuse can there
be for ten?

CARVER. Nine orders of angels and the tenth was mankind
– to replace the fallen ones – you know that – it's the
Proper for the Feast of Saint Michael – so I used ten parts.
It's a wonderful sound . . . a vast blossom . . . like a
complex rose, petal on petal folding and unfolding . . . men
and angels . . .

RICHARDSON. What's the point of these devices if no one
notices?

CARVER. What is the harm in them then? Besides, there are
those who do notice. God notices.

RICHARDSON. The mass is for mankind.

CARVER. It is man's offering to God. If God does not hear
it, it has no purpose.

RICHARDSON. And if man does not understand it, it's no
true offering.

CARVER. I understand it. My singers understand it.

RICHARDSON. And the congregation?

CARVER. They feel it. We don't need to understand
everything. We don't understand God, but we worship
Him. The people still have feeling for it . . . and they have
their own ways; their 'Erse incantations', if you like, and
the street pageants . . .

RICHARDSON. Abominations, all of them.

CARVER. I've heard enough. You'll deprive the people of
any vision they might have of heaven because you insist
that they're like you, hopelessly tied to the earth.

RICHARDSON. I'll find it hard to forget these remarks Robert.

CARVER. Good. You want to marry my sister – yet you speak to me as though I had wasted my life on 'phantasias' – vain delights . . . ah, but of course. She has told you and now you are off the leash like a rat-hound.

RICHARDSON. Told me what?

CARVER. Has she said nothing? Then I am sorry. I have misjudged. But your honesty is unmannerly, to say the least.

Chapel Royal acoustic. RICHARDSON *speaks a little formally throughout.*

JAMES V. So I am to judge between you for the sake of the King of England, is that what you want Richardson?

RICHARDSON. King Henry is fearful of the power of the Pope and he enjoins you to take a like care – even in matters of the choir it is important to see . . .

JAMES V. If King Henry blows too hard in that dust he'll get it in his own eye. Besides, it is mostly the work of his minions. Carver here, whom you so object to, he doesn't write for flatterers. He tells me he writes only for the ear of God.

RICHARDSON. That is the voice of vainglory and the ear is corrupted that listens to it. As for his choir – their snouts are dipped in ale, mouths good only for grunting and squealing.

JAMES V. Voices, ears, snouts, mouths. What about the eyes, Richardson? What about the prick and the arsehole? The spirit is clothed in flesh, man, and there's no use denying it.

RICHARDSON. It is Mammon who is served.

JAMES V (*calls down the Chapel*). To your music Sir Robert – let us hear you rehearse your Motet. You must be patient Richardson.

The Motet Gaude Flore Virginali begins. They listen. The music continues throughout the scene but faded back under speech.

Our Robert is filled with a divine inspiration and he is a credit to Scotland.

RICHARDSON. Not any more, my lord. In France there is a great movement to change the old corrupt orders – to sweep away the lewd and obscure practices of the choirs.

JAMES V. Don't speak to *me* of France. I'm joined in marriage to her. I share her bed and I know her mind and body . . . and I know your Augustinian reforms are coming to nothing. The Abbey of St Victor . . . I am told even they are lapsing into the comfortable old ways.

RICHARDSON. They were terrible to our reformers. Herrings and potage was all they gave them – not even apples, and only a few raisins. When I visited them they were emaciated, and the regular canons bloated and rejoicing at their discomfort.

JAMES V. Herrings and potage are good fare for a priest. The French have softened you. We are not so fat here.

RICHARDSON. But the change is coming. And change must come here too. The people are poor, the church is rich; and the worship of God is turned into an incomprehensible idolatry. The church is corrupt and must yield eventually.

JAMES V. So Sir David Lindsay tells us. He's right . . . and so are you. But you move too fast.

They listen.

Does this music mean nothing to you? Isn't Carver an Austin canon like yourself? You are scarcely loyal.

RICHARDSON (*recklessly*). He's the bastard son of a bishop – a living example of the filthy depravity . . .

JAMES V. You're a fool, man. A mere fool. I've made it my sacred duty to produce as many bastards as can be reasonably expected of a king, and I intend that some of them will be bishops themselves.

RICHARDSON. If they take after their father, the nation will indeed be well stocked . . . but Robert Carver is . . .

JAMES V. Carver is far over your horizon. You are snapping at the shadows of yesterday – here comes my Queen. Marie, let me introduce you.

MARIE DE GUISE. We have already met – both here and in France, (*Teasing*.) but it seems Richardson could not find enough work there.

RICHARDSON. But this is my home. Scotland is my home and it is my privilege . . .

MARIE DE GUISE (*interrupting*). And we have seen that your heart is here also, is it not? The sister to our dear Robert – what is her name?

RICHARDSON. Isobel.

MARIE DE GUISE. And her brother stands between you, I am told?

RICHARDSON. We are not agreed.

JAMES V. Ah! So all this rage about music is over a woman!

RICHARDSON (*with dignity*). It is unjust to say so. It is not in the interest of my love for Isobel that I must denounce her brother's music. I lose much by it: perhaps all hope of her . . . but there's truth in my mission and I am sent by a great king and I cannot, will not and *would* not break my trust to my cause, nor to Isobel – nor will I violate her person to gain possession of her. You will excuse me. I must leave.

RICHARDSON *walks away: short pause*.

MARIE DE GUISE. Ah, vraiment, he is dangerous.

Pause – they listen to the music.

JAMES V. Is this Isobel a girl with long white hair?

MARIE DE GUISE. Yes, James; long hair, long legs, long back and long looks.

JAMES V. Violation? That's not what I would call it – but he is a bit late . . .

MARIE DE GUISE. I hope it is not you who has made her sorrowful.

JAMES V. Sorrowful? Why so? If she comes to bed of a boy I'll find him a bishopric. There must be some religion in his blood with a bishop for a grandfather.

MARIE DE GUISE. This makes me sad for Richardson. Let us move forward where we can hear better . . .

They listen to the music.

This music is in honour of the Holy Virgin – seven verses for her seven Joys. It is a pity such purity seems to attract you to destroy it rather than to honour it.

Fade out music.

Small room acoustic.

MARGARET. You shouldn't get so bothered with Alan. He's not so bad, and he's good with the lad, good to Davie.

CARVER. You know what they say, 'Mony ane kisses the bairn for love o' its nurse'.

MARGARET. Isobel isn't Davie's nurse.

CARVER. No, but she's family, and so is Davie. He's trying to make up now. But he despises us all at heart. He has no eyes, no imagination. 'Plain Dunblane' – that's what Richardson called it. Ah, but the West doorway . . . folds and folds of stone receding in and in to the small dark entrance that opens to the long vagina of the nave . . .

MARGARET. Robert!

CARVER. and at the heart of it is the choir and chalice of the womb. That is where I have planted my seed. That is where *we* conceive. Ah, Maggie: let's try a little religion for old time's sake!

MARGARET. I wish we had had a girl. You wouldn't have spoken like that in the house if we had had a daughter. But it's all boys – men now. Nothing but men. I used to dream of a daughter, Rob. I could even see what she looked like . . .

CARVER. Well . . . ?

MARGARET. Ach . . . (*Exhausted.*) . . . Ach no . . . I'm not saying.

Bell rings three times.

CARVER. So, so. The call again. I suppose if you won't have me I will have to devote myself to Euphemia instead.

MARGARET. You never sang a mass for me.

CARVER. I sing a mass for you every day and for all the souls in Christendom – and beyond it.

MARGARET. I want one for me only. If Euphemia can get one, so can I – especially since she's a hundred and fifty years dead. (*Teasing.*) You should be a hundred and fifty years dead along with her . . . then you would wriggle about in her coffin with your wee worm and not be bothering me with it.

CARVER. Maggie, the only reason I can bother you with my wee worm at all is *because* I sing a mass every day for Euphemia. (*Said pointedly.*) You should pray for her soul and the soul of Robert the Second that left money for the chaplain of Saint Lawrence without putting anything in his will about the chaplain not having a concubine.

MARGARET. Saint Lawrence was roasted on a grid-iron – and so should you be, the things you get up to.

CARVER. I get up to you all right, Maggie. Well up. You can't complain.

ARMOURER *starts hammering steadily, no song or whistle though*.

MARGARET. The altar of Saint Michael is better endowed.

CARVER (*laughing*). Very good! Very good – but Saint Michael's chaplain is allowed no concubines. Come here now and Saint Lawrence will show you how to earn your wages!

MARGARET. Get out of it, you dirty man, and go and bother the dead! I've done enough earning for a lifetime – and what do I get for it? . . . a gaping purse with nothing but bairns put in it.

Fade in distant trumpet calls. Outdoor acoustic.

CARVER. The King is to play Adam. He wants this play to be a lesson to the court.

ISOBEL. Who has he in mind for Cain?

CARVER. No one. That would be too pointed. He left it to me.

RICHARDSON. And Eve? Who is to be the Mother of all our woes?

CARVER. That's not what the *King* asked. He asked who was the most beautiful and he didn't wait for an answer. You will not like this, Richardson. He has asked for Isobel to play Eve.

RICHARDSON. Why should I not like it then . . . indeed, I am flattered.

CARVER. I thought you had told him Isobel.

RICHARDSON. Please explain why I shouldn't feel flattered?

CARVER. You have been flattered more than you know. He expects her to be bare-breasted.

RICHARDSON. Naturally she will refuse.

ISOBEL. What do you expect Eve to look like . . . if the King commands it.

RICHARDSON. I expect her to be fully clothed. The play is not in Eden. The play of Cain and Abel is of where we are now. As we are now.

CARVER (*sickened by the pair of them*). Well, you have your fallen woman if you want her.

ISOBEL. Robert!

RICHARDSON. How dare you speak of her like that – of your own sister. We are all fallen. All.

ISOBEL. You need not worry . . . either of you. I will not play the part . . . not now . . . not even for the King. You can tell him why, Robert. You can tell him why. (*She is bitterly disappointed.*)

CARVER (*angrily*). I think it is time *you* told Richardson why. I see you're dressed for confession – sable and gray – it becomes you.

RICHARDSON. What is this?

DAVIE. Can I play in the play?

CARVER. Davie! Where did you come from?

DAVIE. I want tae play in the play.

CARVER. All the parts are taken, Davie. All except Cain. No one will play Cain. I'd do it myself, but I'm too old for it.

DAVIE. I'll be Cain. I'll play Cain.

CARVER. No. You don't know what it means.

Distant trumpet call.

RICHARDSON. More foolish wars! Your friend Davidson the armourer will be in his glory now!

CARVER. Everybody hates Cain, Davie. Cain was the first evil person in the world.

ISOBEL. Davie has no malice in him. He's perfect for the part. He's the only person innocent enough to play it and not be thought ill of for it.

RICHARDSON. Isobel's right – and Davie's dying to take a part.

ISOBEL. I will teach him his lines.

DAVIE. Ah can learn it. Auntie Isobel'll learn it tae me.

CARVER. People will jeer at you for it.

DAVIE. Ah'm daft so it disnae matter. That no right?

ISOBEL. It'll be his one chance of glory.

CARVER. It's not glory he'll get, that's my worry. If you ask me, Richardson here would be the best Cain – a man that'd set out to destroy his brother's music.

ISOBEL. Please . . . please . . .

RICHARDSON. I can be patient.

Small room acoustic.

What was the meaning of all that, Isobel? What is it I am to be told? Is the King proposing some honour for me that he has chosen you for Eve? I can hardly imagine such a thing. 'You are flattered more than you know.' That's what Robert said. Perhaps the King told Robert first, to spare his feelings before the court. I must say I am surprised. King Henry will be pleased.

ISOBEL. King Henry! King Henry! Who cares for that fat swine? You fool! Bastards . . . all of you . . . bastards. Oh God . . . what have I said? Can't you see what has happened? Do you not see the hem of my skirt is lifting? Who do you think did it? Who do you think did it? It could not have been you. (*Bitterly.*) It never could have

been you. You are too gooooood. To gooood. You had to
wait. Nobody waits! Nobody waits: only you.

RICHARDSON. Just calm yourself and tell me what this is
about.

ISOBEL. I mean, I didn't wait. Oh God, why can't you see?

RICHARDSON. I'm sorry I'm so stupid.

ISOBEL (*through clenched teeth*). All right. All right. I'll tell
it to you so there is no mistaking . . . (*Breathless.*) The King
slept with me . . . (*Viciously.*) Do you understand that? . . .
(*With bitter sense of shame.*) The King slept with me and I
am carrying his child . . . and I would have married you,
yes, I would . . . and not without love either . . . but now
you've wrecked it. You've all wrecked it. (*Sobs.*)

*Very dimly we hear 'L'Homme Arme' whistled. ISOBEL
still sobs. A cat miaows in the room and is ignored.
Gradually we realise RICHARDSON is sobbing also. This
takes over.*

Don't blubber. I can't bear to see you blubber. I can't bear
it. I can't stand this any more. I'm going, Alan. I'm going.
(*Frantic and angry.*)

No response. She leaves.

RICHARDSON. This can't be true. She is saying it to test
me. (*Breaks down again, then controls himself.*)

Tap at the door. Pause. Another. Door opens.

CARVER. I am sorry, Richardson. Truly sorry for this. Of
course you will not want her now . . . I am sorry. (*Silence.*)
Shall I leave? . . . I had better leave . . . I am truly sorry.

RICHARDSON. That is more than she was able to say to me.

CARVER. She is proud and she has been humiliated. To
be commanded to play Eve before the court. She knew
what they would say behind their hands. But it was just so
the King could show off the quality of his latest reject . . .

RICHARDSON. Why didn't she refuse?

CARVER. It is not so easy. He was the first and she was
carrying his child . . . still is. You shouldn't have waited. It
was what she needed from you and you withheld it.

RICHARDSON. How could I not have known? Not have

seen? . . . Eve? Isobel? . . . I should have guessed . . . they were born to deceive us, born to it . . . let her play her part. Let her show herself to the court for what she is.

CARVER. That would cause her much suffering . . .

RICHARDSON. And what of the suffering she has already caused me? Let her suffer for all her sex. You must enjoy this, I suppose. For me to find that my best love has been so misplaced . . . I should never have trusted any woman. Have you encouraged this?

CARVER. No. She has been abused. It happens often. It is as much the men you should mistrust. She needs you more than ever Richardson.

RICHARDSON. She is defiled.

CARVER. The worm is not in every rose, and where it has been it is better to chance upon it as you have done, than tear roses apart to prove it was there.

RICHARDSON. She has shamed me utterly. Before God . . . before the court . . . and then a child . . . not my child . . .

CARVER. It is not in every rose . . . and those it has visited it does not wholly destroy. (*Recedes*.) Not wholly. You have it in you to restore her beauty and her self if you will.

CARVER *goes out, the cat miaows again twice*.

RICHARDSON (*sighing*). I suppose you're hungry. You should have been fed long ago. Long ago.

Outdoor acoustic.

ALEX KYD. There's some that's hopin' the English will win.

STEVIE. Did ye see whit the King had done tae yon gaberlungie man stole a hen?

ALEX. Naw. Tell us.

STEVIE. Well see, they bring this beggar man tae him . . . ay he's stolen the hen aa right – an someone says 'Whit'll we dae wi' 'im Your Majesty?' An' he says (*Spoken in the implacable tones of the King.*) 'Burn 'im – burn 'im alive.'

ALEX. Ye're kiddin'.

STEVIE. Naw, Alex, ah'm no. That's whit he says. An' that's whit they done.

DAVIE. Burnt 'im? Burnt 'im a' tae ashes?

STEVIE. Ay, Davie. Ah nivver want tae see the like o' that again . . . the man . . . he pissed hissel' . . . right there . . . front o' everybody.

ALEX. That widnae pit it oot!

STEVIE. You shut up! There naethin' funny aboot it.

ALEX. They ca' the King a gaberlungie man himsel' . . .

STEVIE. Ay. He plays at that game. Ony lass that's gettin' merrit – 's often as not he's in there first wi' 'er, shakin' the sheets.

DAVIE. Ooooh . . . ooh . . . that sounds guid.

ALEX. That's whit ye'd like Davie, eh? Stark naked under the sheets and a nice wee quine naked beside ye . . . (*Matter-of-fact.*) well ye'll no get it fur yer daft.

DAVIE. Mebbe ah'd get a daft quine. Mebbe she'd be as bonnie as if she had her wits. Mebbe we . . .

STEVIE. It's gone quiet. Nae birds. Nae dugs. Quiet.

DAVIE. Mebbe we'd get daft bairns and be happy.

ALEX. Mebbe ye're no daft efter a'.

STEVIE. It's close. Nae wind.

ALEX. Come oan Davie, let's try anither bit o' the play while we're waitin'. Start where ye light the fire an' it goes a' smoky. You say 'Puff'.

DAVIE. Ay. Ah mind that.
Puff! This smoke does me much shame –
Burn now in the devil's name!
Ah, what devil of hell is it!
Almost had my lungs been split.
Had I blown then one blast more
I had been choked to death full sore.
It stank like the devil in hell,
That longer there I might not dwell.

ALEX. Cain, this is not worth one leek;
Such smokey offering who should seek?

DAVIE. Come kiss the devil right in the arse,
  For this smoke is slow to pass;
  I would that it were in thy throat,
  Fire and sheaf, and wheat and oat.

STEVIE. This is stupid. We havenae ony wheat. 'Sides, oats
  burn easy. Ah've tae pit grass in it tae mak it smoke. It's
  daft.

DAVIE. Mebbe God disnae like oats.

STEVIE. The hail thing is stupid. Naebody can play God.
  An' who's goin' tae be Adam?

ALEX. The King's tae be Adam.

STEVIE. An' we're tae play alongside o' him?

ALEX. It's jist sae he can mak' sport o' us an' he'll seem sae
  bloody clever. Old Father Adam, an' us his wee brats. He
  hisnae ony boys o' his ane. He widnae dae that to *them*.
  Look at that daft bugger on his knees. Whit're ye daein',
  Davie?

DAVIE. Prayin'.

STEVIE. What for?

DAVIE. Ah'm prayin' for ma oats tae burn.

  ALEX *and* STEVIE *howl with laughter.*

ALEX. Aw Christ! That was a good one.

DAVIE (*cross*). It isnae funny.

ALEX. Ach Davie ye dinnae understand – when ye want
  yer oats it's same as wantin' a lassie. Pray awa' man, pray
  awa'.

STEVIE. Naw. Up ye get. Here comes Sir Robert . . . Sir
  Robert, is it right that the King's tae play Adam?

CARVER. Yes, Stevie – as soon as he gets back from the
  wars; so you'd all better be well prepared.

DAVIE. Ah dinnae want tae be burnt.

CARVER. It's not you that gets burnt Davie, it's the
  offering you make.

STEVIE. An' who's tae play God?

CARVER. I am . . . for my sins.

ALEX. Whit aboot Davie's sins. He's no done onything
that deserves him tae be Cain. It isnae right puttin' him for
Cain. He disnae ken whit it means. He's a' confused.

CARVER. But he was keen to do it when no one else would.

ALEX. Awright then. Ah'll dae it. Ah'll swap wi' him.

CARVER. I wish you'd said that before. But it's too late
now. He's learnt his part. Now, Davie. Here's your spade
and when Abel's fire lights on the altar you're to make
believe to kill him with it.

ALEX. Whit for does he need a spade? Could he no pretend
tae use jist his hands?

CARVER. He is meant to be Cain. Cain tilled the ground
like his father, Adam. The King will have a spade too.
Adam and Cain had to use a spade to get the plants to
grow . . . it is a symbol.

DAVIE. Why disnae God like oats?

CARVER. He likes oats, Davie . . . it's not that . . . it's how
they're offered to Him.

DAVIE. Did I no give them right? Is that how come it was a'
smokey?

CARVER. You did well, Davie. It's just a part you play.

DAVIE. Shall ah kill him yet?

CARVER. No. Not yet. You have to say, 'Out, thief, why
burnt thy tithe so clean, When mine smoked . . .'

DAVIE (*interrupting*). Ah remember! Ah remember it!

Out, thief, why burnt thy tithe so clean
When mine but foully smoked
As if it would us both have choked?

ALEX. God's will I trust was here
That made mine burn so clear
If thine smoked am I to blame?

DAVIE. Why yea and thou shalt smart with shame:
With sharp spade 'ere my hand I stay
I shall have torn thy life away

An' then I hit him like this – real hard –

CARVER. DAVIE! NO! OH GOD, NO! NO! NO!

STEVIE. Oh, Jesus . . .

Fade.

Small room acoustic. Sound of things being packed in a chest.

MARGARET (*very matter-of-fact throughout. She is holding off emotion for some other time, so she can be practical and give DAVIE some stability*). I have to go, Robert. You know that yourself . . . I don't know how you could have let the boy take a part like that . . . and a spade . . . how could you all be so foolish? (*Pause.*) You'll not want these if you're eating up at the Palace.

Silence.

If Alex dies they'll hound Davie for the rest of his days . . . so I've decided. I'm going to take him back to Scone. I have a cart arranged for tomorrow.

CARVER. How can you take it like this . . . as though it were just ordinary?

MARGARET. Isobel nearly went mad with it when she was told. Is that what you want me to do? Alan was kind to her . . . and he had no call to be. First she breaks the man's heart, then she asks him for more love than he thought he had in the first place. Maybe he does put chastity before charity – but at least he's *got* charity.

CARVER. I could come with you . . . there is always a place for me at Scone.

MARGARET. No. I don't want that. The Queen has asked you to stay, hasn't she? You men. You are all so careless. There she is expecting a child and the King goes off to Falkland licking his wounds. They say he's in a black depression. Well, it's his own doing. He should never have taken on those wars – but to leave his poor wife like that. She was going to go with him and he wouldn't have it.

CARVER. I know what she feels.

MARGARET. She's returning to Linlithgow tomorrow.

CARVER. I advised against it, you know.

MARGARET. Oh-ho . . . the great counsellor to the Queen.

CARVER. No, no. I advised against Davie playing the part. I had such faith in him. He was getting more and more responsible . . . where is he?

MARGARET. Out with the pigs and the geese. It's comfort for him you know. He's distressed in himself. He knows he's done something wrong, but he has no idea of how he came to do it.

CARVER. Poor lad. He's wise in his own way.

MARGARET. But not in your ways.

CARVER. I'll come and visit you Maggie.

MARGARET. You do that.

CARVER. I'll miss you.

MARGARET. We'll both miss each other, but there's nothing else to be done about it. If anything happens to me, Alan and Isobel say they will take him in.

CARVER. That is very good of them. I suppose I'm no use to him now. Oh, Maggie . . . I've loved you both.

MARGARET. Wheesht. For God's sake wheesht Robert, before my heart breaks altogether . . .

Fade.

Pigs grunting and scuffling in a yard.

DAVIE. Ah didnae mean ony hairm. Honest ah didnae . . . ah kent fine it was make-believe. It was jist that spade sort o' got a swing intae it. But ah didnae mean tae hurt him . . . Mebbe he's a' better now. Here! Get yer snouts intae that.

Sudden noises from the pigs.

Whit's wrang wi' oats? Ah didnae ken God liked blood better'n oats. Heh! There's a notion. Ah could give God blood an' then He'd forgive me. Mebbe it wid be a' better then an ah'd get tae see Alex. He wis nice tae me, wis Alex. Ah like Alex. He could sing tae. Him an' me we werenae clivver but we could sing. He wis good. (*To a pig.*) Go oan get oot o' there. Get oot o' there before we mak black puddings o' ye.

More noises from pigs.

Mebbe pig's blood wid dae for God. 'Stead o' lamb's. It's
a' blood . . . Habbie daes it wi' a knife. That's whit ah'll
dae. Ah'll jist tak' a wee one. They hadnae much blood fir
the play . . . didnae even look like blood.

DAVIE *moves away a bit.*

Whaur a bucket? . . . Here. You (*He grabs at a squealing
pig.*) You'll dae . . . Haud still! (*Pig screams.*) Haud still!
(*Scream dies away to a gurgle then silence.*) Ay. That's
better. This'll mak it a'right an' naebody will be angered at
me ony mair.

Fade.

Chapel Royal acoustic. Scratch of CARVER's *pen.*

MARIE DE GUISE. Why are you working in here in the
Chapel Royal?

CARVER. Well, I usually work at home, but everything is in
turmoil there this evening. The chapel is quiet – and I have
my lectern and my candles.

MARIE DE GUISE. What are you writing?

CARVER. A mass . . . it should be for Margaret . . . you
know . . . she always wanted one just for herself to be sung
in her memory – just like kings and queens – forgive me –

MARIE DE GUISE. No, no, there is no offence.

CARVER. But now . . . well it will be a mass for the sorrows of
the world . . . she has her place in those too . . . we all do . . .

MARIE DE GUISE. Ah. Yes . . . I hear she is leaving
tomorrow, just like me.

CARVER. That is so.

MARIE DE GUISE. I am sorry. It was a terrible accident.
You were not to blame. Nobody was to blame.

CARVER. You have been told?

MARIE DE GUISE. I take an interest in your affairs,
Robert.

CARVER. You are kind to concern yourself. You must have
enough troubles of your own. How is the King?

MARIE DE GUISE (*suddenly weeping*). Oh Robert,
Robert . . .

CARVER. You should not weep . . . you have a young child
. . . ready to be born . . . he will bring you joy.

MARIE DE GUISE. What if I have a girl . . . what if I have
a boy who does not live? I could not bear to lose another
son. It would kill James. He is sick to the heart. He will
not even see me now. I have nothing more that I can give
him, except a healthy son. My James is utterly defeated.

CARVER. The English were stretched, they say. He could
perhaps . . .

MARIE DE GUISE (*incredulous*). Stretched? No . . . no . . .
there was scarcely a fight. More of them drowned
retreating across the Solway than there were killed. They
deserted him. They deserted the King. They deserted
Scotland. There are things I do not understand in this
country. Always James must prove himself – but when
men desert you – then you know you have failed. He is so
sick that I do not even know if I will ever see him again.
My own husband. I have loved him, Robert,
(*Passionately.*) with all my being (*She controls herself.*) and
to be denied him now, of all times . . . it is too hard.
(*Pause.*) Robert, will you say a prayer with me . . . a
prayer for us all?

CARVER. What prayer would you have me say?

MARIE DE GUISE. You know it. You know it well. The
Old King's prayer . . .

CARVER. O bone Jesu, O piissime Jesu, O dulcissime Jesu

MARIE DE GUISE *joins in*.

MARIE DE GUISE/CARVER. O Jesu fili virginis Mariae
plenus pietatis. O dulcis Jesus secumdum misericordiam
tuam miserere mei.

MARIE DE GUISE. O clementissime Jesu deprecor te per
illum. (*She trails off, unable to finish.*) Excuse me. Just
continue with your writing. I shall compose myself a
little.

CARVER *resumes writing*.

Have you enough light for such work?

CARVER. I am used to it.

MARIE DE GUISE. You had a hand in building this chapel, did you not? Someone told me you were apprenticed to the old man in charge . . . that you took his name . . . yes?

CARVER. Yes, it's true. Old David Carver. He taught me . . . he brought me up. (*Pause.*) He knew how to build for voices . . . Every bit of wood he cut and carved was done by the sound of it as much as by measuring it. He said the voice of God was in everything if only we had ears for it.

MARIE DE GUISE. That is a beautiful idea.

CARVER. Yes. I once tried to suggest it myself . . . to make the rose sing to the rhythms of the sea . . .

MARIE DE GUISE. And now? What do you write of now?

CARVER. Oh, I have put off my coat of many colours. I have no glory in the world now.

Sound of pen. CARVER *humming. A door opens softly and closes again.*

MARIE DE GUISE (*whispering to herself at first*). Robert, someone has come into the chapel . . . a young man. Can you see what he is doing?

CARVER. I will look in a minute. It will be one of the altar boys . . . he has probably gone to change the candles.

MARIE DE GUISE (*still whispering*). No. No. I am sure it is David. He is carrying a bowl. He is being very careful. Perhaps it is Holy water. Robert. It is the chalice. He has the chalice in his hands. It is full. He cannot mean to drink it at the altar . . . he has it pressed close to his stomach . . . how strange.

CARVER. Now I can look. Yes, that's Davie. I think he is best left undisturbed. Perhaps he wants to pray. I remember once, he got down on his knees and prayed . . . there seemed to be no reason at the time, but there was something important in his mind. I will put away my things.

MARIE DE GUISE. He is lifting the chalice. (*Normal voice.*) Sacre Dieu! He is pouring it all over the altar cloth.

CARVER (*anxious but not shouting*). Davie? Davie?

MARIE DE GUISE. Oh Mon Dieu! It is not wine, Robert. It is blood!

CARVER. What have you done? What have you done now? Don't run away Davie!

The door opens and closes again. CARVER *and* MARIE DE GUISE *move across the chapel.*

MARIE DE GUISE. He is gone. No. Do not follow him. (*She sighs with relief.*) You need not fear, Robert. It is pig's blood . . . pig's blood only. I would know that smell anywhere. The kitchens at Joinville were never free of it. Ah . . . France . . .

CARVER. The cloth is almost floating in blood.

MARIE DE GUISE. Poor boy. What was he trying to do? Do you have a key, Robert?

CARVER. Yes?

MARIE DE GUISE. Lock the door. We will remove this and clean it ourselves. I will have a new cloth made by one of my ladies. Then no one need know. He will suffer enough without this as well.

CARVER. You are good.

MARIE DE GUISE. I remember his voice. One of the loveliest things I have ever heard.

CARVER. It is broken now.

MARIE DE GUISE. Not in my memory. It will never be broken in my memory. Can you find something we can put this cloth in? I have put the chalice on the floor to catch the drips . . . (*With resigned humour.*) but the cloth drips too . . .

CARVER. This is no place for you, madam . . .

MARIE DE GUISE. It is all right. I have been given strength. (*Confidently.*) I will have a boy. And he will be strong like his father. Yes, that is good. I will put it here.

Fade out on the steady drip of blood into a bowl.

Winter 1543

Small room acoustic. Movement of bodies in bed.

RICHARDSON. The candle's smoking Isobel.

ISOBEL. Can you not reach it from your side of the bed?
Here, I have the trimmer.

RICHARDSON. I was half awake . . . dreaming.

ISOBEL. You shouldn't sleep on your back Alan. What
were you dreaming of?

RICHARDSON. I was travelling in the dark across wet
moorland. All I can see is dead grass and the black line of a
muddy path. It's so dark that a stone stumbled me and it
was white. Then there's this queer noise – a sort of strange
startled bird that whimpers along the line of a choked
ditch. It frightens me. And I feel the pressure of the dead
all about me – and when I look up to the sky for help, the
last darkening tinge of yellow is slipping away high above
all – and then I think that we may never see light again . . .
Isobel.

ISOBEL (*waking again*). Umm?

RICHARDSON. Isobel; you must pray with me against
despair. It is a great sin.

ISOBEL. You seem cocky enough in the day. Why are you
so nervous at night?

RICHARDSON. You torture me! How can I match a King
that slept with every shape of womanhood? I've known
only you – I know no better than what you know of me.

ISOBEL (*almost hysterical*). Why must you mention him?
You torture *me*. Have I not longed to forget him . . .
longed to be free of that reproach. I can't undo it: and I
never lied to you. You always knew . . . and he is dead
now . . . dead . . . he shouldn't hover over us like this . . .

RICHARDSON. You liked it with him, didn't you?

ISOBEL. Yes, yes, yes, why must you make me say so, yes,
it's true . . . but I love you, Alan . . . I love you.

RICHARDSON. Get out! Get out of the bed. I can't bear to
have you beside me. Get out. Get out of this house.

ISOBEL. Alan: it's winter. I have nowhere else.

RICHARDSON. Go to your brother.

ISOBEL. You can't shame me like this. I beg of you. Don't put me out . . . I can't leave the baby . . .

RICHARDSON. I said get out. I can't stand it any more. Get out, get out.

ISOBEL. Alan. I beg of you. I'm on my knees. I beg you. People will see me . . . at least give me my coat.

RICHARDSON. Here, take it.

ISOBEL. What will people think of us. What will they think of you, Alan? You know what happened . . . I'll try to love you, truly I'll try. One man deceived my body . . . but you – you'll deceive my heart; d'you understand, Alan: my heart, my heart . . . oh please, please, please, please . . .

RICHARDSON. How can you say these things to me? 'Yes, I liked it, yes yes yes it's true I liked it, I liked it. I shall try to love you; truly I shall try.'

ISOBEL. You'll wake the baby, Alan . . . please . . . what has got into you?

RICHARDSON. Can't you see how much I need you . . . and night after night you get into the bed and turn your back on me. Night after night I keep that candle lit, hoping your arms will reach over and I will see a look of love and desire in your face.

ISOBEL. Alan . . . Alan!

RICHARDSON. Night after night . . . Oh God . . . I'm sorry . . . if you knew how much I need you and how terrified I am to disappoint you, you'd understand. Here. Come to the fire. You must be frozen cold.

ISOBEL. Need? Need me? Mine is the need Alan.

RICHARDSON. How can you say that yet again?

ISOBEL. No no, that's not what I meant. Listen to me. Let me finish. I mean . . . you can live without me; but without you I am nothing any more but a used-up woman with an unwanted child . . . something to point your finger at and nod sadly. Just like the Queen. We both had girls by the King and we both called them Mary. Mary was forgiven. Perhaps God will forgive me and my little one.

(*Silence*.) Alan, it is I who need you . . . but I am often tired . . . and you know, when you're feeding a baby a woman does not feel the need so much . . . it isn't you Alan. It will be better soon. I promise.

RICHARDSON (*sadly*). When? (*Pause*.) I fear death.

ISOBEL. Why do you say that now? Are you unwell, Alan? Perhaps you're unwell. Let me feel your brow . . . you are quite cool there. You are chilled.

RICHARDSON. No . . . no. But I fear death . . . and the darkness of the world – and all the wrong in it . . . and all my own wrongs – forgive me. Forgive me if you can. You're the one light I can see and yet you're wormwood in my mind . . . don't ever hide your face from me or turn your love elsewhere.

ISOBEL. Where else would my love turn to but you? You rush me Alan. Give me time and learn to be yourself as much with me as with the outer world. Come, come to bed. I'll make you honey with spirits in it.

RICHARDSON. May I make love to you then?

ISOBEL. You should never ask. Should never have to ask.

Stirling 1559

Chapel Royal acoustic.
We hear the start of the closing Agnus Dei of CARVER's *five-part mass.*

CARVER. Good. Good. We'll pause for a minute here.

Music stops: DUNCAN *comes across to* CARVER.

DUNCAN. It's bleak, Robert. That start is bleak.

CARVER. It's meant to be. You know what it's based on, of course . . . fere pessima . . . a wild beast has devoured my son Joseph – but I've given you a chink of light there – just where we stopped.

DUNCAN. . . . . a wild beast. Plagues and wars and reforms . . . but Joseph lived.

CARVER. This next part has the sound of bells. Cheerful bells. And then see here.

DUNCAN. You wrote this for Maggie, didn't you?

CARVER. Well . . . maybe . . . perhaps that's why it's in five parts. The five senses . . . long ago . . . and then the five wounds of Christ on the cross. Our bodies are betrayers, Duncan: and these days our minds are no better. So you see it's for all of us . . . small hopes in darkening days. It ends as bleak as it began.

DUNCAN. She would have been proud to hear it. It's the best thing you've done, but you don't have to sound so . . . apocalyptic about it. It's not the end of the world yet.

CARVER. It is, Duncan, you know fine it is. (*Addressing the choir who reassemble during this speech*.) Now. This may be the last time we'll be able to sing music like this, so you'll not mind my talking to you a little seriously. This final section must be as smooth and dignified as possible. I want all your entries to sound inevitable. You must feel in this a great drama of the soul – but I want no showing off. Dignity. Clarity. (*Tries to mitigate the despondency he himself is spreading*.) Graham! Don't look so sad! Today we will leave a memory in this place . . . I want your thoughts to reach out to an unborn humanity, knowing nothing more about those to come than that they will as surely need our prayers as we do ourselves. So you must sing without anything of your own selves in this except what is eternal and good in you. It is the last and the hardest thing I will ever ask of you . . . you can manage it . . . you are good singers . . . the best . . . the very best. After we've sung tomorrow, you'll all disperse – for a time anyway. The Queen asks me to thank you. She is too ill to attend.

General shuffling and coughing.

DUNCAN. This can't really be the end Robert?

CARVER. I believe it is. Now, Superius lead in from where we left off . . . Dona nobis pacem.

Part of concluding section of the five-part mass, during which CARVER *calls out over the music as per score*.

CARVER. Like bells . . . more like bells. Now grow . . . grow! (*Alerting them to their entries*.) Superius! Tenor!

Fade.

Sound of CARVER *among books. The dust makes him cough but he has a cold anyway.*

CARVER (*coughs. Snuffles and exhales*). Aaah. Here it is. I knew you were lurking in there. Musica Enchiriadis. Where it all began. An old blind Irishman they say – had it copied out for the Franks. Hm. (*Hums a little plainsong.*) Hm. (*Coughs.*) Simple steady stuff for simple steady minds. Davie. Aaah. Davie . . . how long is it now? Twelve years? No . . . the King was alive . . . seventeen. Yes. Just before Solway Moss. Davie'll be in his thirties now . . . they were to be here (*Querulous.*) . . . yesterday. Yesterday they said.

Margaret? . . . so she's dead. They wrote that. She deadened herself to me long ago. That day. And then the blood. The prow of my ship has dipped under a good many waves . . . but that one was cruel. That one left me with a lungful of salt. Never mind. We had good times. Buried at Dunkeld. Well, well, well. 'Go and bother the dead.' That's what she used to say. I don't suppose you'd sing the same tune now Maggie. Musica Enchiriadis. Back you go where you belong (*Sneezes.*) in the dishonoured past. (*Suddenly.*) Who's there?

ISOBEL. Robert! So here you are! My dear Robert. You have a cold.

CARVER. Is there no one with you?

ISOBEL. Davie. Come forward, Davie. Don't be frightened. It's Robert. You remember Robert.

DAVIE. Ay. (*With awakening pleasure.*) Ay. Ah remember ye. Ye've gotten awfy auld.

CARVER. You're older yourself, Davie. Ah. It's good to see you. You look well. And Isobel . . . you are still lovely . . . I hope you are happy . . . and here is Richardson. Well you haven't put on any weight . . .

RICHARDSON. You never could manage to call me Alan, could you?

CARVER. Alan . . . of course . . . forgive me. You look tired.

RICHARDSON. I am tired. The reform occupies my time

. . . I am afraid some are too enthusiastic. I have to watch over everything.

ISOBEL. I see you are among books as usual. We went to your room first.

DAVIE. Ah can read words now.

CARVER. That's good. I knew you would do it one day. You were able to read music quite well.

DAVIE. Isobel and Alan. They learnt me how.

ISOBEL. Taught, Davie.

DAVIE. Ay. They taught me on't.

ISOBEL *laughs pleasantly*.

CARVER. You seem contented, Isobel. I'm glad to see that.

ISOBEL. It's strange to be back here. We were looking out from the rock to see if the view had changed. But it was just the same. Marsh and quagmire and men labouring – and above them all, the graceful birds wheeling free.

RICHARDSON. And the noise of it too – creaking carts: hacking coughs: cursings and shoutings – I don't know how you managed to train such a fine choir out of such a yelling world.

CARVER (*surprised*). Oh! That is generous of you. Well. We're not all delvers and spinners – though I suppose I've delved and spun in my own way – prolation, diminution, perfection, countering, cant organe – all those words we had to learn before we could get at the truth of a beautiful piece of music. I despise theorists. Digging a hole and then planting nothing in it but what they took out of it in the first place.

ISOBEL. Did you have to say that?

RICHARDSON. That's all right.

CARVER. It wasn't directed at you.

RICHARDSON. I know.

Silence.

I expect you'd like to talk to Davie. Isobel and I will take a turn around the walls.

CARVER. You do that. Come on, Davie. Let me show you some of the old places . . . you used to like the bowling green . . . and the terraced gardens . . . Out we go.

Wind. A buzzard mews intermittently. A heavy cart approaches.

CARVER. We'll see you two later . . . in the Chapel . . . Look, Davie! There's the figure of the king up on the corner. Does it remind you of him?

DAVIE. Ah've got books o' ma ane now!

CARVER. That's good.

Heavy cart comes to a halt close by.

ARMOURER (*now driving the cart*). Wey-hey Jess, Tinker. Ca' canny. Here man . . . have I room at the back . . . it's as tight as a goose's arse-hole.

CARVER. I'd know that voice anywhere! Davidson the armourer! Have you stopped your tinkering at last?

ARMOURER. Robert! Robert Carver! My God, man!

CARVER. They haven't given up war have they?

ARMOURER. Na – na – ah lost heart. No siller for decent equipment . . . jist battered cuirasses and washin' the blood and shit off dead men's gear. It's the wine trade now – good stuff this. The best from the Loire. I was sent up to rescue it before the reformers get here. And you. How's yourself, man? Is your wee wet pen still at the scratchin' and dribblin'?

CARVER. The ink's almost dried up on it. It's just a sad old wing beat it gives now and again.

ARMOURER. And Maggie, it was Maggie wasn't it? Any word o' her?

CARVER. She's dead.

ARMOURER. Ay well . . .

CARVER. This is Davie. You remember Davie?

ARMOURER. Davie is it? Man ye've broadened in the shoulders. I could dae wi the likes o you tae humph barrels. Will I get through now?

CARVER. Ay. Keep her straight at that and you'll do. Good to see you.

ARMOURER. Hup! Hup!

Cart moves off and ARMOURER *calls back at them.*

Would ye see me through the lower gate, Davie? There's naebody there. They just left the place wide open.

DAVIE. Ah'll go an help him.

CARVER. Good for you, Davie. Good for you.

Cart rumbles away. Wind.

(*Singing under his breath.*) 'L'homme arme. L'homme arme . . .' (*As the tune rises in pitch he starts coughing badly and gives up. Muttering to himself.*) The world is becoming a fearful place to me . . . and yet the rainbow still rainbows . . . the moon and the tide – they're all known. (*Becoming querulous.*) So what's new to fear?

Pause.

I remember Queen Margaret running barefoot on the close-cropped grass to feed the swans on Lithgow Loch . . . and look what became of her . . . and now the poor Queen so sick. I suppose it was right to try to find a beauty in the air that would ring in the heart . . . and a beauty in the heart that would ring in the air . . . but now look at me . . . as dumb as an English swan and a lot less beautiful! (*Pause.*) Ah! Davie! No need to run.

DAVIE. Ah'm feart. There a big crowd o' folk. They're a' shoutin' an' yellin'. Mebbe they'll be here. Thae gates is open. There's naebody that cares aboot it here.

CARVER. We worry too much. The sun will rise tomorrow. The spring will arrive on time – well, more or less . . .

DAVIE. Ye're nae safe here. Ye're nae safe oot here. We need tae shift.

Very distant crowd noise which continues throughout.

CARVER (*with tired certainty*). Men fear joy. That's it. We have come to fear joy. It's too innocent. It leaves us naked in the world. Remember the gardens here Davie? I used to tell you it was Eden – and the two big beech trees, they were the tree of knowledge and the tree of life. Look at it now. Buzzards above. Burdocks below.

DAVIE. Can ye no hear them?

CARVER. That's a snell wind Davie. I never tire of the view from here, but I'm old. We'll shelter in the Chapel Royal.

They open and close the door of the Chapel Royal. Wind and buzzard cease. The acoustic is more echoey than before.

DAVIE. Whaur's the curtains an' furnishins?

CARVER. They've taken them down the hill. There's no use for this place now – though it is the house of God. At least they left Our Lady and Saint Michael. Too heavy to move, I suppose. Huh. (*Raising his voice to address the statue.*) There's no need for that sword, Saint Michael. Nobody wants to go back. If the gates of Eden were opened they'd toss their heads and walk away. (*He coughs and sniffs.*)

DAVIE. Ye shouldnae leave yer big book here, Sir Robert. They're aye burnin' books.

CARVER. Ah. The book. Books did you no good, did they Davie? All those years hiding away because you played in something out of a book. But you liked the singing.

DAVIE. Will ah no gather the music books? Ah could hide them in the loft o' the pigsty. They're no safe here.

CARVER. You do that, Davie. The sty's still there. No pigs though.

Distant bell rings three times.

It's time for me to pray for the soul of Euphemia down in the parish kirk Davie. I was counting, you know, and I think I've prayed for her soul over ten thousand times – and d'you know Davie, there's still truth in my heart every time I do it.

DAVIE. It's no safe for ye oot there.

CARVER. After all these years, Davie, I'm not going to let the old lady down. I'm fond of Euphemia. And her memory pays my wages.

He goes out. DAVIE shuffles about whistling a tuneless whistle. Then he tries to hum a bit.
Door re-opens.

CARVER. Just gather the books with the music in them Davie. Never mind the theory books . . . fit to be burnt in hell, most of them, anyway.

Door closes.
DAVIE starts looking at books keeping up a tuneless half whistle when he isn't talking to himself.

DAVIE. Lots o' books here . . . Simon Tailler . . . Tetrachordorum. (*Reading with difficulty, especially anything in Latin.*) That's Latin. There nae much music in that. So that's *you* for burnin'. Oh here! That's bonnie! That's a' done in gold. We'll keep you . . . Ordinary in usum Sarum . . . here, ah remember you a' right. They're no goin' tae burn you . . . Jacobi Bassantini Scoti . . . Musica secundum Platonem . . . an' *that's* a' theory . . . ah'll make a wee heap o' them . . . Antiphonary . . . ay, you're for keepin' . . . (*Still half whistling.*) . . .

Door opens. Crowd heard dimly in background.

CARVER. Davie. Davie. They're coming just as you said. There's no time to take all the books out of here. We'll just have to carry what we can.

DAVIE. Have ye no' got a key tae lock the door wi'?

CARVER. Of course, I never thought of it. We'll be safe enough.

DAVIE. Ay? Mebbe.

CARVER *locks door. Crowd can be heard through it coming closer.*

Ah'm feart. Can we no' hide onywhere?

Battering at door starts.

PETER (*outside*). Open! Open in the name of the Lord!

CARVER (*to the people outside*). This is the house of God. It is a sanctuary. (*To DAVIE.*) They must respect that.

JAMES (*outside*). Why waste your time, man. Put your shoulder to it. Here, I'll help.

DAVIE. Can we no' hide?

CARVER. There's no other door, Davie.

PETER *and* JAMES. One! Two! Three!

Door is smashed open. A cheer goes up and people start coming in cheering and jeering. Speeches often overlap.

CARVER. You have no right here. This is the Chapel Royal. The house of God . . .

JAMES (*speaking loudly so the crowd can hear him*). D'ye hear that? The Chapel Royal! The house of a bloated papist queen!

PETER. Here old man. Give us those books.

Crowd start smashing chairs.

CARVER (*scarcely audible in the din*). You have no right! It is theft. Ignorance!

ANDREW. Ignorance? We come in the name of Christ!

CARVER. Leave those chairs!

ANDREW. It is Christ's work that we perform. Leave the chairs, he tells us. But we can burn the books! Heresies and lies!

CROWD. Burn the books! Burn the books!

PETER (*shouting*). Burn all blasphemy!

CARVER. It excites you, doesn't it? Your spittle even reaches my face but you can't defend ignorance with spit you know.

PETER. Will I try my hand to you instead?

DAVIE. Dinna ye dae that or ah'll kill ye!

PETER. Out of my way! Get this idiot out of the way!

CARVER. Leave him alone! He's an innocent.

DAVIE. They're nae like me. They're nae innocent.

PETER. Come on, old man. I'll see you out of here.

DAVIE. Dinnae you touch him. You touch him an ah'll kill ye. You touch him an ah'll kill ye . . . Ah've killed a man . . . Ah've killed a maa . . . (*The word dies on him as he is punched in the stomach.*)

JAMES. That should shut you up!

DAVIE (*his voice receding as he is dragged away*). Ye're a' stupid! Stupid! Stupid! Stu . . . (*He is hit again.*)

CARVER (*calling out*). Don't hurt him! He's a child . . . can't you see that.

ANDREW. We don't need you to tell us!

CARVER (*calling out*). Leave that statue. That is St Michael.

ANDREW (*laughing*). Saint Michael? It's a block of stone! A graven image! Haul it down!

JAMES. We need a rope to it. Good man. Ay. Throw it over!

ANDREW. Stand back there! It's moving. Easy . . . easy . . .

JAMES. Haul away! Here he comes.

A heavy crash is followed by a cheer.

ANDREW. Now for the other one!

Breaking window.

PETER. Ay. You may break the glass too. It's stained with iniquity.

RICHARDSON *comes in.*

CARVER. Richardson! For God's sake put an end to this!

RICHARDSON (*cutting across* CARVER *with commanding power*). Andrew! . . . James! . . . Peter!? All of you! Stop this at once. This is a disgrace to the reform. I want every one of you to leave NOW. This is the house of God.

ANDREW. It is the house of the ungodly. It has been turned into a den of iniquity and idolatry!

RICHARDSON. One might ask by whom, Andrew. No, don't scowl at me. You are all beginners merely. You will reform nothing by this! Look at this shambles. This is not the work of Christ!

PETER. Christ whipped the traders in the temple!

RICHARDSON. And you are Christ, are you? No, no, no . . .

CARVER. And we are not money-changers.

PETER. You are *all* money-changers! Priests, canons, bishops . . . fat money-changers!

RICHARDSON. Enough! Leave this to me, Peter. (*To the crowd.*) I am prepared to forget this sorry episode. I will not report it. But you must all leave now.

General shuffling and murmuring as people start to leave.

(*Quieter.*) I will deal with this man. James! fetch water and put out that fire. Now go . . . *all* of you . . . go.

CARVER. Thank you. Thank you Alan . . . where is Davie?

JAMES. Reform? You are as bad as the rest of them . . . feart when it comes to the bit.

RICHARDSON. Robert, I am utterly ashamed. This was never intended.

CARVER. Can you see Davie anywhere?

JAMES (*roughly*). There's a man girning away over there.

RICHARDSON (*calling out*). Davie? Are you all right?

CARVER. Did they hurt you Davie?

ISOBEL. Is it safe to come in?

RICHARDSON. Isobel! Yes, yes. I was too late. You can see . . . too late . . .

They have moved across to DAVIE.

ISOBEL. Is that you, Davie?

CARVER. Are you hurt, Davie?

DAVIE. Ah'm no right. Ah'm no feelin' awfy guid . . . There's yer big music book. Ah kent fine ye cared for that yin special.

ISOBEL. Don't talk! Don't try to talk.

DAVIE. Ah protectit it for ye . . . it's in ma satchel.

CARVER. Good lad, Davie. You needn't worry about it now.

RICHARDSON. I don't like it. He's too pale.

DAVIE. They didnae think a daftie wad keep a big book, but ah'm no sae daft an ah kept it for ye.

ISOBEL. Where do you hurt, Davie? Where is it sore?

DAVIE (*his voice beginning to weaken*). They kicked me . . . ah'm no sae guid . . .

CARVER. Can you point to where it hurts?

DAVIE (*suddenly impatient*). Ach it hurts everywhere man . . . ah'm no feelin' right. (*He faints.*)

ISOBEL. Here's some water.

RICHARDSON. He's passing out. Hold up his head.

ISOBEL. I can't get him to drink it.

CARVER (*very gently*). Davie? Davie?

RICHARDSON (*suddenly tired*). It's no use, Robert. He must be bleeding to death. How could this have happened?

ISOBEL (*her voice receding as though trying to follow him, ending up with gentle sobbing as the men speak*). Davie! . . . Davie . . . Davie . . .

RICHARDSON. He's leaving us for a better world . . .

CARVER (*very quietly and while* RICHARDSON *is speaking*). In nomine domini et filii patri et spiritu sancto . . .

RICHARDSON . . . I'll close his eyes now, Isobel.

ISOBEL *sobs quietly. The men also are near breaking down.*

CARVER. If only I hadn't asked him to gather up the books . . . how could they? . . . how could they do such a thing?

RICHARDSON (*bitterly upset*). We had better take care of *this* book then, had we not . . . I trust you think it was worth it . . .

ISOBEL (*remonstrating*). Alan!

CARVER. Davie thought so . . .

ISOBEL. How can you talk about a book when Davie lies here dead at your feet? What kind of humans are you? (*Her sobbing redoubles and then subsides.*)

RICHARDSON (*clearly under stress and actually restraining himself*). I suspect Robert here thinks a book is worth a life, don't you Robert?

Pause.

CARVER (*very slowly and quietly*). Davie gave his life for that book. Don't take his giving away from him. Don't ever either of you take away from what he has done. It was his giving. It could never have been yours. It is not yours to touch or diminish.

ISOBEL (*with agonised bitterness*). His gift! His gift! What use ever had he for such a book. What good are such things to him now . . . you selfish, selfish, selfish . . .

CARVER (*almost shouted*). He *sang* from it. (*His cry of protest starts off his cough but he becomes calm again.*) He loved it. It was the one thing in the whole world that he could do that few others could. It was through his singing that he found such little nobility as he could ever find in the eyes and ears of others and now he has done something more noble than any of us will ever encounter. You taught him to read. You believed in that. I taught him to read music. Good or bad, he had faith in it. (*He nearly breaks down.*)

RICHARDSON. The book is valueless. But what Davie did is noble indeed. You are right to say so.

ISOBEL. I wish it had never been made.

RICHARDSON. You are upset. We are all upset. The book can do no more harm than it has done already . . . it's not as though such music is likely to be heard again anyway. We will have to move him – I will go and get help . . .

CARVER. I can help you . . .

RICHARDSON. No, Robert. You're frail and you are not well. (*Pause.*) There's no hope of identifying who is responsible for it of course. Come with me Isobel. I'll be back soon, Robert.

CARVER. Thank you Alan. Thank you.

RICHARDSON *and* ISOBEL *leave*.

Ah Davie. When the great door opens you won't have to sneak in. They'll meet you there and take you to the heart of the rose . . . to the very heart . . .

CARVER *sighs deeply then begins to pray, at first the words are scarcely audible but become recognisable at 'Sanguinem' and are at almost normal voice level at 'et in me respicias miserum'. Fade out on the final paragraph.*

O bone Jesu. O clementissime Jesu deprecor te per illum sanguinem pretiosum quem pro peccatoribus effundere voluisti ut abluas iniquitatem meam et in me respicias miserum et indignum peccatorum et hoc nomen Jesum invocantem

O nomen Jesu, nomen dulce, nomen dilectabile, nomen Jesu, nomen suave . . .

Fade in central climax of 'O Bone Jesu' then fade to closing announcements.

IN THE NATIVE STATE

by Tom Stoppard

for Felicity Kendal

Tom Stoppard has written for radio, television, stage and film. His work for radio includes: *The Dissolution of Dominic Boot* (1964); *M is for Moon Among Other Things* (1964); *If You're Glad, I'll Be Frank* (1966); *Albert's Bridge* (1967, Italia Prize Winner); *Where Are They Now?* (1976) and *The Dog It Was That Died* (1983). For television he has written *A Walk on Water* (1963, later re-written for the stage as *Enter a Free Man*, 1968); *A Separate Peace* (1966); *Teeth* (1967); *Another Moon Called Earth* (1967, the seed of *Jumpers*); *Neutral Ground* (1968); *Artist Descending a Staircase* (1972); *Three Men in a Boat* (1975); *The Boundary* (1975 with Clive Exton); *Professional Foul* (1977 Bafta and Broadcasting Press Guild Awards); and *Squaring the Circle* (1984). His stage plays include: *Rosencrantz and Guildenstern are Dead* (1966; Evening Standard and Tony Awards; he also directed and wrote the screenplay for the film which won the Prix d'Or at the Venice Film Festival 1990 for Best Film); *The Real Inspector Hound* (1968); *After Magritte* (1970); *Jumpers* (1972; Evening Standard Award Winner); *Travesties* (1974; Evening Standard and Tony Awards); *Dirty Linen* (1976); *Every Good Boy Deserves Favour* (1977); *Night and Day* (1978; Evening Standard Award Winner) and *The Real Thing* (1982; Evening Standard and Tony Awards) and *Hapgood* (1988). He has also written screenplays for *Despair*; *The Romantic Englishwoman*; *The Human Factor*; *Brazil*; *Empire of the Sun*; *The Russia House* and *Billy Bathgate*.

In the Native State was first broadcast on BBC Radio 3 as the 'Sunday Play' on 21 April 1991. The cast was as follows:

FLORA CREWE aged thirty-five	Felicity Kendal
NIRAD DAS aged thirty-three	Sam Dastor
MRS SWAN aged eighty-three	Peggy Ashcroft
ANISH DAS aged forty	Lyndham Gregory
DAVID DURANCE about thirty, officer class	Simon Treves
NELL (Mrs Swan) aged twenty-three, middle-class bluestocking	Emma Gregory
NAZRUL young or middle-aged, a Muslim, speaks no English	Amerjit Deu
PIKE age not crucial (thirty-five to fifty-five), educated American, Southern accent	William Hootkins
COOMARASWAMI, middle-aged, fat, cheerful, Indian accent	Renu Setnar
RESIDENT aged forty-plus, Winchester and Cambridge	Brett Usher
RAJAH aged late fifties, educated at Harrow	Saeed Jaffrey
FRANCIS Englishman, thirty-three, Indian Civil Service	Mark Straker

EMILY EDEN Englishwoman
  (a real person) was
  forty-two in 1839   Auriol Smith

In addition:
Indian QUESTIONER
Club SERVANT
English MAN and WOMAN at the Club

Director: John Tydeman
Running time, as broadcast: 135 mins

Note:
The play is set in two places and periods: India in 1930, and England in the present day.

  We come to learn that Nirad Das was educated initially at a 'vernacular school', unlike Anish Das, who went to a 'convent school'. The significance of this is that Nirad speaks English with a stronger Indian accent than Anish.

Scene One: India

The verandah of a guesthouse. Jummapur would be a considerable town, but the guesthouse is conceived as being set somewhat on its own; the ambient sound would not be urban. There are references to monkeys, parrots, dogs, chickens. The surround would be sandy, not metalled.

FLORA (*interior voice*).
   'Yes, I am in heat like a bride in a bath,
   without secrets, soaked in heated air
   that liquifies to the touch and floods,
   shortening the breath, yes,
   I am discovered, heat has found me out,
   a stain that stops at nothing,
   not the squeezed gates or soft gutters,
   it brims as I shift,
   it webs my fingers round my pen,
   yes, think of a woman in a blue dress
   sat on a straight-backed chair at a plain table
   on the verandah of a guesthouse,
   writing about the weather.
   Or think, if you prefer, of bitches,
   cats, goats, monkeys at it like knives
   in the jacaranda – '

NIRAD DAS. Do you want me to stop, Miss Crewe?

FLORA. What?

DAS. Would you like to rest?

FLORA. No, I don't want to rest. Do you?

DAS. Not at all, but you crossed your legs, and I thought perhaps –

FLORA. Oh! I'm so sorry! So I did. There. Is that how I was?

DAS. You are patient with me. I think your nature is very kind.

FLORA. Do you think so, Mr Das?

DAS. I am sure of it. May I ask you a personal question?

FLORA. That *is* a personal question.

DAS. Oh, my goodness, is it?

FLORA. I always think so. It always feels like one. *Carte blanche* is what you're asking, Mr Das. Am I to lay myself bare before you?

DAS (*panicking slightly*). My question was only about your poem!

FLORA. At least you knew it was personal.

DAS. I will not ask it now, of course.

FLORA. On that understanding I will answer it. My poem is about heat.

DAS. Oh. Thank you.

FLORA. I resume my pose. Pen to paper. Legs uncrossed. You know, you are the first man to paint my toenails.

DAS. Actually, I am occupied in the folds of your skirt.

FLORA. Ah. In that you are not the first.

DAS. You have been painted before? But of course you have! Many times, I expect!

FLORA. You know, Mr Das, your nature is much kinder than mine.

Scene Two: England

Interior. We come to learn that MRS SWAN *is serving tea (on a brass table-top) in a bungalow in Shepperton, a garden's length from the (quiet) road.*

MRS SWAN. Do you think you take after your father?

ANISH. I don't know. I would like to think so. But my

father was a man who suffered for his beliefs, and I have never had to do that, so . . .

MRS SWAN. I meant being a painter. You are a painter like your father.

ANISH. Oh . . . yes. Yes, I am a painter like my father. Though not at all like my father, of course.

MRS SWAN. Your father was an Indian painter, you mean?

ANISH. An Indian painter? Well, I'm as Indian as he was. But yes. I suppose I am not a particularly *Indian* painter . . . not an Indian painter *particularly*, or rather . . .

MRS SWAN. Not particularly an Indian painter.

ANISH. Yes. But then, nor was he. Apart from being Indian.

MRS SWAN. As you are.

ANISH. Yes.

MRS SWAN (*pouring tea*). Though you are not at all like him.

ANISH. No. Yes. Perhaps if you had seen my work . . . (*Accepting the teacup.*) Oh, thank you.

MRS SWAN. Of course, *you* are a successful painter.

ANISH. I didn't mean that, Mrs Swan . . . only that my father was a quite different kind of artist, a portrait painter, as you know . . .

MRS SWAN. I can't say I do, Mr Das. Until I received your letter your father was unknown to me. In fact, the attribution 'unknown Indian artist' summed up the situation, exactly, if indeed it was your father who made the portrait of my sister.

ANISH. Oh, the portrait is certainly my father's work, Mrs Swan! And I have brought the evidence to show you! I have been in such a state! I have done no work for a week! You simply cannot imagine my feelings when I saw the book in the shop window – my excitement! You see, I carry my copy everywhere.

MRS SWAN. Well, I hope there'll be lots like *you*, Mr Das.

ANISH. There will be no one like me, Mrs Swan! It was not

the book, of course, but the painting on the jacket and the same on the frontispiece inside! My father was not 'unknown' in Jummapur. Surely the publishers or somebody . . .

MRS SWAN. They made inquiries by letter, but it was all sixty years ago.

ANISH. Yes. If only my father could have known that one day his portrait of Flora Crewe would . . .

MRS SWAN. By the way, what *were* your father's beliefs?

ANISH (*surprised*). Why . . . we are Hindu . . .

MRS SWAN. You said he had suffered for his beliefs.

ANISH. Oh. I meant his opinions. For which he suffered imprisonment.

MRS SWAN. Who put him in prison?

ANISH. You did.

MRS SWAN. I did?

ANISH. I mean, the British.

MRS SWAN. Oh, I see. *We* did. But how did we know what his opinions were?

ANISH. Well . . . (*Uncertainly.*) I suppose he took part in various actions . . .

MRS SWAN. Then he was imprisoned for his actions not his opinions, Mr Das, and obviously deserved what he got. Will you have a slice of cake?

ANISH. Thank you.

MRS SWAN. Victoria sponge or Battenberg?

ANISH. Oh . . .

MRS SWAN. The sponge is my own, the raspberry jam too.

ANISH. I would love some.

A clock chimes in the room.

MRS SWAN. Ignore it. The clock has decided to be merely decorative. It chimes at random. There we are, then . . .

ANISH. Thank you.

MRS SWAN. But all that must have been before you were born . . . Independence . . .

ANISH. Oh, yes, long before. I was the child of my father's second marriage. I was born in '49, and these events took place in Jummapur in 1930.

MRS SWAN. 1930! But that was when Flora was in Jummapur!

ANISH. Yes, I know. That is why I am here.

Scene Three: India

On the verandah.

FLORA. Mr Das, I am considering whether to ask you a delicate question, as between friends and artists.

DAS. Oh, Miss Crewe, I am transported beyond my most fantastical hopes of our fellowship! This is a red-letter day without dispute!

FLORA. If you are going to be so Indian I shan't ask it.

DAS. But I cannot be less Indian than I am.

FLORA. You could if you tried. I'm not sure I'm going to ask you now.

DAS. Then you need not, dear Miss Crewe! You considered. The unasked, the almost asked question, united us for a moment in its intimacy, we came together in your mind like a spark in a vacuum glass, and the redness of the day's letter will not be denied.

FLORA. You are still doing it, Mr Das.

DAS. You wish me to be less Indian?

FLORA. I did say that but I think what I meant was for you to be *more* Indian, or at any rate *Indian*, not Englished-up and all over me like a labrador and knocking things off tables with your tail – so *waggish* of you, Mr Das, to compare my mind to a vacuum. You only do it with us. I don't believe that left to yourself you can't have an ordinary conversation without jumping backwards through hoops of delight, *with* whoops of delight, I think I mean; actually I do know what I mean, I want you to be with me as you would be if *I* were Indian.

DAS. An Indian, Miss Crewe! Oh dear, that is a mental construction which has no counterpart in the material world.

FLORA. A *unicorn* is a mental construction which has no counterpart in the material world but you can imagine it.

DAS. You can imagine it but you cannot mount it.

FLORA. Imagining it was all I was asking in my case.

DAS (*terribly discomfited*). Oh! Oh, my gracious! I had no intention – I assure you –

FLORA (*amused*). No, no, you cannot unwag your very best wag. You cleared the table, the bric-à-brac is on the parquet – the specimen vase, the snuff box, the souvenir of Broadstairs – (*But she has misjudged.*)

DAS (*anguished*). You are cruel to me, Miss Crewe!

FLORA (*instantly repentant*). Oh! I'm so sorry. I didn't want to be. It's my nature. Please come out from behind your easel – look at me.

DAS. May we fall silent, please. I prefer to work in silence.

FLORA. I've spoiled everything. I'm very sorry.

DAS. The shadow has moved. I must correct it.

FLORA. Yes, it has moved. It cannot be corrected. We must wait for tomorrow. I'm so sorry.

Scene Four: England

ANISH. When my father met Flora Crewe he had been a widower for several years, although he was still quite a young man, a year or two younger than her, yes . . . the beginning of the Hot Weather in 1930: he would have been not yet thirty-four. He had lost his wife to cholera and he was childless. I knew nothing of my father's life before Swaraj. The British Empire was prehistory to me. By the time I was old enough to be curious, my father was over sixty, an old gentleman who spoke very little except when he sometimes read aloud to me. I say read to me but really he read to himself, with me in attendance. He liked to read in English. Robert Browning, Tennyson, Macaulay's *Lays of Ancient Rome*, and Dickens, of course . . .

MRS SWAN. How surprising.

ANISH. Oh, yes. (*Meaning 'no'.*) He went from a vernacular school to Elphinstone College in Bombay, and you only have to look at Elphinstone College to know it was built to give us a proper British education.

MRS SWAN. I really meant, how surprising in view of his 'opinions'. But I spoke without thinking. Your father resented the British and loved English literature, which was perfectly consistent of him, and I have interrupted you. You haven't mentioned your mother.

ANISH. My mother speaks no English. She is from a village, peasant farmers, no, plot-holders. She was born in the year Flora Crewe came to Jummapur, and she married when she was sixteen. It was not from her that I learned . . . that . . .

MRS SWAN. That . . . ?

ANISH. That my father was a thorn in the flesh of the British; and was still remembered for it – I might say, is honoured for it.

MRS SWAN. By whom?

ANISH. By his son.

MRS SWAN. It does you credit.

ANISH. In Bengal and the United Provinces, all over British India, of course, there were thousands of people who did as much and more, and went to gaol, but in Jummapur we were 'loyal', as you would say, we had been loyal to the British right through the First War of Independence.

MRS SWAN. The . . . ? What war was that?

ANISH. The Rising of 1857.

MRS SWAN. Oh, you mean the Mutiny. *What* did you call it?

ANISH. Dear Mrs Swan, imperial history is only the view from . . . no, no – please let us not argue. I promise you I didn't come to give you a history lesson.

MRS SWAN. You seem ill-equipped to do so. We were your Romans, you know. We might have been your Normans.

ANISH. And did you expect us to be grateful?

MRS SWAN. That's neither here nor there. I don't suppose
I'd have been grateful if a lot of Romans turned up and
started laying down the law and the language and telling us
we were all one country now, so Wessex had to stop
fighting Mercia, and so forth. 'What a cheek,' is probably
what I would have thought. 'Go away, and take your
roads and your baths with you.' It doesn't matter what I
would have thought. It's what I think now that matters.
You speak English better than most young people I meet.
Did you go to school here?

ANISH. No, I went to a convent school in . . . You are
spreading a net for me, Mrs Swan.

MRS SWAN. What net would that be? Have some more
cake.

ANISH. Mrs Swan, you are a very wicked woman. You
advance a preposterous argument and try to fill my mouth
with cake so I cannot answer you. I will resist you and
your cake. *We* were the Romans! We were up to date
when you were a backward nation. The foreigners who
invaded *you* found a third-world country! Even when you
discovered India in the age of Shakespeare, we already had
our Shakespeares. And our science, architecture, our
literature and art, we had a culture older and more
splendid, we were rich! After all, that's why you came.
(*But he has misjudged.*)

MRS SWAN (*angrily*). We made you a proper country! And
when we left you fell straight to pieces like Humpty
Dumpty! Look at the map! You should feel nothing but
shame!

ANISH. Oh, yes . . . I am ashamed. I am a guest in your
house and I have been . . .

MRS SWAN. . . . no, only provocative. We will change the
subject.

ANISH. I'm sorry.

The clock chimes.

MRS SWAN. That clock has gone quite mad. It has gained
twenty minutes since this morning . . . There seems no
point in putting it back.

ANISH. No, we cannot put it back. I'm so sorry.

Scene Five: India

FLORA. While having tiffin on the verandah of my
    bungalow I spilled kedgeree on my dungarees and had to
    go to the gymkhana in my pyjamas looking like a coolie.

DAS. I was buying chutney in the bazaar when a thug who
    had escaped from the choky ran amuck and killed a box-
    wallah for his loot, creating a hullabaloo and landing
    himself in the mulligatawny.

FLORA. I went doolally at the durbar and was sent back to
    Blighty in a dooley feeling rather dikki with a cup of char
    and a chit for a chotapeg.

DAS. Yes, and the burra sahib who looked so pukka in his
    topi sent a coolie to the memsahib –

FLORA. No, no. You can't have memsahib *and* sahib, that's
    cheating – and anyway, I've already said coolie.

DAS. I concede, Miss Crewe. You are the Hobson-Jobson
    champion!

FLORA. You are chivalrous, Mr Das. So I'll confess I had
    help. I found a whole list of Anglo-Indian words in my
    bedside drawer, for the benefit of travellers.

DAS. But I know both languages, so you still win on
    handicap.

FLORA. Where did you learn everything, Mr Das?

DAS. From books. I like Dickens and Browning and
    Shakespeare of course – but my favourite is Agatha
    Christie! *The Mysterious Affair at Styles*! Oh, the woman
    is a genius! But I would like to write like Macaulay.

FLORA. Oh dear.

DAS. I have to thank Lord Macaulay for English, you know.
    It was his idea when he was in the government of India
    that English should be taught to us all. He wanted to
    supply the East India Company with clerks, but he was
    sowing dragon's teeth. Instead of babus he produced
    lawyers, journalists, civil servants – he produced Gandhi!
    We have so many, many languages, you know, that
    English is the only language the nationalists can
    communicate in! That is a very good joke on Macaulay,
    don't you think?

FLORA. Are *you* a nationalist, Mr Das?

DAS. Ah, that is a very interesting question! But we shouldn't have stopped. It's getting late for you. I must work more quickly.

FLORA. It's only half-past ten.

DAS. No, it's nearly April, and that is becoming late.

FLORA. Yes, it seems hotter than ever. Would you like some more lemonade?

DAS. No, thank you, no lemonade. Miss Crewe, you haven't looked at my painting yet.

FLORA. No. Not yet. I never look. Do you mind?

DAS. No.

FLORA. You do really. But I once asked a painter, 'Can I look?' and he said, 'Why? When I paint a table I don't have to show it to the table.'

DAS. I said you had been painted before.

FLORA. Only once.

DAS. A portrait?

FLORA. Not in the way you mean. It was a nude.

DAS. Oh.

FLORA. Unusually. He painted his friends clothed. For nudes he used models. I believe I was his friend. But perhaps not. Perhaps a used model only. It hardly matters. He was dead so soon afterwards. He was not so kind to me as you are. I had to lie with my shoulders flat but my hips twisted towards the canvas. I could hardly move afterwards.

DAS. Do you have the painting?

FLORA. No.

DAS. Where is it?

FLORA. Nowhere. A man I thought I might marry destroyed it. So after that, I didn't want to be painted again.

DAS. Oh . . .

FLORA. But luckily I forgot that, when you asked me. I must have got over it without realizing. My goodness, what a red-letter day you are having. There's a man on a horse.

DURANCE (*off*). Good morning! Miss Crewe, I think!

FLORA. Yes, good morning! (*Aside to* DAS.) Do you know him? (*To* DURANCE.) How do you do!

DAS. He is the Assistant.

DURANCE (*off*). May I get down a moment?

FLORA. Of course. What a beautiful animal! (*Aside to* DAS.) Assistant what?

DAS. Captain Durance!

DURANCE. Thank you!

FLORA. Come on up, do join us.

We have heard the horse walking forward, perhaps snorting, and DURANCE *dismounting, and now coming up the three or four wooden steps on to the verandah.*

DURANCE (*arriving*). Oh, it's Mr Das, isn't it?

DAS. Good morning, sir. But we have never met.

DURANCE. Oh, but I know you. And Miss Crewe, your fame precedes you.

FLORA. Thank you . . . but . . .

DURANCE. I'm from the Residency. David Durance.

FLORA. How do you do?

DURANCE. Oh, but look here – I'm interrupting the artist.

FLORA. We had stopped.

DURANCE. May one look? Oh, I say! Coming along jolly well! Don't you think so, Miss Crewe?

DAS. I must be going. I have overstayed my time today.

FLORA. But we'll continue tomorrow?

DAS. Yes. Perhaps a little earlier if it suits you. I will leave everything just inside the door, if that is all right . . . and the easel . . .

DAS *is moving the objects, bumping them down in the interior.*

FLORA. Yes, of course. Why don't you leave the canvas too? It will be quite safe.

DAS. I . . . yes . . . I have a drape for it. Thank you. There.

FLORA. Like shutting up the parrot for the night.

DAS. There we are. Thank you for the lemonade, Miss Crewe. An absolute treat. I promise you! Goodbye, sir – and – yes – and until tomorrow . . .

He goes down the steps to the outside and mounts a bicycle and pedals away.

FLORA. Yes . . . goodbye! (*To* DURANCE.) I'll put my shoes on. Sorry about my toes, but I like to wriggle them when I'm working.

DURANCE. I'll only stay a moment. My chief asked me to look in. Just to make sure there's nothing we can do for you.

FLORA. There's a servant who seems to come with the guesthouse, though he has a way of disappearing, but would you like some tea?

DURANCE. No, nothing for me. Really. We might have found you more comfortable quarters, you know, not quite so in-the-town.

FLORA. How did you know I was here?

DURANCE. Now there's a point. Usually we know of arrivals because the first thing they do is drop in a card, but in your case . . . rumours in the bazaar, so to speak. Are you an old hand here, Miss Crewe?

FLORA. No, I've never been to India before. I came up from Bombay just a few days ago.

DURANCE. But you have friends here, perhaps?

FLORA. No. I got on a boat and I came, knowing no one. I have friends in England who have friends here. Actually, one friend.

DURANCE. In Jummapur, this friend?

FLORA. No – the *friend* – my friend – is in London, of

course; *his* friends are in different places in Rajputana, and I will also be going to Delhi and then up to the Punjab, I hope.

DURANCE. Now I see. And your friend in London has friends in Jummapur?

FLORA. Yes.

DURANCE. Like Mr Das?

FLORA. No. Are you a policeman of some kind, Mr Durance?

DURANCE. Me? No. I'm sorry if I sound like one.

FLORA. Well, you do a bit. I'm travelling with letters of introduction from Mr Joshua Chamberlain to a number of social clubs and literary societies. I speak on the subject of 'Literary Life in London', in return for board and lodging . . . So you see I couldn't have taken advantage of your kindness without giving offence to my hosts.

DURANCE. The game is different here. By putting up at the Residency you would have gained respect, not lost it.

FLORA. Thank you, but what about *self* respect?

DURANCE. Well . . . as long as all is well. So you are following in Chamberlain's footsteps. All is explained.

FLORA. I don't think *I* explained it. But yes, I am. He spoke in Jummapur three years ago, on the subject of Empire.

DURANCE. Yes. Is he a good friend?

FLORA. Yes.

DURANCE. Did you know he was some sort of Communist?

FLORA. I thought he might be. He stood twice for Parliament as the Communist candidate.

DURANCE (*unoffended, pleasant as before*). I amuse you. That's all right, amusing our distinguished visitors is among my duties.

FLORA. Well, don't be so stuffy. And call again if you like.

DURANCE. Thank you. How long will you be with us?

FLORA. I'm expected in Jaipur but they don't mind when I come.

DURANCE. I'm sure you'll have a marvellous time. There are wonderful things to see. Meanwhile, please consider yourself an honorary member of the Club – mention my name, but I'll put you in the book.

FLORA. Thank you.

DURANCE. Well . . .

FLORA. I wish I had a lump of sugar for your horse. Next time.

DURANCE. He's my main indulgence. I wish I'd been here when a good horse went with the job.

FLORA. Yes . . . what *is* your job? You mentioned your chief.

DURANCE. The Resident. He represents the government here.

FLORA. The British government?

DURANCE. Delhi. The Viceroy, in fact. Jummapur is not British India . . . you understand that?

FLORA. Yes . . . but it's all the Empire, isn't it?

DURANCE. Oh, yes. Absolutely. But there's about five hundred rajahs and maharajahs and nabobs and so on who run bits of it, well, nearly half of it actually, by treaty. And we're here to make sure they don't get up to mischief.

FLORA. I knew you were a kind of policeman.

DURANCE (*laughs*). Miss Crewe, would you have dinner with us while you are here?

FLORA. With you and your wife, do you mean?

DURANCE. No . . . at the Club. Us. With me. I don't run to a wife, I'm afraid. But do come. We're a reasonably civilized lot, and there's usually dancing on Saturdays; only a gramophone but lots of fun.

FLORA. I'd love to. On Saturday, then.

DURANCE. Oh . . . splendid! I'll come by. (*He mounts his horse.*)

FLORA. I haven't got a horse, you know.

DURANCE. We have a Daimler at the Residency. I'll see if I can wangle it. Pick you up about eight?

FLORA. Yes.

DURANCE. We don't dress, normally, except on dress nights. (*Laughs at himself.*) Obviously.

FLORA. I'll be ready.

DURANCE. Jolly good.

FLORA. Goodbye.

DURANCE. Goodbye.

FLORA (*calling out*). Wangle the Daimler!

Scene Six: England

ANISH. I apologize if I was rude. *You* didn't put my father in gaol, after all.

MRS SWAN. Not in any sense. Jummapur was a native state, so your father was put in gaol by his own people.

ANISH (*cautiously*). Well . . .

MRS SWAN (*firmly*). Whatever your father may have done, the Resident would have had no authority to imprison an Indian. The Rajah of Jummapur had his own justice.

ANISH. Even so, you – (*Corrects himself.*) the British . . .

MRS SWAN. Oh, I'm not saying we wouldn't have boxed his ears and sent him packing if he forgot which side his bread was buttered, but facts are facts. The Rajah put your father in the choky. How long for, by the way?

ANISH. Six months, actually.

MRS SWAN. There you are. In Bengal or the UP he would have got a year at least. After the war it may have been different. With Independence round the corner, people were queuing up to go to prison; it was their ticket to the show. They'd do their bit of civil disobedience and hop into the paddy-wagon thoroughly pleased with themselves. Francis – that's my husband – would let them off with a small fine if he thought they were Johnny-come-latelies, and they'd be furious. That was when Francis had his District. We were right up near Nepal . . .

ANISH. Yes, I noticed your . . .

MRS SWAN. Of course you did. In India we had pictures of coaching inns and fox hunting, and chintz covers from Liberty's and all sorts of knick-knackery from home . . . and now I've landed up in Shepperton I've got elephants and prayer-wheels cluttering up the window ledges, and the tea table is Nepalese brass. One could make a comment about human nature, but have a slice of Battenberg instead.

ANISH. Thank you.

MRS SWAN. I got it specially, an artistic sort of cake, I always think. What kind of paintings are they, these paintings that are not like your father's. Describe your latest. Like the cake?

ANISH (*eating*). Delicious. Thank you.

MRS SWAN. No, are they like the cake?

ANISH. Oh. No. They are all . . . like each other really. I can't *describe* them.

MRS SWAN. Indescribable, then. But modern, I suppose?

ANISH (*becoming slightly impatient*). It's not *my* paintings I have come about.

MRS SWAN. No, of course. You recognized your father's work in the window of a bookshop. Still, he might have been more pleased to be in one art gallery than in a hundred bookshops.

ANISH. Perhaps not. I'm sure my father never had a single one of his paintings reproduced, and that is an extraordinary pleasure for an artist. I know! The painting under one's hand is everything, of course . . . unique. But replication! *That* is popularity! If we are allowed a little worldly pride, put us on thousands and thousands of book jackets – on calendars – biscuit tins!

MRS SWAN. Well, it's only *three* thousand of the *Selected Letters*, but America is still to come. Mr Pike thinks Flora's letters will do very well in America, and he should know, being an American himself.

ANISH. Mr Pike?

MRS SWAN. The editor. He put the book together. A serious man, Mr Pike, with a surprising *Gone with the Wind* sort of accent.

ANISH. Editor? Oh, yes. So he is. 'Edited with an introduction by Eldon Cooper Pike.' What does it mean – edited – exactly? Are there more letters that are not in the book?

MRS SWAN. Naturally. *Selected Letters of Flora Crewe*, that is what it means. And then there's the footnotes. Mr Pike did those too.

ANISH. Oh yes . . . the footnotes.

MRS SWAN. Far too much of a good thing, the footnotes, in my opinion; to be constantly interrupted in a Southern drawl by someone telling you things you already know or don't need to know at that moment. I hear Mr Pike's voice every time I go to the bits at the bottom of the page. He teaches Flora Crewe at a university in Maryland. It makes her sound like a subject, doesn't it? Like biology, or in her case, botany. Flora is widely taught in America. I have been written to, even visited, and on one occasion telephoned by young women doing Flora Crewe.

ANISH. Always young women?

MRS SWAN. Almost always, yes. She has become quite a heroine. Which she always was to me. I was only five when Mother died, so it was Flora who . . . oh dear, I'm going to need a hanky.

ANISH. Oh, I say! I'm sorry if I –

MRS SWAN (*snuffling*). Found it. (*She blows her nose.*) It makes me so cross that she missed it all, the *Collected Poems*, and now the *Letters*, with her name all over the place and students and professors so *interested* and so sweet about her poetry. Nobody gave tuppence about her while she was alive except to get her knickers off. Never mind, how is your tea?

ANISH. Erm . . . sorry. Very nice, very nice tea.

MRS SWAN. I'll have to go and repair myself. Yes, I like it well enough but I can't get the tea here to taste as it should. I expect it's the water. A reservoir near Staines

won't have the makings of a good cup of tea compared to
the water we got in the Hills. It came straight off the
Himalayas.

*With the help of a stick she has walked to the door and
closed it behind her.*

Scene Seven: India

FLORA (*interior voice*).
'Yes, I am in heat like a corpse in a ditch,
my skin stained and porous as a photograph
under a magnifying lens that shows each hair
a lily stem straggling out of a poisoned swamp.
Heat has had its way with me,
yes, I know this ditch, I have been left for dead before,
my lips gone slack and the wild iris
flickers in the drooling cavity, insects
crawl like tears from behind my eyes – '

Oh, fiddlesticks! May we stop for a moment. (*She gets up.*)
I'm sticking to myself.

DAS. Of course! Forgive me!

FLORA. You mustn't take responsibility for the climate too,
Mr Das.

DAS. No, I . . .

FLORA. No, I'm sorry. I'm bad-tempered. Should we have
some tea? I wouldn't mind something to eat too. (*Calls
out.*) Nazrul! Am I saying his name right? There's a jar of
duck pâté in the refrigerator . . .

NAZRUL *is a male servant. He speaks Urdu.*

Oh, Nazrul . . . char and . . .

NAZRUL (*in Urdu*). Yes, madam, I will bring tea
immediately . . .

FLORA. . . . bread . . . and in the fridge, no, don't go, listen
to me –

DAS. Would you allow me, please?

DAS *and* NAZRUL *speak in Urdu. DAS orders bread and
butter and the duck pâté from the fridge. But NAZRUL
has dramatic and tragic disclosures to make. Thieves have
stolen the pâté. DAS berates him.*

FLORA (*over the conversation*). . . . a jar with a picture of a *duck* . . .

NAZRUL *is promising to fetch bread and butter and cake, and he leaves.*

What was all that?

DAS. He will bring tea, and bread and butter and cake. The pâté has been taken by robbers.

FLORA. What?

DAS (*gravely*). Just so, I'm afraid.

FLORA. But the fridge is padlocked. Mr Coomaraswami pointed it out to me particularly.

DAS. Where do you keep the key?

FLORA. Nazrul keeps it, of course.

DAS. Ah well . . . the whole thing is a great mystery.

FLORA *splutters into laughter and* DAS *joins in.*

FLORA. But surely, isn't it against his religion?

DAS. Oh, certainly. I should say so. Not that I'm saying Nazrul stole the pâté, but stealing would be against his religion, undoubtedly.

FLORA. I don't mean stealing, I mean the pork.

DAS. But I thought you said it was duck.

FLORA. One must read the small print, Mr Das. 'Duck pâté' in large letters, 'with pork' in small letters. It's normal commercial practice.

DAS. Yes, I see.

FLORA. We must hope he only got the duck part . . .

DAS. That is your true nature speaking, Miss Crewe!

FLORA. . . . though of course, if they use one pig for every duck, Nazrul will have been lucky to get any duck at all.

DAS. The truth will never be known, only to God, who is merciful.

FLORA. Yes. Which God do you mean?

DAS. Yours if you wish, by all means.

FLORA. Now, Mr Das, there is such a thing as being too polite. Yours was here first.

DAS. Oh, but we Hindus can afford to be generous; we have gods to spare, one for every occasion. And Krishna said, 'Whichever god a man worships, it is I who answer the prayer.'

FLORA. I wasn't sure whether Krishna was a god or a person.

DAS. Oh, he was most certainly a god, one of the ten incarnations of Vishnu, and a favourite subject of the old Rajasthani painters. He had a great love affair, you see, with a married lady, Radha, who was the most beautiful of the herdswomen. Radha fell passionately in love with Krishna and she would often escape from her husband to meet him in secret.

FLORA. I think that's what confused me. Come and sit down, Mr Das. Take the cane chair. I'll keep mine for posture.

DAS (*sitting*). Thank you.

FLORA. I've been looking at temples with Mr Coomaraswami.

DAS. Yes. Do you find them interesting?

FLORA. I like some of the sculptures. The women have such serene faces. I mean, the goddesses.

DAS. Yes, they are beautiful.

FLORA. Breasts like melons, and baby-bearing hips. You must think me ill-favoured.

DAS. No. My wife was slightly built.

FLORA. Oh . . .

NAZRUL *arrives with a noisy tray*.

Thank you, Nazrul. Two kinds of cake!

NAZRUL *leaves, saying in Urdu that he will return with bread and butter*.

DAS. He will return with bread and butter.

FLORA (*arranging teacups*). How is your painting today?

DAS. Altered. Your face . . . I think your work was troublesome.

FLORA. Yes.

DAS. Is it the rhyming that is difficult?

FLORA. No.

DAS. The metre?

FLORA. No. The . . . emotion won't harmonize. I'm afraid I'm not much good at talking about it.

DAS. I'm sorry.

FLORA. That's why I don't keep nipping round to your side of the easel. If I don't look there's nothing to say. I think that that's better.

DAS. Yes. It is better to wait. My painting has no *rasa* today.

FLORA. What is *rasa*?

DAS. *Rasa* is juice. Its taste. Its essence. A painting must have its *rasa* . . . which is not *in* the painting exactly. *Rasa* is what you must feel when you see a painting, or hear music; it is the emotion which the artist must arouse in you.

FLORA. And poetry? Does a poem have *rasa*?

DAS. Oh yes! Without *rasa* it is not a poem, only words. That is a famous dictum of Vishvanata, a great teacher of poetry, six hundred years ago.

FLORA. *Rasa* . . . yes. My poem has no *rasa*.

DAS. Or perhaps it has two *rasas* which are in conflict.

FLORA. Oh . . .

DAS. There are nine *rasas*, each one a different colour. I should say mood. But each mood has its colour . . . white for laughter and fun, red for anger, grey for sorrow . . . each one has its own name, and its own god, too.

FLORA. And some don't get on. Is that it?

DAS. Yes. That is it. Some do and some don't. If you arouse emotions which are in opposition to each other the *rasas* will not . . . harmonize, you said.

FLORA. Yes.

DAS. Your poem is about heat.

FLORA. Yes.

DAS. But its *rasa* is perhaps . . . anger?

FLORA. Sex.

DAS (*unhesitatingly*). The *rasa* of erotic love is called Shringara. Its god is Vishnu, and its colour is *shyama*, which is blue-black. Vishvanata in his book on poetics tells us: Shringara requires, naturally, a lover and his loved one, who may be a courtesan if she is sincerely enamoured, and it is aroused by, for example, the moon, the scent of sandalwood, or being in an empty house. Shringara goes harmoniously with all other *rasas* and their complementary emotions, with the exception of cruelty, disgust and sloth.

FLORA. I see. Thank you. Empty house is very good. Mr Das, you sounded just like somebody else. Yourself, I expect. I knew you could. The other one reminded me of Dr Aziz in Forster's novel. Have you read it yet? I kept wanting to kick him.

DAS (*offended*). Oh . . .

FLORA. For not knowing his worth.

DAS. Then perhaps you didn't finish it.

FLORA. Yes, perhaps. Does he improve?

DAS. He alters.

FLORA. What is your opinion of *A Passage to India*?

DAS. Was that the delicate question you considered to ask me?

FLORA (*laughs happily*). Oh, Mr Das!

Scene Eight: England

MRS SWAN *re-enters the room.*

MRS SWAN. There . . . that's better . . .

ANISH. I was looking at your photographs. I hope you don't mind.

MRS SWAN. I took that one myself, in Venice, the summer before Flora went to India. I had a Kodak which let down in front in pleats. It took very good snaps; I wonder what happened to it? That was the day Diaghilev died. But we didn't know that till afterwards. We crossed to the Lido to have dinner with him at the hotel and he was dead.

ANISH. Is this one your husband?

MRS SWAN. Yes. That's Francis in Rawalpindi before we were married. Have you been up there?

ANISH. No. We have always lived in Rajasthan.

MRS SWAN. But you do not live there now?

ANISH. No. I live here now.

MRS SWAN. You wrote from St John's Wood.

ANISH. Yes. London is my home now. I have spent half my life here. I married here.

MRS SWAN. An English girl?

ANISH. Yes. Australian.

MRS SWAN. What an odd reply.

ANISH. Yes. I suppose so. Mrs Swan, it says in the book that your sister's portrait is reproduced by your permission. Does that mean you have it?

MRS SWAN. Yes.

ANISH. Here? In the house?

MRS SWAN. Oh, yes. Would you like to see it?

ANISH. Very much! I half expected to see it the moment I entered.

MRS SWAN. Pride of place, you thought. That's because you're a painter. Flora would not have cared to be on show. The portrait has always fended for itself rather . . .

ANISH. I understand. Where do you keep it?

MRS SWAN. Nowhere particularly. We always took it around with us from house to house and sometimes it ended up on top of a wardrobe. Oh dear, that must seem rather rude.

ANISH. It's all right.

MRS SWAN. Come along. It's in the bedroom, wrapped up.

You're lucky. It only just came back from being
photographed for the book. You can unwrap it for me.
Where's my stick? Has it fallen down?

ANISH. Here . . . let me . . .

MRS SWAN. Thank you.

ANISH. Do you need me to help you?

MRS SWAN. I hope not. Otherwise what would I do when
you'd gone? But you may open the door. You can see why
I got a bungalow.

*They are moving now, she with her stick. They enter
another room.*

I wonder what we called bungalows before India, and
verandahs and so on. It must have made certain
conversations quite awkward. 'I'm looking for a house
with no upstairs and an outside-inside bit stuck on the
front . . .'
Well, there you are! Rather well wrapped up. Will you
need the kitchen scissors, do you think?

ANISH. We'll see. What is in the boxes?

MRS SWAN. Flora's letters. Mr Pike had them
photographed too. Try to save the brown paper – it looks
a good size to be useful.

ANISH. Yes, I will . . .

MRS SWAN. Oh, it's quite easy . . . that's it . . .

The painting is unwrapped.

Well, there she is.

ANISH. Oh . . .

MRS SWAN. Yes, a bit much, isn't it?

ANISH. Oh . . . it's . . . so vibrant . . .

MRS SWAN. Vibrant. Yes . . . Oh . . . I say, *you're* not
going to blub too, are you?

ANISH (*weeping*). I'm sorry.

MRS SWAN. Don't worry. Borrow my hanky . . . It just
goes to show, you need an eye. And your father, after all,
was, like you, an Indian painter.

Scene Nine: India

FLORA. 'Jummapur. April 5th. Darling Nell, I'm having my portrait painted by an artist I met here, and I'm not using the historical present, I mean he's at it as I write, so if you see a painting of me in my cornflower dress sitting writing on a verandah you'll know I was writing *this* – some of the time anyway. He thinks I'm writing a poem. Posing as a poet, you see, just as the Enemy once said of me in his rotten rag.'

PIKE's *voice, which does sound rather like Clark Gable in* Gone with the Wind, *comes in immediately, intimate and slightly hushed, rather in the manner of the continuity voice which introduces live concerts on the radio.*

PIKE. 'The Enemy' was J. C. Squire (1884–1958), poet, critic, literary editor of the *New Statesman*, and editor of the London *Mercury*. FC is evidently referring to an anonymous editorial in the London *Mercury* (April 1920) complaining about, 'an outbreak of versifying flappers who should stop posing as poets and confine themselves to posing as railway stations'. The magazine was sued by the poets Elizabeth Paddington (1901–88) and Lavinia Clapham (1899–1929), both cases being settled out of court. FC poured a pint of beer over Squire's head in the Fitzroy Tavern in January 1921.

FLORA. 'I am installed in a little house with a verandah and three good-sized rooms under a tin roof. The verandah is at the front and you go into the main room which has an electric ceiling-fan and electric light, and an oil lamp which I prefer even when the electricity hasn't failed. There's a nice big window at the back, looking out at a rather hopeless garden, and then there is a nice plain bedroom with a big bed and desk and one wooden chair and a wash-stand, and through another door a little bathroom with a Victorian bath and also a shower which is, alas, contemporary makeshift. Over on the other side is a kitchen bit with a fridge, but my cook and bottle-washer disregards the electric stove and makes his own arrangements on a little verandah of his own. And all this is under a big green tree with monkeys and parrots in the branches and it's called a duck bungalow – '

PIKE. Dak bungalow, literally post-house.

FLORA. ' – although there is not a duck to be seen, only some scrawny chickens and a peahen. This is my first proper stop since I got off the boat and posted my Bombay letter. Yours overtook me and was waiting for me – why didn't I think of posting myself overland? – and thank you for it, but, darling, you mustn't expect me to be Intelligence from Abroad, as the *Times* used to say – you obviously know much more than I do about the Salt March – '

PIKE. Gandhi's 'March to the Sea' to protest the salt tax began at Ahmedabad on March 12th. He reached the sea on the day this letter was written.

FLORA. ' – nobody has mentioned it to me – and you'd better explain to Josh that the earthshaking sensations of Lord Beaverbrook's new Empire Party, etc. – '

PIKE. See Appendix G.

FLORA. ' – cause little stir in Jummapur. Sorry to disappoint.'

The appropriate sound effects creep in to illustrate Flora's letter, so here we begin to hear a slow steam train, followed in due course by the hubbub of the station, the clip-clop of the horse pulling the buggy as mentioned and the bicycle bells etc. which accompany the ride into town. Further down the letter, it is intended that Flora's questioner at her lecture will be heard in the appropriate physical ambience. In general, Flora's letter becomes an immediate presence – we can hear her pen scratching now and then, and insects, distant life, etc. – but when her letter takes us into an event, the sound-plot turns into the appropriate accompaniment.

'I arrived here on a huffing and puffing local with as many people riding on the roof as inside, and the entire committee of the Jummapur Theosophical Society was on the platform, bunch of flowers at the ready, not quite a red carpet and brass band but almost, and I thought there must be someone important on the train and it turned out to be me – '

COOMARASWAMI. Miss Crewe! Welcome to Jummapur!

FLORA. Thank you! How nice!
' – which was very agreeable.'

Are you Mr Coomaraswami?

COOMARASWAMI. That is me! Is this suitcase your only luggage?

FLORA. 'And in no time at all they put me in a buggy and the President of the Theosophical sat beside me holding a yellow parasol while the committee bicycled alongside, sometimes two to a bike, and here I came in triumph, like Britannia in a carnival float representing Empire, or, depending on how you look at it, the Oppression of the Indian People, which is how you *will* look at it and no doubt you're right but I never saw anyone less oppressed than Mr Coomaraswami, whose entire twenty stone shakes with laughter all the time. The Hot Weather, they tell me, is about to start, but I can't imagine anything hotter than this, and it will be followed by the Wet Season, though I already feel as though I am sitting in a puddle. Everything which requires movement must be accomplished between sunrise and breakfast, by which time inside is too hot to move and outside is too hot to think. My bedroom, apart from the ceiling fan, also has a punkah, which is like a line of washing worked by a punkah-wallah who sits outside and flaps the thing by a system of ropes and pulleys – or would if he were ever here, which he isn't. At sundown, gentle movement may be contemplated, and on Monday I was brought forth to deliver my lecture to a packed house, Mr C's house, in fact, and a much more sensible house than mine – built round a square courtyard, with a flat roof all around so I had an audience in the gods like gods in the audience, and though I say it myself I did a good one, encouraged by the sight of several copies of *Venus* and *Nymph*, in the front rows, and it all went terribly well except for a nasty moment when questions were invited and the very first one went – '

QUESTIONER. Miss Crewe, it is said you were an intimate friend of Mr H. G. Wells . . .

FLORA. ' – and I thought, God, how unfair! – to have come all this way to be gossiped about as if one were still in the Queen's Elm – '

PIKE. A public house in the Fulham area of Chelsea.

FLORA. ' – but it turned out nothing was meant by it except – '

QUESTIONER. Does Mr Wells write his famous books with a typewriter or with pen and ink?

FLORA (*firmly*). With pen and ink, a Waterman fountain pen, a present from his wife.
'Not that I had the least idea – Herbert did damn little writing when I was around, and made sure I did even less.'

PIKE. FC's liaison with Wells began no earlier than November 1929 and was therefore short, possibly the weekend of December 7th and 8th.

FLORA. 'After which there was a reception with lemonade and whisky and delicious snacks and conversation – darling, it's so moving, they read the *New Statesman* and *Time and Tide* and the *TLS* as if they were the Bible in parts (well, I don't mean the *Bible* but you know what I mean) and they know who wrote what about whom; it's like children with their faces jammed to the railings of an unattainable park. They say to me – '

QUESTIONER. What is your opinion of Gertrude Stein, Miss Crewe?

FLORA. ' – and I can't bring myself to say she's a poisonous old baggage who's travelling on a platform ticket – '

PIKE. FC's animosity towards Gertrude Stein should not lend credence to Hemingway's fanciful assertion (in a letter to Marlene Dietrich) that Stein threatened to scratch FC's or (the possessive pronoun is ambiguous) Alice Toklas's eyes out. If FC over-praised the chocolate cake, it would have been only out of politeness. (See 'Bunfight at 27 Rue de Fleurus' by E. C. Pike, Maryland Monographs, UMP, 1983.)

FLORA. ' – but anyway that's when I met my artist.'

DAS. Miss Crewe, may I congratulate you on your lecture. I found it most interesting!

FLORA. Thank you . . . !

DAS. I was surprised you did not mention Virginia Woolf.

FLORA. I seldom do.

DAS. Have you met George Bernard Shaw?

FLORA. Yes. I was nearly in one of his plays once.

DAS. But you are not an actress . . . ?

FLORA. No, that was the trouble.

DAS. What do you think of Jummapur?

FLORA. Well, I only arrived on Saturday but –

DAS. Of course. How absurd of me!

FLORA. Not at all. I was going to say that my first impressions –

DAS. Jummapur is not in any case to be compared with London. Do you live in Bloomsbury?

FLORA. No, I live in Chelsea.

DAS. Chelsea – of course! My favourite part of London!

FLORA. Oh! You . . . ?

DAS. I hope to visit London one of these days. The Chelsea of Turner and the Pre-Raphaelite Brotherhood! Rossetti lived in Cheen Walk! Holman Hunt lived in Old Church Street! 'The Hireling Shepherd' was *painted* in Old Church Street! What an inspiration it would be to me to visit Chelsea!

FLORA. You are a painter!

DAS. Yes! Nirad Das.

FLORA. How do you do?

DAS. I am top hole. Thank you. May I give you a present?

FLORA. Oh . . .

DAS. Please do not judge it too harshly, Miss Crewe . . .

FLORA. But it's wonderful. Thank you.
  ' – and he gave me a pencil sketch of myself holding forth on the literary life, and the next thing I knew I'd agreed to sit for him. He is charming and eager and looks like a rosewood Charlie Chaplin, not the jumpy one in the films, the real one who was at Iris's tennis party.'

PIKE. Iris Tree was the daughter of Sir Herbert Beerbohm Tree, who, soon after the Crewe family arrived in London, gave FC her first employment, fleetingly as a cockney bystander in the original production of *Pygmalion*, and, after objections from Mrs Patrick Campbell, more permanently 'in the office'. It was this connection which brought FC into the orbit of Iris and her friend Nancy Cunard, and thence to the Sitwells, and arguably to the writing of poetry. FC's first poems, written in 1914–15, now lost, were submitted to the Sitwell magazine *Wheels*, and although they were not accepted (how they could have been worse than Miss Tree's contributions to *Wheels* is difficult to imagine), FC remained to become a loyal footsoldier in the Sitwells' war against 'the Enemy'.

FLORA. 'He is rather virile in a compact sort of way, with curly hair and hot brown eyes; he smiles a lot, he's got the teeth for it, white as his pyjamas.'

DAS, *painting, is heard grunting in exasperation.*

'Not that he's smiling at the moment. When I glance up I can see him frowning at me and then at the canvas as if one of us had misbehaved. By the way, I don't mean I've seen him in his pyjamas, darling, it's what he goes about in. At the Theosophical there was everything from loincloths like Gandhi to collars and ties. Which reminds me, I had a visit from a clean young Englishman who has asked me to dinner tonight at the Brits' Club. It was a bit of an afterthought really. I think I made a gaffe by not announcing myself to the Resident, the Senior Brit, and the young man, he was on a horse, was sent to look me over. I think he ticked me off but he was so nice it was hard to tell.'

DAS *is heard sighing.*

'I've a feeling I'm going to have to stop in a minute. My poem, the one I'm not writing, is about sitting still and being hot. It got defeated by its subject matter. Ask Dr Guppy – '

PIKE. Dr Alfred Guppy had been the Crewe family doctor since the move from Ashbourne to London in 1913. His notes on FC's illness, with references to pulmonary congestion, are first dated 1926.

FLORA. ' – if this is what he meant by a warm climate.'

DAS. Oh, fiddlesticks!

FLORA. I'm sorry. Is it my fault?

DAS. No, how can it be?

FLORA. Is that so silly?

DAS. No . . . forgive me! Oh dear, Miss Crewe! Yesterday I felt . . . a communion and today –

FLORA. Oh! It *is* my fault! Yesterday I was writing a poem, and today I have been writing a letter. That's what it is.

DAS. A letter?

FLORA. I am not the same sitter. How thoughtless of me. How could I expect to be the same writing to my sister as for writing my poem.

DAS. Yes. Yes.

FLORA. Are you angry?

DAS. I don't know. Can we stop now? I would like a cigarette. Would you care for a cigarette? They are Goldflake.

FLORA. No. But I'd like you to smoke.

DAS. Thank you. You were writing to your sister? She is in England, of course.

FLORA. Yes. Her name is Eleanor. She is much younger than me; only twenty-three.

DAS. Then she cannot be so much younger.

FLORA. Routine gallantry is disappointing in a man.

DAS. I'm sorry.

FLORA. I am thirty-five and I look well enough on it.

DAS. I guessed your age to be thirty-two, if it is all right to say so.

FLORA. Yes, it is all right to say so.

DAS. Where does your sister live?

FLORA. That's almost the first thing you asked *me*. Would it mean anything to you?

DAS *is loosening up again, regaining his normal good nature*.

DAS. Oh, I have the whole of London spread out in my imagination. Challenge me, you will see!

FLORA. All right, she lives in Holborn.

DAS (*pause*). Oh. Which part of London is that?

FLORA. Well, it's – oh dear – between the Gray's Inn Road and –

DAS. Holl-born!

FLORA. Yes. Holborn.

DAS. But of course I know Holl-born! Charles Dickens lived in Doughty Street!

FLORA. Yes. Eleanor lives in Doughty Street.

DAS. But, Miss Crewe, *Oliver Twist* was written in that very street!

FLORA. Well, that's where Eleanor lives, near her work. She is the secretary to the editor of a weekly, the *Flag*.

DAS. The *Flag*!

FLORA. You surely have never read that too?

DAS. No, but I have met the editor of the *Flag* –

FLORA (*realizing*). Yes, of course you have! That is how I came to be here. Mr Chamberlain gave me letters of introduction.

DAS. His lecture in Jummapur caused the Theosophical Society to be suspended for one year.

FLORA. I'm sorry. But it's not for me to apologize for the Raj.

DAS. Oh, it was not the Raj but the Rajah! His Highness is our only capitalist! Do you agree with Mr Chamberlain's theory of Empire? I was not persuaded. Of course I am not an economist.

FLORA. That wouldn't deter Mr Chamberlain.

DAS. It is not my impression that England's imperial adventure is simply to buy time against revolution at home.

FLORA. I try to keep an open mind. Political theories are often, and perhaps entirely, a function of temperament. Eleanor and Mr Chamberlain are well suited.

DAS. Your sister shares Mr Chamberlain's opinions?

FLORA. Naturally. For reasons I have implied.

DAS. Yes. Being his secretary, you mean.

FLORA. Being his mistress.

DAS. Oh.

FLORA. You should have been a barrister, Mr Das.

DAS. I am justly rebuked!

FLORA. It was not a rebuke. An unintended slight, perhaps.

DAS. I am very sorry about your sister. It must be a great sadness for you.

FLORA. I am very happy for her.

DAS. But she will never be married now! Unless Mr Chamberlain marries her.

FLORA. He is already married, otherwise he might.

DAS. Oh my goodness. How different things are. Here, you see, your sister would have been cast out – for bringing shame on her father's house.

FLORA *chuckles and he becomes angry*.

Yes, perhaps we are not so enlightened as you.

FLORA. I'm sorry. I was only laughing because the difference is not the one you think. My father cast Eleanor out but the shame for him was Mr Chamberlain's politics. Poor father. A poet and a Communist . . . he must have felt like King Lear. Well, you have had your cigarette. Are we going to continue?

DAS. No, not today.

FLORA. I'll go back to my poem.

DAS. I have an appointment I had forgotten.

FLORA. Oh.

DAS. Actually you mustn't feel obliged . . .

DAS *is heard gathering together his paraphernalia, apparently in a hurry now*.

FLORA. What have I done?

DAS. Done? What should you have done?

FLORA. Stop it. Please. Stop being Indian. (*Pause.*) Oh, I understand. (*Pause.*) Yes, yes. I did look.

DAS. Yes.

FLORA. I had a peep. Why not? You wanted me to.

DAS. Yes, why not? You looked at the painting and you decided to spend the time writing letters. Why not?

FLORA. I'm sorry.

DAS. You still have said nothing about the painting.

FLORA. I know.

DAS. I cannot continue today.

FLORA. I understand. Will we try again tomorrow?

DAS. Tomorrow is Sunday.

FLORA. The next day.

DAS. Perhaps I cannot continue at all.

FLORA. Oh. And all because I said nothing. Are you at the mercy of every breeze that blows? Or fails to blow? Are you an artist at all?

DAS. Perhaps not! A mere sketcher – a hack painter who should be working in the bazaar!

FLORA. Stop it.

DAS. Or in chalks on the ghat.

FLORA. Stop! I'm ashamed of you. And don't cry.

DAS. I will if I wish. Excuse me. I cannot manage the easel on my bicycle. I will send for it.

It becomes a physical tussle, a struggle. She begins to gasp as she speaks.

FLORA. You will not! And you will not take your box either. Give it to me – put it back –

DAS. I do not want to continue, Miss Crewe. Please let go!

FLORA. I *won't* let you give in –

DAS. Let go, damn you, someone will see us!

FLORA *falls over, gasping for breath.*

Oh . . . oh, Miss Crewe – oh, my God – let me help you. I'm sorry. Please. Here, sit down –

She has had an attack of breathlessness. He is helping her to a chair. FLORA *speaks with difficulty.*

FLORA (*her voice coming back*). Really, I'm all right. (*Pause.*) There.

DAS. What happened?

FLORA. I'm not allowed to wrestle with people. It's a considerable loss. My lungs are bad, you see.

DAS. Let me move the cushion.

FLORA. It's all right. I'm back now. Panic over. I'm here for my health, you see. Well, not *here* . . . I'll stay longer in the Hills.

DAS. Yes, that will be better. You must go high.

FLORA. Yes. In a day or two.

DAS. What is the matter with you?

FLORA. Oh, sloshing about inside. Can't breath under water. I'm sorry if I frightened you.

DAS. You did frighten me. Would you allow me to remain a little while?

FLORA. Yes. I would like you to. I'm soaking.

DAS. You must change your clothes.

FLORA. Yes. I'll go in now. I've got a shiver. Pull me up. Thank you. Ugh. I need to be rubbed down like a horse.

DAS. Perhaps some tea . . . I'll go to the kitchen and tell –

FLORA. Yes. Would you? I'll have a shower and get into my Wendy House.

DAS. Your . . . ?

FLORA. My mosquito net. I love my mosquito net. My big towel is on the kitchen verandah – would you ask Nazrul to put it in the bedroom?

DAS *is shouting for* NAZRUL *in the inner part of the house. The action stays with* FLORA *as she goes into the interior, undressing, and through a door. She turns a squeaky tap. There is no sound of water, only a thumping in the pipes.*

Oh, damn, come on, damn you.

DAS (*off*). Miss Crewe! I'm sorry, there's –

FLORA. Yes, no water.

DAS (*off*). It's the electricity for the pump.

FLORA. Yes. (*She turns the tap again. The thumping in the pipes ceases.*) I have to lie down. (*She moves.*) There's water in the pitcher, on the washstand.

DAS. Nazrul is not – oh! Oh, I'm so sorry! –

FLORA. I'm sorry, Mr Das, but really I feel too peculiar to mind at the moment.

DAS. Please take the towel.

FLORA. Thank you. No, please, get the water jug and my face cloth from the wash-stand.

He moves; he lifts the jug.

Is there any water?

DAS. Yes, it's full . . . Here –

FLORA. Thank you. Hold the towel. (*She pours a little water over herself.*) Oh, heaven. Would you pour it – over my back, not too much at a time. Oh, thank you. I'm terribly sorry about this. And my head. Oh, that's good. I feel as weak as a kitten.

The water splashes down over her and on to the floor.

DAS. I'm afraid that's all.

FLORA. Thank you.

DAS. Here . . . should I dry you?

FLORA. My back please. Rub hard. Thank you. (*Her voice comes out shivery.*) Thank you. Stop a minute.

She takes the towel. She uses it and gives it back to DAS.

There. Thank you. And my legs. Thank you.

DAS. There was no one in the kitchen. And no water for tea.

FLORA. Never mind. I'll get into bed now.

She does so. She has to draw the net aside.

DAS. Do you have soda water?

FLORA. I think so.

DAS. I will fetch it.

FLORA. Yes please. In the fridge.

DAS. Yes. Oh, but is it locked?

FLORA. Oh . . . perhaps. Now I'm hot again, and no electricity for the fan. The sheet's too hot. It's too late for modesty. Anyway, I'm your model.

DAS. I will fetch soda water.

FLORA. That was the thing I was going to ask you.

DAS. When?

FLORA. The delicate question . . . whether you would prefer to paint me nude.

DAS. Oh.

FLORA. I preferred it. It had more what-do-you-call-it.

DAS. *Rasa.*

FLORA (*laughs quietly*). Yes, *rasa.*

Scene Ten: England

MRS SWAN. I remember the frock. It was not quite such a royal blue. Her cornflower dress, she called it.

ANISH. And her? Is it a good likeness?

MRS SWAN. Well, it's certainly Flora. She always sat upright and square to the table; she hated slouchers. She would have made a good schoolmistress, except for the feet. She always slipped her shoes off to work, and placed them neatly to one side like that. Yes, it's a very faithful portrait.

ANISH. But unfinished.

MRS SWAN. Is it? Why do you say that?

ANISH. It wasn't clear from the book, the way they cropped the painting. See here, my father has only indicated the tree – and the monkey – especially the doorway beyond . . .

MRS SWAN. Oh, but it's a portrait of *her*.

ANISH. Yes but he wasn't satisfied with her. He would have gone back to complete the background only when he considered the figure finished. Believe me. My father abandoned this portrait. I wondered why he hadn't signed it. Now I know. Thank you for showing it to me.

MRS SWAN. Mr Das, you said you had come to show *me* something. *Evidence* you said –

ANISH. Yes! I did. Come into the hall, Mrs Swan. Can you guess what it is?

MRS SWAN. A photograph of your father looking like Charlie Chaplin.

ANISH (*off*). No, better evidence than that. You may be shocked.

MRS SWAN (*approaching*). Oh dear, then you had better prepare me.

ANISH. It's a painting of course . . . wrapped up in this paper for sixty years.

He unwraps the paper.

We need a flat surface, in the light –

MRS SWAN. The table in the bay . . .

ANISH. Yes, please come to the window –

They are moving, she with her stick.

May I use the elephants? To hold it flat.

MRS SWAN. Very suitable.

ANISH. And there you are, then.

MRS SWAN (*taken aback*). Oh, good heavens.

ANISH. A second portrait of Flora Crewe.

MRS SWAN. Oh . . . How like Flora.

ANISH. More than a good likeness, Mrs Swan.

MRS SWAN. No . . . I mean *how like Flora*!

Scene Eleven: India

DAS (*approaching*). Nazrul has returned, most fortunately. I was able to unlock the refrigerator. I have the soda water.

FLORA. Thank you. You must have some too.

DAS. I will put it on the table.

FLORA. Yes. No – no, the table by me. It's quite safe, I've covered myself.

DAS. May I move this book?

FLORA. Thank you. Do you know it? I found it here.

DAS. *Up the Country* . . . No. It looks old.

FLORA. A hundred years before my time, but it's just my book.

DAS. Oh – let me – let me pour the water for you.

FLORA. Thank you.

DAS (*while pouring water from the bottle into a glass*). Nazrul was delayed at the shops by a riot, he says. The police charged the mob with lathis, he could have easily been killed, but by heroism and inspired by his loyalty to the memsahib he managed to return only an hour late with all the food you gave him money for except two chickens which were torn from his grasp.

FLORA. Oh dear . . . you thanked him, I hope.

DAS. I struck him, of course. You should fine him for the chickens.

FLORA (*drinking*). Oh, that's nice. It's still cold. Perhaps there really was a riot.

DAS. Oh, yes. Very probably. I have sent Nazrul to fetch the dhobi – you must have fresh linen for the bed. Nazrul will bring water but you must not drink it.

FLORA. Thank you.

The noise of the punkah begins quietly.

DAS. I'm sure the electricity will return soon and the fan will be working.

FLORA. What's that? Oh, the punkah!

DAS. I have found a boy to be punkah-wallah.

FLORA. Yes, it makes a draught. Thank you. A *little* boy?

DAS. Don't worry about him. I've told him the memsahib is sick.

FLORA. The memsahib. Oh dear.

DAS. Yes, you are memsahib. Are you all right now, Miss Crewe?

FLORA. Oh yes. I'm only shamming now.

DAS. May I return later to make certain?

FLORA. Are you leaving now? Yes, I've made you late.

DAS. No, not at all. There is no one waiting for me. But the servant will return and . . . we Indians are frightful gossips, you see.

FLORA. Oh.

DAS. It is for yourself, not me.

FLORA. I don't believe you, Mr Das, not entirely.

DAS. To tell you the truth, this is the first time I have been alone in a room with an Englishwoman.

FLORA. Oh. Well, you certainly started at the deep end.

DAS. We need not refer to it again. It was an accident.

FLORA. I didn't think you blushed.

DAS (*coldly*). Oh, yes. I assure you our physiology is exactly the same as yours.

FLORA. Well said, but I didn't mean that. I was being personal. I didn't expect an artist to blush.

DAS. Then perhaps I am not an artist, as you said.

FLORA. I did not. All I did was hold my tongue and you wanted to cut and run. What would you have done in the ordinary rough and tumble of literary life in London – on which, as you know, I am an expert. I give lectures on it. I expect you would have hanged yourself by now. When *Nymph In Her Orisons* came out one of the reviewers called it *Nymph In Her Mania*, and made some play with 'free verse' and 'free love', as if my poems, which I had found so hard to write, were a kind of dalliance, no more than that. *I* cried a bit too. *I* wanted to cut and run. Oh, the dreadful authority of print. It's bogus. If free verse and free love have anything in common it's a distrust of promiscuity. Quite apart from it not applying to me . . .

DAS. Of course not!

FLORA. Bogus and ignorant. My poems are not free verse.

DAS. Oh . . .

FLORA. I met my critic somewhere a few months later and poured his drink over his head and went home and wrote a poem. So that was all right. But he'd taken weeks away from me and I mind that now.

DAS. Oh! You're not dying are you?

FLORA. I expect so, but I intend to take years and years about it. You'll be dead too, one day, so let it be a lesson to you. Ignore everything, including silence. I was silent about your painting, if you want to know, because I thought you'd be an *Indian* artist.

DAS. An Indian artist?

FLORA. Yes. You *are* an Indian artist, aren't you? Stick up for yourself. Why do you like everything English?

DAS. I do not like everything English.

FLORA. Yes, you do. You're enthralled. Chelsea, Bloomsbury, *Oliver Twist*, Goldflake cigarettes . . . even painting in oils, that's not Indian. You're trying to paint me from my point of view instead of yours – what you *think* is my point of view. You *deserve* the bloody Empire!

DAS (*sharply*). May I sit down, please?

FLORA. Yes, do. Flora is herself again.

DAS. I will move the chair near the door.

FLORA. You can move the chair on to the verandah if you like, so the servants won't –

DAS. I would like to smoke, that is what I meant.

FLORA. Oh. I'm sorry. Thank you. In that case, can you see me through the net from over there?

DAS. Barely.

FLORA. Is that no or yes? Oof! That's better! That's what I

love about my little house – you can see out but you can't
see in.

DAS (*passionately*). But you are looking out at such a house!
The bloody Empire finished off Indian painting! (*Pause*.)
Excuse me.

FLORA. No, I prefer your bark.

DAS. Perhaps your sister is right. And Mr Chamberlain.
Perhaps we have been robbed. Yes; when the books are
balanced. The women here wear saris made in Lancashire.
The cotton is Indian but we cannot compete in the
weaving. Mr Chamberlain explained it all to us in simple
Marxist language. Actually, he caused some offence.

FLORA. Yes, you mean the Rajah . . .

DAS. No, no – he didn't realize we had Marxists of our own,
many of them in the Jummapur Theosophical Society. For
some, Marx is the god whose wisdom the Society honours
in its title!

FLORA. Mr Coomaraswami . . . ?

DAS. No, not Mr Coomaraswami. *His* criticism is that you
haven't exploited India *enough*. 'Where are the cotton
mills? The steel mills? No investment, no planning. The
Empire has failed us!' That is Mr Coomaraswami. Well,
the Empire will one day be gone, like the Mughal Empire
before it, and only their monuments remain – the visions
of Shah Jahan! – of Sir Edwin Lutyens!

FLORA. 'Look on my works, ye mighty, and despair!'

DAS (*delighted*). Oh, yes! Finally like the empire of
Ozymandias! Entirely forgotten except in a poem by an
English poet. You see how privileged we are, Miss Crewe.
Only in art can empires cheat oblivion, because only the
artist can say, 'Look on my works, ye mighty, and
despair!'

FLORA. Well, it helps if he happens to be Shelley.

DAS. There are Mughal paintings in the museum in London.

FLORA. Yes. Rajput miniatures in the Victoria and Albert.

DAS. You have seen them?

FLORA. Yes.

DAS. And you like them, of course.

FLORA. Yes. Very much.

DAS. Eighteenth and early nineteenth century, or earlier, nothing much good later.

FLORA. I didn't mean I expected you to paint like that. I just didn't like you thinking English was better because it was English. If that is what you were thinking. Did you consider my question?

DAS. What question?

FLORA. Can't you paint me without thinking of Rossetti or Millais? Especially without thinking of Holman Hunt. Would your nudes be Pre-Raphaelite too?

DAS. The Pre-Raphaelites did not paint nudes. Their models were clothed.

FLORA. Oh, yes, weren't they though! The Brotherhood painted life as if it were a costume drama put on by Beerbohm Tree. I knew him, you know. He gave me my first job. And my second. All right, Alma-Tadema, then. I bet you like Alma-Tadema.

DAS. Yes, very much. When you stood . . . with the pitcher of water, you were an Alma-Tadema.

FLORA. Well, I don't want to be painted like that either – that's C. B. Cochran, if only he dared.

DAS. I don't understand why you are angry with me.

FLORA. You were painting me as a gift, to please me.

DAS. Yes. Yes, it was a gift for you.

FLORA. If you don't start learning to *take* you'll never be shot of us. Who whom? Nothing else counts. Mr Chamberlain is bosh. Mr Coomaraswami is bosh. It's your country, and we've got it. Everything else is bosh. When I was Modi's model I might as well have *been* a table. 'Lie down – thrust your hips.' When he was satisfied, he got rid of me. There was no question who whom. You'd never change his colour on a map. But please light your Goldflake.

Pause. DAS *lights his cigarette with a match.*

DAS. I like the Pre-Raphaelites because they tell stories. That is my tradition too. I am Rajasthani. Our art is narrative art, stories from the legends and romances. The English painters had the Bible and Shakespeare, King Arthur . . . We had the Bhagavata Purana, and the Rasikpriya, which was written exactly when Shakespeare had his first play. And long before Chaucer we had the Chaurapanchasika, from Kashmir, which is poems of love written by the poet of the court on his way to his execution for falling in love with the king's daughter, and the king liked the poems so very much he pardoned the poet and allowed the lovers to marry.

FLORA. Oh . . .

DAS. But the favourite book of the Rajput painters was the Gita Govinda, which tells the story of Krishna and Radha, the most beautiful of the herdswomen.

The ceiling-fan starts working.

FLORA. The fan has started. The electricity is on.

DAS. You will be a little cooler now.

FLORA. Yes. I might have a sleep.

DAS. That would be good.

FLORA. Mr Durance has invited me to dinner at the Club.

DAS. Will you be well enough?

FLORA. I am well now.

DAS. That is good. Goodbye, then.

FLORA. Were Krishna and Radha punished in the story?

DAS. What for?

FLORA. I should have come here years ago. The punkah boy can stop now. Will you give him a rupee? I'll return it tomorrow.

DAS. I will give him an anna. A rupee would upset the market.

Scene Twelve: England

ANISH. I was in England when my father died. It was Christmas day, 1967. My first Christmas in London, in a house of student bedsits in Ladbroke Grove. An unhappy day.

MRS SWAN. Yes, of course.

ANISH. I mean it was already unhappy. The house was cold and empty. All the other students had gone home to their families, naturally. I was the only one left. No one had invited me.

MRS SWAN. Well, having a Hindu for Christmas can be tricky. Francis would invite his Assistant for Christmas lunch, and I always felt I should be apologizing for rubbing something in which left him out, if you follow me. It quite spoiled the business of the paper hats too. There's nothing like having an Indian at table for making one feel like a complete ass handing round the vegetables in a pink paper fez. That was after I-zation, of course.

ANISH. I heard the telephone . . .

MRS SWAN. Did you? Well, it's stopped now. The mistletoe was another problem.

ANISH. . . . no, there was a coin box in the hall. I could hear it ringing all day. It would stop and then start again. I ignored it. The phone was never for me. But finally I went up and answered it, and it was my uncle calling from Jummapur to say my father was dead.

MRS SWAN. Oh, how sad. Did you go home?

ANISH. Yes. There was great sadness in our house.

MRS SWAN. Of course . . .

ANISH. I'm ashamed of it but I found the rituals of death and grief distasteful. I wanted to return to England. And I did, as soon as permitted. There were legal matters which I was grateful to leave to my father's elder brother. So I was in England again when I learned that I had a legacy from my father. He had left me his tin trunk which had always stood at the foot of his bed.

MRS SWAN. Ah, yes . . .

ANISH. It arrived finally and it was locked. There had been no mention of a key. So I broke the hasp. There was nothing of value in the trunk that I could see.

MRS SWAN. You were disappointed?

ANISH. Well, yes. It was mainly letters and old bills, my report cards from school, and so on. But at the bottom of everything was a painting rolled up in paper. An extraordinary painting, a nude, a portrait of a woman. Even more amazing, a European woman, apparently painted many years before. I couldn't imagine who she was or what it meant.

MRS SWAN. Did you ask anyone? Your uncle?

ANISH. No. It was clear that this was something my father was sharing with me alone. A secret he was passing on. So I rolled the picture up again and put it away. I never hung it, of course. I never showed it to anyone, until years later I showed it to my wife.

MRS SWAN. Until now.

ANISH. Yes, until a week ago. The book in the shop window. It was like seeing a ghost. Not her ghost; his. It was my father's hand – his work – I had grown up watching him work, his portrait-work, in oils – local bigwigs, daughters of well-to-do businessmen. I had seen a hundred original Nirad Dases, and here was his work, not once, but repeated twenty times over. It filled the window of the bookshop, a special display . . . *The Selected Letters of Flora Crewe*, and in the next instant I saw it was the same woman.

MRS SWAN. Yes. Oh, yes, it's Flora. It's as particular as an English miniature. A watercolour, isn't it?

ANISH. Watercolour and gouache, on paper.

MRS SWAN. It's fascinating. It looks Indian but he hasn't made *her* Indian.

ANISH. Well, she was *not* Indian.

MRS SWAN. Yes, I know. I'm not gaga, I'm only old. I mean he hasn't painted her flat. But everything else looks Indian, like enamel . . . the moon and stars done with a pastry cutter. And the birds singing in the border. Or is that the ceiling of the room, that line?

ANISH. I'm not sure.

MRS SWAN. And the foliage in bloom, so bright. Is it day or night? I know what's odd. The different parts are on different scales. The tree is far too small, or it's the right size too close. You can't tell if the painter is in the house or outside looking in.

ANISH. She is in a house within a house . . . look.

MRS SWAN. This edge must be the floor. Flora wrote about animals scratching about under the bungalow. There's a snake, look. Oh, but there couldn't have been gazelles under the house, could there? Perhaps it's a border after all . . . or a touch of fancy.

ANISH. Symbolism, yes.

MRS SWAN. I like the book on the pillow. That's Flora.

ANISH. And a pitcher on the table next to her, and bread on the plate . . . Do you see the lettering on the book?

MRS SWAN. Too small. I could find a magnifying glass . . .

ANISH. It says 'Eden'.

MRS SWAN. Eden? . . . (*Understanding.*) Oh!

ANISH. A book of verses underneath the bough, a jug of wine, a loaf of bread and thou beside me singing in the wilderness!

MRS SWAN. That's not Indian.

ANISH. No. The Mughals brought miniature painting from Persia when they made their Indian empire. But Muslim and Hindu art are different. The Muslim artists were realists. To a Hindu every object has an inner meaning, everything is to be interpreted in a language of symbols –

MRS SWAN. Which you understand, Mr Das?

ANISH. Not in detail. I'd have to look it up.

MRS SWAN (*amused*). Look it up! (*Apologizing.*) Oh, I'm sorry.

ANISH. But this flowering vine that winds itself around the dark trunk of the tree . . .

MRS SWAN. Oh . . .

ANISH. The vine is shedding its leaves and petals, look where they're falling to the ground. I think my father knew your sister was dying.

MRS SWAN. It upsets me, to see her nakedness.

ANISH. Yes . . . it's unguarded; she is not posing but resting –

MRS SWAN. No, I did not mean that. I don't make presumptions.

ANISH. Oh . . . but . . .

MRS SWAN. I was not there to nurse her . . . bathe her . . . I never saw her body at the end.

ANISH. Yes. Let me put it away now.

MRS SWAN. No, leave it, please. I want to look at it more. Yes. Such a pretty painting.

ANISH. It was done with great love.

MRS SWAN. He was certainly taken with her. Whether she posed for him, or whether it's a work of the imagination . . .

ANISH. Oh . . . but the symbolism clearly –

MRS SWAN. Codswallop. Your 'house within a house', as anyone can see, is a mosquito net. I had one which was gathered at the top in exactly that way. And a drink and a sandwich don't add up to the *Rubáiyát of Omar Khayyám* by a long chalk. Eden, indeed! Why would a Hindu call it Eden?

ANISH. *Her* paradise, not his –

MRS SWAN. Don't be a fool. The book is a volume of Indian travels. It was Flora's beside reading. She mentions it in one of her letters – you should read the footnotes.

Scene Thirteen: India

FLORA. 'Jummapur. Sunday. April 6th. Darling Nell, I posted a letter only hours ago – at least I put it in the box at the Club last night and no doubt it's still there – but I'll make this the next page of my journal and probably post it when I leave Jummapur. We had an excitement in town yesterday morning, a riot, and half a street of shops burned to the ground, with the police out in force – the Rajah's police. The Rajah of Jummapur is Hindu (otherwise it would more likely be Jumma*bad* – not – *pur*) but the Muslims got the best of it according to my cook, who was in the heat of the battle. The Brits here shake their heads and ask where will it all end when we've gone, because going we are. That's official. Tell Josh. I got it from the Resident, whose view is that (a) it is our moral duty to remain and (b) we will shirk it. So now it's Sunday after breakfast, and I've been horse riding! – in a long skirt like the Viceroy's daughters twenty years ago, the first women to ride astride in India. Do you remember Llandudno? No, you surely can't. I think that was the last time I was ever on anything resembling a horse.'

PIKE. The Crewe family spent August at the seaside resort in North Wales from 1904 until 1911, the year of Mrs Crewe's elopement. FC's allusion is evidently to donkey rides on the sands, and her comment is of some interest, since, if she is right, a recently published photograph described as showing FC and Maynard Keynes on horseback at Garsington in 1924 (*Ottoline Morrell and Her Circle in Hell*, by Toshiro Kurasaki, 1988) misidentifies her; if not him.

FLORA. 'If I start coming over a bit dated it's because in my bungalow, which is not duck but dak, i.e. for travellers (as Josh has probably told you by now), I have discovered among a box of dilapidated railway novels a book of letters written from India a hundred years ago by an English spinster – hand on my heart – to her sister Eleanor in London, and this is now my only reading.'

PIKE. The spinster was Emily Eden and the book was *Up the Country*, 1866. The Hon. Miss Eden was accompanying her brother, the Governor-General Lord Auckland, on an official progress up country. The tour, supported by a caravan of ten thousand people, including Auckland's French chef, and almost as many animals, lasted thirty months, from October 1837, and Emily wrote hundreds of letters to sisters and friends at home, happily unaware that the expedition's diplomatic and strategic accomplishment was to set the stage for the greatest military disaster ever to befall the British under arms, the destruction of the army in Afghanistan.

FLORA. 'I shall steal the book when I leave here in a day or two and pick up Emily's trail in Delhi and Simla and up into the Punjab, where the literary societies are holding their breath. Speaking of which, I am doing pretty well with mine, well enough to go dancing last night. My suitor (I suppose I must call him that, though I swear I did

nothing to encourage him) came to fetch me in an
enormous open Daimler which drew a crowd.'

Sound of the Daimler and the crowd.

(*Calling out from off.*) You wangled it!

Sounds of DURANCE *opening the driver's door and
closing it again.* FLORA *has opened the passenger door,
got into the car and slammed the door. The ambience is the
hubbub of Indian voices, children, dogs, chickens . . .
general excitement.*

Can I drive?

DURANCE. Next time. Is that a bargain?

FLORA. It's a bargain.

DURANCE. Done. By the way, I hope you'll call me
David. First names are generally the drill with us.

FLORA. David.

Sounds of DURANCE *shouting in Urdu, to clear a path.
The car honks its horn and moves.*

'And off we went, pushing through the mob of curiosity
seekers, scattering children and dogs and chickens right
and left, rather like leaving Bow Street in a police van. My
God, how strange; that was ten years ago almost to the
day.'

PIKE. In fact, nine. See 'The Woman Who Wrote What She
Knew', by E. C. Pike (Maryland Monographs, UMP,
1981).

FLORA. 'I fully expected the Club to be like a commercial
hotel in the hotter part of Guildford, but not at all – it's
huge and white and pillared, just like the house of your
first memory, perhaps – poor mama's nearly-house, which
was ours for six months and then no more. I've never been
back to Maybrook, perhaps we should make a pilgrimage
one day.'

PIKE. The Crewe family met Sir George Dewe-Lovett of
Maybrook Hall, Lancashire, on the promenade at
Llandudno in August 1911. Catherine Crewe never
returned to the house at Ashbourne. She eloped with
Dewe-Lovett, a director of the White Star Shipping Line,
and took her daughters, who were aged four and sixteen,

to live at Maybrook. Percival Crewe proved to be unacrimonious and divorce proceedings were under way when the girls returned to Ashbourne to stay with their father for the Easter holidays of 1912, while their mother joined Dewe-Lovett at Southampton. The *Titanic* sailed on April 10th and FC never saw her mother or Maybrook again.

FLORA. 'And everyone at the Club was very friendly, going out of their way to explain that although they didn't go in much for poetry, they had nothing against it, so that was all right, and dinner was soup, boiled fish, lamb cutlets, sherry trifle and sardines on toast – eight of us at the Resident's table – '

WOMAN. Are you writing a poem about India, Flora?

FLORA. Trying to.

MAN. Kipling – there was a poet! 'And the dawn comes up like thunder on the road to Mandalay!'

WOMAN. I thought that was a *song*.

FLORA. 'The Resident was a different matter – '

RESIDENT. The only poet I *know* is Alfred Housman. I expect you've come across him.

FLORA. Of course!

RESIDENT. How is he nowadays?

FLORA. Oh – come *across* him –

RESIDENT. He hauled me through *Ars Amatoria* when I was up at Trinity –

FLORA. *The Art of Love*?

RESIDENT. When it comes to love, he said, you're either an Ovid man or a Virgil man. *Omnia vincit amor* – that's Virgil – 'Love wins every time, and we give way to love' – *et nos cedamus amori*. Housman was an Ovid man – *et mihi cedet amor* – 'Love gives way to me'.

FLORA. I'm a Virgil man.

RESIDENT. Are you? Well, you meet more people that way.

FLORA. ' – and his sources of information were impressive.'

RESIDENT. I believe you're here on doctor's orders.

FLORA. Why . . . yes . . . how . . . ?

RESIDENT. If there's anything you need or want, you tell
David – right, David?

DURANCE. Yes, sir.

FLORA. Thank you. He's already promised me a go in the
Daimler.

DURANCE (*embarrassed*). Oh . . .

RESIDENT. If you like cars, the Rajah has got about eighty-
six of them – Rollses, the lot. With about ten miles on the
clock. Collects them like stamps. Well, don't let me stop
you enjoying yourselves.

DURANCE. Would you like to dance, Flora?

FLORA. 'And it turned out to be an easy evening to get
through, which only goes to show, when in Rome, etc.,
and I wish I'd remembered that when I *was* in Rome.'

PIKE. FC was in Rome twice, in 1920 and 1926, en route to
Capri in each case. It is unclear what she means here.

FLORA. 'Interrupted!'

*The gramophone dance music, which has been in the
background, becomes the dominant sound as DURANCE
and FLORA begin to dance.*

DURANCE. Do you mean you've come to India for your
health?

FLORA. Is that amusing?

DURANCE. Well, it is rather. Have you seen the English
cemetery?

FLORA. No.

DURANCE. I must take you there.

FLORA. Oh.

DURANCE. People here drop like flies – cholera, typhoid,
malaria – men, women and children, here one day, gone
the next. Are you sure the doctor said India? Perhaps he
said Switzerland and you weren't paying attention.

FLORA. He didn't say India. He said a sea voyage and somewhere warm – but I wanted to come to India.

DURANCE. Then good for you. Live dangerously, why not?

FLORA. Oh – you're too energetic for me – slow down!

DURANCE. Well, I suppose this is somewhere warm. In a month you can't imagine it – but you'll be gone to the hills, so you'll be all right.

FLORA. Yes. Let's sit down.

DURANCE. Slow one coming up . . . ?

FLORA. No, I'm out of puff.

They stop dancing.

DURANCE. Yes, of course. You're not really bad, are you, Flora?

FLORA. No, but I'd rather sit down. Do you think there might be more air outside?

DURANCE. On the verandah? Any air that's going. Should we take a peg with us?

He calls to a SERVANT.

Koi-hai! Thank you – two burra pegs.

SERVANT. Yes, sir.

FLORA. Lots of soda with mine, please.

They move further away from the music, which has continued and come to the exterior, which makes its own noise, crickets, insects, leaves . . .

DURANCE. There we are. Long-sleever? Good for putting the feet up.

FLORA. Yes – long-sleever. Thank you. How pretty the lanterns . . .

DURANCE. I hope you don't mind the moths.

FLORA. No, I like moths.

DURANCE. If they make a whining noise, kill them.

FLORA. It's a nice Club.

DURANCE. Yes, it's decent enough. There are not so many British here so we tend to mix more.

FLORA. With the Indians?

DURANCE. No. In India proper, I mean *our* India, there'd be two or three Clubs. The box-wallahs would have their own and the government people would stick together, you know how it is – and the Army . . .

FLORA. Mr Das called you Captain.

DURANCE. Yes, I'm Army. Seconded, of course. There are two of us Juniors – political agents we call ourselves when we're on tour round the states. Jummapur is not one of your twenty-one gun salute states, you see – my Chief is in charge of half-a-dozen native states.

FLORA. In charge?

DURANCE. Oh yes.

FLORA. Is he Army? No – how silly –

DURANCE. He's ICS. The heaven-born. A Brahmin.

FLORA. Not seriously?

DURANCE. Yes, seriously. Oh no, not a Brahmin seriously. But it might come to that with I-zation.

FLORA *is puzzled by the word.*

Indianization. It's all over, you know. We have Indian officers in the Regiment now. My fellow Junior here is Indian, too, terribly nice chap – he's ICS, passed the exam, did his year at Cambridge, learned polo and knives-and-forks, and here he is, a pukka sahib in the Indian Civil Service.

FLORA. But he's not here.

DURANCE. At the Club? No, he can't come into the Club.

The SERVANT *arrives.*

Ah, here we are. Thank you . . .

The SERVANT *leaves.*

Cheers. Your health, Flora. I drink to your health for which you came. I wish you were staying longer. I mean, only for my sake, Flora.

FLORA. Yes, but I'm not. So that's that. Don't look hangdog. You might like me less and less as you got to know me.

DURANCE. Will you come riding in the morning?

FLORA. Seriously.

DURANCE. Yes, seriously. Will you?

FLORA. In the Daimler?

DURANCE. No. Say you will. We'll have to go inside in a minute if no one comes out.

FLORA. Why?

DURANCE. There's nothing to do here except gossip, you see. Everyone is agog about you. One of the wives claims ... Were you in the papers at home? Some scandal about one of your books, something like that?

FLORA. I can see why you're nervous, being trapped out here with me – let's go in –

DURANCE. No – I'm sorry. Flora . . . ? Pax? Please.

FLORA. All right. Pax.

He kisses her, uninvited, tentatively.

DURANCE. Sealed with a kiss.

FLORA. No more. I mean it, David. Think of your career.

DURANCE. Are you really a scandalous woman?

FLORA. I was for a while. I was up in court, you know. Bow Street.

DURANCE (*alarmed*). Oh, not really?

FLORA. Almost really. I was a witness. The publisher was in the dock, but it was my poems – *Venus In Her Season*, my first book.

DURANCE. Oh, I say.

FLORA. The case was dismissed on a technicality, and the policemen were awfully sweet; they got me away through the crowd in a van. It was all most enjoyable actually, and it gave me an entrée to several writers I admired, most of whom, it turned out, were hoping it worked the other way round. My sister was asked to leave school. But that was mostly my own fault – the magistrate asked me why all the poems seemed to be about sex, and I said, 'Write what you know' – just showing off, I was practically a virgin, but it got me so thoroughly into the newspapers my name rings a bell even with the wife of a bloody jute planter or something in the middle of Rajputana, damn, damn, damn. No, let's go inside.

DURANCE. Sit down, that's an order. How's your whisky?

FLORA. Excellent. All the better for being forbidden. My God, where did that moon come from?

DURANCE. Better. I love this country, don't you?

FLORA. Yes, I think I do. What's going to happen to it? The riot in town this morning . . . does that happen often?

DURANCE. Not here, no. The gaols are filling up in British India.

FLORA. Well, then.

DURANCE. It wasn't against us, it was Hindu and Muslim. Gandhi's salt march reached the sea today, did you hear? Our Congress Hindus closed their shops in sympathy, and the Muslims wouldn't join in, that's all it was about. The Indian National Congress is all very well, but to the Muslims, Congress means Gandhi . . . a Hindu party in all but name.

FLORA. Will Gandhi be arrested?

DURANCE. No, no. The salt tax is a lot of nonsense actually.

FLORA. Yes, it does seem hard in a country like this.

DURANCE. Not that sort of nonsense. It works out at about four annas a year. Most Indians didn't even know there *was* a salt tax.

FLORA. Well, they do now.

DURANCE. Yes. They do now. Would you like one more turn round the floor before they play the King?

FLORA. No, I'm tiring. (*She gets up.*) Will you finish my whisky? I'd like to go back to my little house.

DURANCE. Yes, of course. Would you mind saying goodnight to my Chief? It would go down well.

FLORA. I'd like to. The Brahmin.

DURANCE. Yes. The highest caste of Hindu, you see, and the ICS are the highest caste of Anglo-India. There's about twelve hundred ICS and they run the continent. That's three for every million Indians.

FLORA. Why do the Indians let them?

DURANCE. Why not? They're better at it.

FLORA. Are they?

DURANCE. Ask them.

FLORA. Who?

DURANCE. The natives. Ask them. We've pulled this country together. It's taken a hundred years with a hiccup or two but the place now works.

FLORA. That's what you love, then? What you created?

DURANCE. Oh no, it's India I love. I'll show you.

A sudden combination of animal noises are heard – buffalo snorting, horses whinnying, FLORA crying out. FLORA and DURANCE on horseback.

DURANCE. Did he frighten you? He's big but harmless.

FLORA. Oh my!

DURANCE. We surprised him in his bath.

FLORA. He's immense! Thank you!

DURANCE. Me?

FLORA. He was *my* surprise really.

DURANCE. Oh yes. Just for you.

FLORA. I've never been given a buffalo before.

DURANCE. Look – sand grouse! (*He makes a noise to represent the firing of a shotgun, both barrels.*) A nice left and right!

FLORA. Don't shoot them, they're mine.

Her interior voice comes in, 'inside' the scene itself.

'Where life began at the lake's edge,
water and mud convulsed,
reared itself and became shaped

into buffalo.
The beast stood dismayed,
smeared with birth, streaming
from his muzzle like an infant, celebrated
with lily flowers about his horns.
So he walked away to meet his death
among peacocks, parrots, antelopes.
We watched him go, taller than he,
mounted astride, superior beasts.'

DURANCE. Time to trot – sun's up.

FLORA. Oops – David – I'll have to tell you – stop! It's my
first time on a horse, you see.

DURANCE. Yes, I could tell.

FLORA (*miffed*). Could you? Even walking? I felt so proud
when we were walking.

DURANCE. No, no good, I'm afraid.

FLORA. Oh, damn you. I'm going to get off.

DURANCE. No, no, just sit. He's a chair. Breathe in. India
smells wonderful, doesn't it?

FLORA. Out here it does.

DURANCE. You should smell chapattis cooking on a
camel-dung fire out in the Thar Desert. Perfume!

FLORA. What were you doing out there?

DURANCE. Cooking chapattis on a camel-dung fire.
(*Laughs*.) I'll tell you where it all went wrong with us and
India. It was the Suez Canal. It let the women in.

FLORA. Oh!

DURANCE. Absolutely. When you had to sail round the
Cape this was a man's country and we mucked in with the
natives. The memsahibs put a stop to that. The memsahib
won't muck in, won't even be alone in a room with an
Indian.

FLORA. Oh . . .

DURANCE. Don't point your toes out. May I ask you a
personal question?

FLORA. No.

DURANCE. All right.

FLORA. I wanted to ask *you* something. How did the Resident know I came to India for my health?

DURANCE. It's his business to know. Shoulders back. Reins too slack.

FLORA. But I didn't tell anybody.

DURANCE. Obviously you did.

FLORA. Only Mr Das.

DURANCE. Oh, well, say no more. Jolly friendly of you, of course, sharing a confidence, lemonade, all that, but they can't help themselves bragging about it, telling all they know.

FLORA (*furious*). Rubbish!

DURANCE. Well . . . I stand corrected.

FLORA. I'm sorry. I don't believe you, though.

DURANCE. Righto.

FLORA. I'm sorry. Pax.

DURANCE. Flora.

FLORA. No.

DURANCE. Would you marry me?

FLORA. No.

DURANCE. Would you think about it?

FLORA. No. Thank you.

DURANCE. Love at first sight, you see. Forgive me.

FLORA. Oh, David.

DURANCE. Knees together.

FLORA. 'Fraid so.

She laughs without malice but unrestrainedly. He punishes her without malice by breaking his horse into a trot. Her horse follows, trotting. FLORA squealing with fright and laughing.

Scene Fourteen: India

Inside the bungalow.

FLORA. 'Next day. Oh dear, guess what? You won't approve. Quite right. So I think it's time to go. Love 'em and leave 'em.'

PIKE. What, if anything, came of this is not known. The man was most probably the Junior Political Agent at the Residency, Captain David Arthur Durance, who took FC dancing and horse riding. He was killed in Malaya in 1942 during the Japanese advance on Singapore.

FLORA. 'I feel tons better, though. The juices are starting to flow again, as you can see from the enclosed.'

PIKE. 'Buffalo' and 'Pearl', included in *Indian Ink*, 1932.

FLORA. 'I'll keep sending you fair copies of anything I finish in case I get carried away by monsoons or tigers, and if I do, look after the comma after "astride", please, it's just the sort of thing they leave out – printers have taken more years off my life than pulmonary congestion, I can tell you. Send 'Buffalo' to *Blackwood's* and 'Pearl' to *Transition*, and if you get a pound for them put it in the Sacha Fund.'

PIKE. The reference is obscure.

FLORA. 'I'm writing this at my table on the verandah, looking longingly to the hills I can't see. The dak menagerie is subdued by the heat, except for a pi-dog barking under the house – and I'd better start with what interrupted me yesterday after my early morning ride – which was a Rolls Royce *circa* 1912 but brand new, as it were, driven by a Sikh in a turban called Singh – '

PIKE. A tautology: all Sikhs are named Singh (however, not all people named Singh are Sikhs).

FLORA. Oh, shut up!

She is shouting at the dog, which is responding. She manages to get rid of the dog – clapping her hands and generally making a dog-dismissing row. The dog departs, whining and yelping.

'He was a chauffeur with a note from His Highness the Rajah of Jummapur, inquiring after my health and assuring

me that the spiritual beauty of Jummapur had been
increased a thousandfold by my presence, and asking my
indulgence towards his undistinguished collection of
motor cars, which nevertheless might be worthy of my
interest during an idle hour since he understood I was a
connoisseur of the automobile . . . Well, what is a poor girl
to do? Hop into the back of the Rolls, that's what.'

Sound of FLORA *getting into the Rolls.*

Thank you!

The car moves, etc.

'The Rajah's palace didn't exactly have a garage, more of a
cavalry barracks with the Motor Show thrown in, and he
himself was there to greet me.'

RAJAH. Miss Crewe! How delightful that you were able to
come!

FLORA. Oh, how sweet of you to ask me . . . your
Highness . . . oh – sorry!

RAJAH. Please!

FLORA. 'And I made a mess of that, sticking my hand out
at his bow, bowing at his hand – '
What a wonderful sight!
' – but he was very sporting about it, and there were all these
cars gleaming in the courtyard – with a dozen grooms
standing by, one couldn't think of them as mechanics.'

RAJAH. Let me show you one or two.

FLORA. Thank you! Oh – a Hispano-Suiza!
'He's a large soft-looking man with beautiful eyes like a
seal and wearing a long buttoned-up brocade coat over
white leggings, no jewellery except a yellow diamond ring
not much bigger than my engagement ring from Gus, only
real, I suppose – '

PIKE. Augustus de Boucheron enjoyed brief celebrity as a
millionaire philanthropist and patron of the arts. FC met
him, and received his proposal of marriage, on October
11th 1918, at a party given for the Russian Ballet by the
Sitwells at Swan Walk (it was at the same party that
Maynard Keynes met the ballerina Lopokova). FC had
returned from France only hours earlier and was wearing
her auxiliary nurse's uniform. Her fortunes were at their

lowest ebb, for she was supporting her sister, still at
school, and also her father, who, since being invalided out
of the Army, had given up the Bar and enjoyed few
periods of lucidity. The engagement to de Boucheron was
announced on January 1st 1919 and ended on August 1st
in a furniture store (see note on page 334).

FLORA. ' – and he knew very little about cars, he just liked
the look of them, which was endearing, and I know how
badly this must be going down in Doughty Street but we
soon got on to politics – he was at school with Winston
Churchill.'

RAJAH. But I'm afraid I can't remember him at all. Look at
this one! I couldn't resist the headlamps! So enormous,
like the eggs of a mythical bird!

FLORA. Yes – a Brancusi!

RAJAH. Is it? I don't know their names. All the same, I read
Churchill's speeches with great interest. He is right in
what he says, don't you agree, Miss Crewe? The loss of
India would reduce Britain to a minor power.

FLORA. That may be, but one must consider India's
interests too.

RAJAH. But what about Jummapur's interests?

FLORA. Yes, of course, but aren't they the same thing?

RAJAH. No, no. Independence would be the beginning of
the end for the Native States. Though in a sense you are
right too – Independence may be the beginning of the end
for Indian nationalism too. Only yesterday, you may have
heard about the hullabaloo in town.

FLORA. Yes.

RAJAH. The Princes stood firm with the British during the
First Uprising in my grandfather's day –

FLORA. The . . . ?

RAJAH. In '57 the danger was from fundamentalists –

FLORA. The Mutiny . . .

RAJAH. – today it is the progressives. Marxism. Civil
disobedience. But I told the Viceroy, you have to fight
them the same way, you won't win by playing cricket. (*He*

presses a bulb-horn, which honks.) My father drove this one. It's a Bentley.

FLORA. Yes.

RAJAH. He won it at Monte Carlo. He spent much of his time in the south of France, for his health. (*He laughs.*) But *you* have come to India for *your* health!

FLORA (*not pleased*). Well . . . yes, your Highness. Everybody seems to know everything about me.

RAJAH. Should we have some refreshment? (*He opens the door of a car.*)

FLORA (*puzzled*). Oh . . . thank you.

RAJAH. After you.

FLORA. You mean in the car?

RAJAH. Do you like this one?

FLORA. I . . . yes, of course. It's a Packard.

RAJAH. It's quite a step to my apartments. Why walk in the sun when we have so many motorcars?

FLORA. Oh I see. Thank you. (*She gets into the car.*)

RAJAH. I keep them all ready. Would you care to drive?

FLORA. Yes, I'd love to. I'll slip over.

She moves over to the steering wheel. The RAJAH *gets into the car and closes the door.*

RAJAH. Jolly good, we'll have some tiffin. When do you leave Jummapur?

FLORA. ' – and we drove all of two hundred yards past saluting sentries, into the palace proper, which had a fountain inside, and we walked through a series of little gardens into his reception room, where we had sherbet – you can imagine the rest, can't you? – me sat on silk cushions being peeped at by giggling ladies of the harem through the latticework of carved marble – well, no such thing. We had tea and cold cuts and little iced cakes, and the furniture was from Heals, three-piece suite and all, and I know it was Heals because the sofa was absolutely the one I broke my engagement on when I took Gus to the

French Pictures – my God, I thought, that's the Modigliani sofa!'

PIKE. The exhibition of Modern French Art at Heal and Sons in the Tottenham Court Road enlivened the hot early-August days of 1919. Modigliani was one of several newer artists shown with the better-known Matisse, Picasso and Derain, and it was his nudes, including the 'Peasant Girl', now in the Tate Gallery, which provoked such comments in the press as that the show was glorifying in prostitution. FC had met Modigliani in Paris at his first show, on December 3rd 1917 (the date is fixed by the fact that the show was closed by the police on the opening day) and she sat, or rather reclined, for the artist soon afterwards. Concurrently with the French pictures, Messrs Heals were showing a model flat. FC arrived at Heals with de Boucheron, expecting to see her portrait, only to discover that her fiancé had bought the painting from the artist and, as he triumphantly confessed, burned it. The ensuing row moved from the gallery to the model flat, and it was on the sofa of the model sitting-room that FC returned de Boucheron's engagement ring (though not the lease on the Flood Street house, which was to be the Crewes' London home from then on). De Boucheron, under his real name, Perkins Butcher, went to prison in 1925 for issuing a false prospectus. His end is unknown.

FLORA. 'I started to tell his Highness about Heals but when I said French pictures he got hold of the wrong end of the stick entirely – '

RAJAH. French pictures?

FLORA. Yes. There was a tremendous fuss – the pictures were wallowing in prostitution, that sort of thing. And of course those of us who defended them were simply admitting our depravity!

RAJAH. My dear Miss Crewe, you are quite the emancipated woman!

FLORA. Not at all. What has being a woman got to do with it?

RAJAH. Oh, I agree with you! I was guilty of male prejudice!

FLORA. In fact they are probably more to my taste than yours – surely it's more a matter of culture than gender?

RAJAH. Ah, but we have 'French pictures' of our own. Of course, you have never seen them.

FLORA. I'm not sure that I understand.

RAJAH. In *our* culture, you see, erotic art has a long history and a most serious purpose. (*Walking away*.) These drawings, for example – if I may be so bold – are the depictions not of depravity . . . (*Walking back*.) but of precepts towards a proper fulfilment of that side of life which . . .

FLORA. 'And he produced an album of exquisite water colours – medieval, I think – which we admired solemnly together, he determined to acknowledge me as an enlightened woman, I determined to be one. Really what a muddle, and not entirely honest, of course – he insisted I chose one as a gift – '
No, really, I couldn't –

RAJAH. Yes, yes – which one would you like?

FLORA. ' – like pondering a big box of chocolates – should one go for the Turkish Delight or plump for the nut cluster?'
Well, this one is rather sweet . . .

RAJAH. Ah, yes . . .

FLORA. How very kind.
' – and he invited me to move into the palace for the remainder of my visit but I got away finally in a yellow Studebaker and was brought home at lamp-lighting time . . .'

Sounds of the Studebaker arriving, FLORA getting out and closing the car door; the car leaving. FLORA calls out.

Thank you very much, Mr Singh!

She comes up the wooden steps to the verandah.

Oh, Mr Das!

DAS. Good evening, Miss Crewe! I'm sorry if we frightened you.

FLORA. And Mr Coomaraswami!

COOMARASWAMI. Yes, it is me, Miss Crewe.

FLORA. Good evening. What a surprise.

COOMARASWAMI. I assure you – I beg you – we have not come to presume on your hospitality –

FLORA. I wish I had some whisky to offer you, but will you come inside.

COOMARASWAMI. It will be cooler for you to remain on the verandah.

FLORA. Let me find Nazrul.

COOMARASWAMI. He is not here, evidently. But perhaps now that the mistress has returned it is permitted to light the lamp?

FLORA. Yes, of course.

COOMARASWAMI. So much more pleasant than sitting in the electric light. (*He lights the oil lamp.*) There we are. And the moon will clear the house tops in a few minutes . . . but where is it? Perhaps on the wrong side of the house. Never mind.

FLORA. Please sit down.

COOMARASWAMI. May I take this chair?

FLORA. No, that's Mr Das's chair. And this is mine. So that leaves you with the sofa.

COOMARASWAMI. Ah, never, never has my fatness received more charming, more delicate acknowledgement! (*He sits down.*) Oh yes, very comfortable. Thank you, Miss Crewe. Mr Das told me that I was exceeding our rights of acquaintance with you in coming to see you without proper arrangement, and even more so to lie in wait for you like *mulaquatis*. If it is so, he is blameless. Please direct your displeasure at me.

DAS. Miss Crewe does not understand *mulaquatis*.

COOMARASWAMI. Petitioners!

FLORA. In my house you are always friends.

COOMARASWAMI. Mr Das, what did I tell you!

FLORA. But what can I do for you?

DAS. Nothing at all. We require nothing!

FLORA. Oh . . .

COOMARASWAMI. Have you had a pleasant day, Miss Crewe?

FLORA. Extremely interesting. I have been visiting his Highness the Rajah.

COOMARASWAMI. My goodness!

FLORA. I believe you knew that, Mr Coomaraswami.

COOMARASWAMI. Oh, you have found me out!

FLORA. He showed me his cars . . . and we had an interesting conversation, about art . . .

COOMARASWAMI. And poetry, of course.

FLORA. And politics.

COOMARASWAMI. Politics, yes. I hope, we both hope – that your association with, that our association with, in fact – if we caused you embarrassment, if you thought for a moment that I personally would have knowingly brought upon you, compromised you, by association with –

FLORA. Stop, stop. Mr Das, I am going to ask *you*. What is the matter?

DAS. The matter?

FLORA. I shall be absolutely furious in a moment.

DAS. Yes, yes, quite so. My friend Coomaraswami, speaking as President of the Theosophical Society, wishes to say that if his Highness reproached you or engaged you in any unwelcome conversation regarding your connection with the Society, he feels responsible, and yet at the same time wishes you to know that –

FLORA. His Highness never mentioned the Theosophical Society.

DAS. Ah.

COOMARASWAMI. Not at all, Miss Crewe?

FLORA. Not at all.

COOMARASWAMI. Oh . . . well, jolly good!

FLORA. What has happened?

COOMARASWAMI. Ah well, it is really of no interest. I am very sorry to have mentioned it. And we must leave you, it was not right to trouble you after all. Will you come, Mr Das?

FLORA. I hope it is nothing to do with my lecture?

COOMARASWAMI (*getting up*). Oh no! Certainly not!

DAS. Nothing!

COOMARASWAMI. Mr Das said we should not mention the thing, and how truly he spoke. I am sorry. Goodnight, Miss Crewe.

He shouts towards somebody distant, in Urdu, and the explanation is an approaching jingle of harness, horse and buggy. He goes down the steps to meet it and climbs aboard.

DAS. I am coming, Mr Coomaraswami. Please wait for me a moment.

FLORA. If you expect to be my friends, you must behave like friends and not whatever-you-called it. Tell me what has happened.

COOMARASWAMI (*off*). Mr Das!

DAS (*shouts*). Please wait!

FLORA. Well?

DAS. The Theosophical Society has been banned, you see. The order came to Mr Coomaraswami's house last night.

FLORA. But why?

DAS. Because of the disturbances in the town.

FLORA. The riot?

DAS. Yes, the riot.

FLORA. I know about it. The Hindus wanted the Muslims to close their shops. What has that to do with the Theosophical Society?

COOMARASWAMI (*off*). I am going, Mr Das!

DAS (*shouts*). I come now!

Mr Coomaraswami is a man with many hats! And his
Highness the Rajah is not a nationalist. I must leave you,
Miss Crewe. But may I step inside to fetch my painting
away?

FLORA. If you like.

DAS. I do not have my bicycle this evening, so I can manage
the easel also.

FLORA. Mr Das, did you tell people I was ill?

DAS. What do you mean?

FLORA. That I came to India for my health?

COOMARASWAMI (off). I cannot wait, Mr Das!

DAS (shouts). A moment!

Why do you ask me that?

FLORA. He is leaving you behind.

The horse and buggy are heard departing.

DAS. I will walk, then.

FLORA. It seems that everyone from the Rajah to the
Resident knows all about me. I told no one except you. If
I want people to know things, I tell them myself, you see.
I'm sorry to mention it but if there's something wrong
between two friends I always think it is better to say what
it is.

DAS. Oh . . . my dear Miss Crewe . . . it was known long
before you arrived in Jummapur. Mr Chamberlain's letter
said exactly why you were coming. Mr Coomaraswami
told me himself when I began to paint your portrait. But,
you see, I already knew from talking with others. This is
how it is with us, I'm afraid. The information was not
considered to be private, only something to be treated with
tact.

FLORA. Oh . . .

DAS. As for the Rajah and the Resident, I am sure they
knew before anybody. A letter from England to Mr
Coomaraswami would certainly be opened.

FLORA. Oh . . . (*She is merely making sounds, close to
tears.*)

DAS. You must not blame yourself. Please.

FLORA. Oh, Mr Das . . . I'm so glad . . . and so sorry. Oh dear, have you got a hanky?

DAS. Yes . . . certainly.

FLORA. Thank you. How stupid I am.

DAS opens the door to the interior.

DAS. I will fetch the canvas.

We go with him. He moves the easel, folds it, etc.

FLORA (*off*). Don't take it. (*Approaching.*) If it is still a gift, I would like to keep it, just as it is.

DAS. Unfinished?

FLORA. Yes. All portraits should be unfinished. Otherwise it's like looking at a stopped clock. Your handkerchief smells faintly of . . . something nice. Is it cinnamon?

DAS. Possibly not. The portrait is yours, if you would like it. Of course. I must take it off the stretcher for you, or it will not travel easily in your luggage. Perhaps I can find a knife in the kitchen, to take out the little nails.

FLORA. There are scissors on the table.

DAS. Ah – yes. Thank you. No – I think I would damage them. May I call Nazrul?

FLORA. I thought –

DAS. Yes – Mr Coomaraswami sent him away, he is suspicious of everyone. I'm sorry.

FLORA. It doesn't matter.

DAS. No. There is no hurry.

FLORA. No. But I am leaving tomorrow.

DAS. Tomorrow?

FLORA. I think I must. Every day seems hotter than the day before. Even at dawn.

DAS. Yes, you are right of course.

FLORA. But I will see you again, because I'll come back this way to Bombay, by July 10th at the latest. My boat sails on the 12th.

DAS. You may take a later boat.

FLORA. No, I cannot. My sister . . . oh, you'll be horrified, but never mind; my sister is having a baby in October.

DAS. That is joyful news.

FLORA. Oh, good.

DAS. I can keep the painting for you until you come back if you like.

FLORA. No, I'd like to have it with me.

DAS. Miss Crewe . . . actually I have brought something to show you. I decided I must not show it to you after all, but if we are friends again . . . I would like you to see it.

FLORA. What is it?

DAS. I left it in my briefcase outside.

FLORA. I would like to see it.

DAS (*hesitates*). Well . . . I will bring it.

FLORA. All right.

> DAS *walks the few steps back to the verandah, and returns, speaking.*

DAS. I have wrapped it, although it is itself only a sheet of paper.

FLORA. Oh . . . shall I open it?

DAS. You must look at it in the light. Let me –

FLORA. No – not the electric light. I seldom cry, but never in the electric light. Do you mind? There is enough light in the other window; Mr Coomaraswami was quite right about the moon. (*She moves. She unwraps the paper.*) It's going to be a drawing, isn't it? Oh!

DAS (*nervous, bright*). Yes! A good joke, is it not? A Rajput miniature, by Nirad Das!

FLORA (*not heeding him*). Oh . . . it's the most beautiful thing . . .

DAS (*brightly*). I'm so pleased you like it! A quite witty pastiche –

FLORA (*heeding him now*). Are you going to be Indian?
Please don't.

DAS (*heeding her*). I . . . I am Indian.

FLORA. An Indian artist.

DAS. Yes.

FLORA. Yes. This one is for yourself.

DAS. You are not offended?

FLORA. No, I'm pleased. It has *rasa*.

DAS. I think so. Yes. I hope so.

FLORA. I forget its name.

DAS (*pause*). Shringara.

FLORA. Yes. Shringara. The *rasa* of erotic love. Whose god
is Vishnu.

DAS. Yes.

FLORA. Whose colour is blue-black.

DAS. Shyama. Yes.

FLORA. It seemed a strange colour for love.

DAS. Krishna was often painted shyama.

FLORA. Yes. I can see that now. It's the colour he looked in
the moonlight.

Scene Fifteen: England

MRS SWAN. 'Which only goes to show, when in Rome,
etc., and I wish I'd remembered that when I *was* in Rome.
Interrupted! Next day. Oh dear, guess what? You won't
approve. Quite right. So I think it's time to go. Love 'em
and leave 'em . . .'

ANISH. May I see?

MRS SWAN. It's no different from what you can read in the
book. Though it's a relief not to have Clark Gable butting
in all the time. I decided not to tell Mr Pike about Rome,
even though it was several Popes ago and Norman
Douglas wouldn't have given a hoot. Let sleeping dogs lie,
that's what I say.

ANISH. 'You won't approve . . . Oh dear, guess what? You won't approve . . .'

MRS SWAN. I wish I'd kept the envelopes, they'd be worth something now to a collector, a philatelist, I mean.

ANISH. Mr Pike's footnote talks about the political agent, Captain Durance.

MRS SWAN. Gratuitously.

ANISH. Yes! Why wouldn't you approve of Captain Durance? Surely it's more likely she meant . . .

MRS SWAN. Meant what, Mr Das?

ANISH. I don't mean any offence.

MRS SWAN. Then you must take care not to give it.

ANISH. Would you have disapproved of a British Army officer – Mrs Swan? – more than an Indian painter?

MRS SWAN. Certainly. Mr Pike is spot-on there. In 1930 I was working for a Communist newspaper. Which goes to show that people are surprising. But you know that from your father, don't you?

ANISH. Why?

MRS SWAN. He must have surprised you too. The thorn in the lion's paw.

ANISH. Yes. Yes, I was surprised.

MRS SWAN. In any case, if you read Flora's words simply for what they say, you would see that when she said I wouldn't *approve*, she did not mean this man or that man. Flora was ill. As it turned out she was dying. Cigarettes, whisky and men, and for that matter the hundred-yard dash, were not on the menu. She didn't need Dr Guppy to tell her that. No, I would not have approved. But Flora's weakness was always romance. To call it that.

ANISH. She had a romance with my father, then.

MRS SWAN. Quite possibly. Or with Captain Durance. Or his Highness the Rajah of Jummapur. Or someone else entirely. It hardly matters, looking back. Men were not really important to Flora. If they had been, they would have been fewer. She used them like batteries. When things went flat, she'd put in a new one.

Scene Sixteen: India

FLORA. 'Heat collects and holds as a pearl at my throat,
lets go and slides like a tongue-tip
down a Modigliani,
spills into the delta, now in the salt-lick,
lost in the mangroves and the airless moisture,
a seed-pearl returning to the oyster –
et nos cedamus amori – '

> *She is on the verandah, at dawn. The Daimler car is approaching.*
>
> (*Hearing the car.*) Oh . . .
>
> *The Daimler arrives. The engine is cut, the car door opens.*
>
> David . . . ?

DURANCE. You're up!

FLORA. Up with the dawn. What on earth are *you* doing?

DURANCE (*approaching*). I'm afraid I came to wake you. Don't you sleep?

FLORA. Yes, I slept early and woke early.

DURANCE. The grapevine says you're leaving today.

FLORA. Yes.

DURANCE. I promised you a turn with the Daimler – remember?

FLORA. Yes.

DURANCE. I wanted to show you the sunrise. There's a pretty place for it only ten minute down the road. Will you come?

FLORA. Can I go in my dressing-gown?

DURANCE. Well . . . better not.

FLORA. Righto. I'll get dressed.

DURANCE. Good.

FLORA. Come up.

> DURANCE *comes up the verandah steps.*

DURANCE. Writing a poem?

FLORA. Writing *out* a poem, to send to my sister. (*Going.*) I'll be quick.

DURANCE. The damnedest thing happened to me just now.

FLORA (*inside*). Can't hear you! Come in, it's quite safe.

DURANCE also enters the interior. He is now in the living-room. FLORA is further within the bungalow.

DURANCE. That fellow Das was on the road. I'm sure it was him.

FLORA (*off*). Well . . . why not?

DURANCE. He cut me.

FLORA (*off*). What?

DURANCE. I gave him a wave and he turned his back. I thought – 'Well, that's a first!'

FLORA (*further off*). Oh! There's hope for him yet.

DURANCE. They'll be throwing stones next. What did you say?

FLORA (*further off*). Wait – I'm going into the shower!

DURANCE. Oh. Do you want any help?

FLORA (*further off*). No, thank you, not today.

After a few moments the shower is turned off.

(*In the bathroom.*) Oh – yes, I do – my towel is in there – will you bung it on the bed?

DURANCE does this. He enters the bedroom. FLORA's voice is still beyond a closed door.

DURANCE. It's very damp.

FLORA. Yes. Second shower today. Out you go.

DURANCE. Oh . . . !

FLORA. What?

DURANCE. You're reading Emily Eden. I read it years ago.

FLORA. We'll miss the sunrise.

DURANCE (*with the book*). There's a bit somewhere . . . she reminds me of you. 'Off with their heads!'

FLORA (*off*). Whose heads? Are you out?

DURANCE leaves the bedroom and enters the living-room.

DURANCE. Yes, I'm out. I'll see if I can find it.

Now FLORA is in the bedroom.

FLORA (*off*). I'll be two shakes.

DURANCE. Here it is – listen! – 'Simla, Saturday, May 25th, 1839. The Queen's Ball "came off" yesterday with great success . . .' Oh!

FLORA (*off*). What!

DURANCE. Nothing. I found your bookmark.

FLORA (*off*). Oh . . . (*Now she enters the living-room.*) I'm sort of decent – wet hair will have to do. It's not my bookmark – I put it in the book for safekeeping.

DURANCE. Where did you get such a thing?

FLORA. His Highness gave it to me.

DURANCE. Why?

FLORA (*reacting to his tone*). Because he is a Rajah. Because he was feeling generous. Because he hoped I'd go to bed with him. I don't know.

DURANCE. But how could he . . . feel himself in such intimacy with you? Had you met him before?

FLORA. No, David – it was a muddle –

DURANCE. But my dear girl, in accepting a gift like this don't you see – (*Pause.*) Well, it's your look-out, of course . . .

FLORA. Shall we go?

DURANCE. . . . but I'm in a frightfully difficult position now.

FLORA. Why?

DURANCE. Did he visit you?

FLORA. I visited him.

DURANCE. I know. Did he visit you?

FLORA. Mind your own business.

DURANCE. But it is my business.

FLORA. Because you think you love me?

DURANCE. No, I . . . Keeping tabs on what his Highness is up to is one of my . . . I mean I write reports to Delhi.

FLORA (*amused*). Oh, heavens!

DURANCE. You're a politically sensitive person, actually, by assocation with Chamberlain . . . I mean this sort of thing –

FLORA. Oh, darling policeman.

DURANCE. How can I ignore it?

FLORA. Don't ignore it. Report what you like. I don't mind, you see. *You* mind. But I don't. I have never minded.

She steps on to the verandah.

(*In despair.*) Oh – look at the sky! We're going to be too late!

DURANCE (*to hell with it*). Come on! Our road is due west – if you know how to drive a car we'll make it.

They dash to the car, which roars into life and takes off at what sounds like a dangerous speed.

FLORA. 'My suitor came to say goodbye, and now I'm packed, portrait and all, and waiting for Mr Coomaraswami to take me to the station in his chariot. I'll post this in Jaipur as soon as I get there – I'm not going to post it here because I'm not. I feel fit as two lops this morning, and happy too, because something good happened here which made me feel half-way better about Modi and Gus and getting back to Paris too late – a sin which I'll carry to my grave.'

PIKE. This appears to be about the portrait. FC had arranged to return to France to sit for Modigliani in the autumn of 1919, but she delayed, arriving only on the morning of January 23rd, unaware that Modigliani had been taken to hospital. He died on the following evening without regaining consciousness, of tuberculosis, aged thirty-five. Thus, the frontispiece of this book shows the only known portrait of Flora Crewe, by an unknown Indian artist.

Scene Seventeen: England

MRS SWAN *opens her front door from inside.*

MRS SWAN. Goodbye, Mr Das.

ANISH. Goodbye, Mrs Swan – thank you.

MRS SWAN. If you change your mind, I'm sure Flora wouldn't mind . . .

ANISH. No. Thank you, but it's my father I'm thinking of. He really wouldn't want it, not even in a footnote. So we'll say nothing to Mr Pike.

MRS SWAN. Well, don't put it away in a trunk either.

ANISH. Oh no! It will be on the wall at home, and I'll tell my children too. Thank you for tea – the Victoria sponge was best!

MRS SWAN. I'm baking again tomorrow. I still have raspberries left to pick and the plums to come, look. I always loved the fruit trees at home.

Walking from front door to the gate. A quiet street.

ANISH. At home?

MRS SWAN. Orchards of apricot – almond – plum – I never cared for the southern fruits, mango, paw-paw and such like. But up in the North-West . . . I was quite unprepared for it when I first arrived. It was early summer. There was a wind blowing.

Cross-fading, wind.

And I had never seen such blossom, it blew everywhere, there were drifts of snow-white flowers piled up against the walls of the graveyard. I had to kneel on the ground and sweep the petals off her stone to read her name.

Scene Eighteen: India

NELL. 'Florence Edith Crewe . . . Born March 21st 1895 . . . Died June 10th 1930. *Requiescat in Pacem.*'

FRANCIS. I'm afraid it's very simple. I hope that's all right.

NELL. Yes. It was good of you.

FRANCIS. Oh no, we look after our own. Of course.

NELL. I think she would have liked 'Poet' under her name. If I left some money here to pay for it . . . ?

FRANCIS. There are funds within my discretion. You may count on it, Miss Crewe. Poet. I should have thought of that. It is how *we* remember your sister.

NELL. Really?

FRANCIS. She read one evening. The Club has a habit of asking guests to sing for their supper and Miss Crewe read to us . . . from her work.

NELL. Oh dear.

FRANCIS (*laughs gently*). Yes. Well, we're a bit behind the times, I expect. But we all liked her very much. We didn't know what to expect because we understood she was a protégée of Mr Chamberlain, who had lectured in the town some years before. Perhaps you know him.

NELL. Yes. I'm not really in touch with him nowadays.

FRANCIS. Ah. It was just about this time of year when she was here, wasn't it? It was clear she wasn't well – these steps we just climbed, for instance, she could hardly manage them. Even so. Death in India is often more unexpected, despite being more common, if you understand me. I'm talking far too much. I'm so sorry. I'll wait at the gate. Please stay as long as you wish, I have no one waiting for me.

NELL. I won't be a moment. Flora didn't like mopers.

FRANCIS *leaves her*.

(*Quietly*.) Bye bye, darling . . . oh – damn! (. . . *because she has burst into sobs. She weeps unrestrainedly*.)

FRANCIS (*returning*). Oh . . . oh, I say . . .

NELL. Oh, I'm sorry.

FRANCIS. No – please . . . can I . . . ?

NELL *stops crying after a few moments*.

NELL. I've messed up your coat. I've got a hanky somewhere.

FRANCIS. Would you like to . . . ? Here . . .

NELL. Yes. Thank you. (*She uses his handkerchief.*) I came too soon after all. I hated waiting a whole year but . . . well, anyway. Thank you, it's a bit wet. Should I keep it? Oh, look, I've found mine, we can swap.

FRANCIS. Don't you worry about anything. What a shame you had to come on your own. You have another sister, I believe. Or a brother?

NELL. No. Why?

FRANCIS. Oh. Flora was anxious to return to England to be an aunt, she said.

NELL. Yes. I had a baby in October. He only lived a little while, unfortunately. There was something wrong.

FRANCIS. Oh. I'm so sorry.

NELL. It's why I couldn't come before.

FRANCIS. Yes, I see. What rotten luck. What was his name?

NELL. Alexander. Sacha Alexander Percival Crewe. How nice of you to ask. Nobody ever does. I say, how about that blossom!

They start to walk.

FRANCIS. Yes, it's quite a spot, isn't it? I hope you stay a while. First time in India?

NELL. Yes.

FRANCIS. Mind the loose stone here. May I . . . ?

NELL. Thank you. I'm sorry I blubbed, Mr Swan.

FRANCIS. I won't tell anyone. Do call me Francis, by the way. Nobody calls me Mr Swan.

NELL. Francis, then.

FRANCIS. Do you like cricket?

NELL (*laughs*). Well, I don't play a *lot*.

FRANCIS. There's a match tomorrow.

NELL. *Here?*

FRANCIS. Oh, yes. We're going to field a Test team next year, you know.

NELL. We?

FRANCIS. India.

NELL. Oh.

Scene Nineteen

EMILY EDEN. 'Simla, Saturday, May 25th, 1839. The Queen's Ball "came off" yesterday with great success . . . Between the two tents there was a boarded platform for dancing, roped and arched in with flowers and then in different parts of the valley, wherever the trees would allow of it, there was "Victoria", "God Save The Queen" and "Candahar" in immense letters twelve feet high. There was a very old Hindu temple also prettily lit up. Vishnu, to whom I believe it really belonged, must have been affronted. We dined at six, then had fireworks, and coffee, and then they all danced till twelve. It was the most beautiful evening; such a moon, and the mountains looked so soft and *grave*, after all the fireworks and glare. Twenty years ago no European had ever been here, and there we were with a band playing, and observing that St Cloup's *Potage à la Julienne* was perhaps better than his other soups, and that some of the ladies' sleeves were too tight according to the overland fashions for March, and so on, and all this in the face of those high hills, and we one hundred and five Europeans being surrounded by at least three thousand mountaineers, who, wrapped up in their hill blankets, looked on at what we call our polite amusements, and bowed to the ground if a European came near them. I sometimes wonder they do not cut all our heads off and say nothing more about it.'

MICKEY MOOKEY

One of Colonel Throckmorton's WHOPPERS

by Steve Walker

Steve Walker, whose epic theological comedy *The Pope's Brother* won a Giles Cooper Award last year, was born in the very house depicted in *Mickey Mookey* as belonging to Granny Dwindley. Four years later he made his stage debut singing extracts from *The Threepenny Opera* in a nightclub, at about which time he also met Mickey Mookey for the first time, but, being good, was never taken away by him. There have been sixty-four one-man shows of Walker's paintings and drawings. His pictures hang in collections all over the world, including in the Kremlin, in a room which itself is depicted in his forthcoming radio play *Holus-Bolus*, which with *The Pope's Brother* and *Oates after his Fingers* completes his *Pymlot and Everything Trilogy*.

Whoppers is a series of six plays, *Mickey Mookey* being the second, which describe the worldwide adventures of the 704-year-old storyteller Colonel Digby Throckmorton and his suicidal sidekick Binsley. Throckmorton tells outrageously impossible and lie-filled stories which somehow turn out to be true and transform our inner landscapes on the way. A visitor to Tunbridge Wells may meet the Colonel by standing on any corner and shouting WHOPPERS! for several days. A new series of *Whoppers* is to be broadcast next year, as will Walker's history of the next century *21st Century Blues*, and listeners to the World Service will find his *The Pipsqueak*. Walker played Hoss Cartwright in *Bonanza* for three years, after the untimely death of Dan Blocker. He is currently working on a book about his experiences as a member of the Polish Government.

Mickey Mookey was first broadcast as part two of a six-part series called *Whoppers* on BBC Radio 5 on 2 October 1991. The cast was as follows:

Whopperizers:

Stuck in the Elevator:

COLONEL DIGBY THROCKMORTON (our 704-year-old Whopperteller)	Norman Jones
NORMAN C BINSLEY (the failed accountant)	Richard Tate
MRS HILDA LIPPE (a screaming woman)	Kathleen Helme
DOUGLAS WIVERTONSON III (a bankrupt rabbit-breeder)	Ronnie Herdman

At loose in the Whopper:

FRED BULLEN (a burglar)	John Hollis
JOSH BULLEN (an apprentice burglar and bad egg in the making)	Nicholas Gatt
HECTOR FLOOGE-SNIPPIT (toffee-nosed house owner)	Norman Jones
CONSTABLE BLOOMSBURIED (an unbent policemen)	Richard Tate
GRANNY DWINDLEY (Josh's Granny)	Kathleen Helme

LUCIANO VON ALLIEYOWLER S.J. (a singing cat)	Richard Tate
DOREEN HUDSPITH (a horrible Geordie girl)	Sue Sheridan
MR HUDSPITH (Doreen's Grandad)	Ronnie Herdman
MICKEY MOOKEY (you'll know him when you see him)	Tom Georgeson
DENNIS BLINT (a bad boy)	Sue Sheridan
CHESTER EVANS (an innocent bad boy)	Neil Roberts
MILLIE WHOPPERINGTON-ARKLE (a bad girl who likes horses)	Sue Sheridan
HUW (the horriblest boy in Wales)	Neil Roberts
MR SNAVELTHOMAS (a librarian)	Ronnie Herdman
THE MAP MAKER (a map maker lost in his work)	Richard Tate

Mickey Mookey appears by permission of the International League of Boogeymen and Allied Trades.

Director: Sally Avens
Running time, as broadcast: 30 mins

Ludicrous 1950s-ish 'going shopping' music.

THROCKMORTON (*in a hurry, extra fast*). I never go shopping, you know . . . I usually send my horse. He completely ignores my shopping-lists, always brings back the wrong things. I have three rooms full of saddles at home . . . a saddle for each of my 704 birthdays! And all those toasters he buys from that man in the betting-shop! But today my horse is running in the Grand National – he'll hate me saying this, but he hasn't a chance – so I'm doing the shopping myself. For some odd reason I've bought another saddle. I'm wrestling with it on one of those stupid elevators . . .

Effort of THROCKMORTON *lifting saddle, the tinkle of stirrups.*

. . . and there's nowhere near enough room for it.

Acoustic of moving elevator. Herb Alpert is providing muzak.

BINSLEY. Here, watch where you're sticking that saddle!

THROCKMORTON. Dreadfully sorry.

Clatter and bump of THROCKMORTON *moving his saddle.*

MRS LIPPE. Ooooh!

THROCKMORTON. Do excuse me, madam.

MR WIVERTONSON (*a tiny, irritating voice*). Careful with that whopping-great saddle! It's up against all the buttons!

A fizz, a clank, a bigger clank, a boing, the whizzzzzzsht of the lift sticking between floors. The muzak dies with a slow groan, then continues strangled.

MRS LIPPE. The lift's stopped!!! Stopped!!! We're stuck! Arrrrhhhhhhh!

BINSLEY. We'll die! They'll never get us out! (*He wailingly weeps.*) It's the end of all my dreams!

MR WIVERTONSON (*teeth chattering*). I saw it in a film once. These people were in a lift and the cable snapped and when they opened the door after it hit the bottom there was nothing but warm marmalade bubbling on the floor. (*Simpers.*)

THROCKMORTON (*no-nonsense, taking charge militarily*). I am Colonel Digby Throckmorton. I am 704 years old. I was born in the year 1297 in what today is Tunbridge Wells. I have served my country in 4,621 wars and I assure you, madam and sirs, that the authorities will shortly engineer our release from this sticky conveyance. Perhaps, while we are waiting, I might tell you all a story.

Threatening creak of the lift.

MRS LIPPE. We'll never hear the end!!!! We'll all be marmalade, any minute!!!!

THROCKMORTON. Piffle-and-squeak! (*Ponders.*) Mmmmmm . . . mmmm . . . yes, I know! I'll tell you about my great-great-great-great-great-great-great-great-great-great-great-great-great-great nephew, Joshua Bullen . . . an absolutely monstrous boy!

BINSLEY. Does he have long tentacles and eat tractors?

THROCKMORTON. Pardon?

BINSLEY. I heard about a boy in Swindon like that.

THROCKMORTON. Look, I'm telling this story, not you! No, he hasn't a single tentacle and has hardly ever eaten a tractor. He is a perfectly normal boy! Except . . . well: he does have freckles. In my regiment in Kuala Lumpur I once shot a man for having freckles. But apart from the freckles and the burglaries he was perfectly normal. Did I say he was a burglar? Truth be told, his father was the burglar. He just took Josh along to help, to climb through bathroom windows, that sort of thing.

Interior acoustic. A poky room. Big BULLEN *and* JOSH *are eating their dinner. Clink of plates. They both talk with their mouths full. Continually glugging beer and belching.*

JOSH *has the voice of a 10-year-old Michael Caine,* BULLEN *the voice of a recently-hanged mass-murderer gargling with gravel.*

JOSH. Dad? Dad? We going out tonight, are we? Eh?

BULLEN. Shut up, Bullen's kid! Eat yer kidneys!

JOSH. We is, isn't wees?

BULLEN. Shut up, Bullen's kid. Eat yer liver!

JOSH. I knows when you're thinking about a burglarizing. I can see the house wot you're thinking about burglarizing in the fog of your glass eye.

BULLEN. Shutuuuuuurpppppppppppppppppppp, Bullen's kid.

JOSH. Where are we going? West End? Hampstead?

BULLEN (*chuckles devilishly*). Here, Bullen's kid, hold my eye for me.

A sucking plop as the eye comes out. He rolls it across the table.

BULLEN. Look inside the eye, son. Can yerh see the house what wees gwan to do over tonight?

JOSH. I sees it! I sees it! A big white house behind a high wall.

BULLEN. Can yerh sees inside, son? Through the winders.

JOSH. Paintings of fat women with no clothes on. Bet one's got a safe behind her, eh, Dad? . . . And I sees a tremendacious sideboard-thingy full of silver cups and dishes.

BULLEN (*suddenly angry*). Eat yerh beans, Bullen's kid! Or I'll shove the lot up yerh nose! (*Benevolent again.*) Heh-heh-heh. For breakfast tomorrar yerh can eat yerh beans off a silver plate. (*Barks.*) Here! Gis moy eye back!

Faint Herb Alpert lift-muzak during
THROCKMORTON's *narration.*

THROCKMORTON. So Josh and his Father went out that
night to burglarize a house. They wore striped pullovers,
false beards, little black masks and carried bags with
SWAG written on them in big black letters.

Crash of JOSH *falling through a window, knocking bottles
of cosmetics all over a bathroom, and a splash of him
falling into the toilet.*

*Silence. Owl hoots. Distant peep of traffic and faraway
London.*

BULLEN (*hushed*). You all right, Bullen's kid?

JOSH (*from inside, calls hushed*). I fell straight into the
toilet.

Slosh of toilet water.

BULLEN. Heh-heh-heh. Hurry up and open the front door
for your old Dad.

Sound of BULLEN *hurrying around to the front of the
house on a gravel path. He softly sings 'By the Light of the
Silvery Moon'.*

BULLEN (*to himself*). Hurry up, Bullen's kid! Hurry up!

A click as the door opens.

JOSH (*a rasping whisper*). Dad! Hurry on in, Dad!

BULLEN (*hurrying in*). Well done, boy.

Door clicks shut behind them. Absolute silence.

JOSH (*in normal voice*). The cups are through here . . .

BULLEN. Shhhhhhh!

JOSH (*Shhhhed*). . . . . I reckons the safe's in the room with
the books, behind a picture of a fat lady having a bath.

BULLEN (*hushed*). You get the cups, Bullen's kid. I'll look
behind the fat lady.

JOSH *walks off, his footsteps creak loudly.*

BULLEN (*calling him back with a rasp*). Here . . . here . . . can you see the combination of the safe in me eye.

JOSH (*looking carefully*). Sorry, Dad . . . Yeah! – it's there, very faint though. 42 left, 61 right, 11 left, 5 right.

BULLEN. Good boy. (*Mutters as he goes.*) 42 left, 61 right . . .

JOSH. Good luck, Dad.

BULLEN. Fill them sacks, kid!

We go with BULLEN, *his footsteps creaking into the room with the safe. He belches.*

BULLEN (*close, intimate*). Excuse my manners! What am I excusing meeself for . . . there's only me here and I don't care if I burps me head off. (*Belches hugely.*) Hello darlin!

Grunts as he pulls at picture, it creaks softly open.

Gotta be careful not to slosh yerh water for yerh . . . Arhhhhh, looka that! Whopping great safe, big as a fridge! What were them numbers again?

We hear the clinking turning of the safe's combination dial.

42 left . . . 61 right . . . 11 left . . . 5 right. (*Heave of effort from* BULLEN *and a heavy creak from the safe.*). Corrrrrrrrrr! Luvly dosh! (*With awe.*) Enough ter buy all the chicken legs in the world!

A clatter of JOSH *running in dragging a swag-bag full of silver cups.*

JOSH (*a hushed shout*). Dad! Dad! Someone's coming down the stairs!

BULLEN. Shut yerh clatter!

Silence except for their breathing.
Then . . . a Rottweiler's growl.

JOSH. Dad, it's one of them Rottenweileralsationdouberhounds.

BULLEN. I sees it. And the other one behind it. And the four more in the doorway . . . Wot luvly toothypegs they've got.

A hound growls.

When I says the word, Bullen's kid . . . scarper. Take this

dosh with yer and go and stay with yerh Granny in Gateshead.

JOSH (*tearfully*). What about you, Dad?

BULLEN (*barks*). Do as yerh told!!!!!

BULLEN's bark sets the Rotweilers barking. He shouts above the barking.

BULLEN. SCARPER, KID!!!! SCARPER!!!!!

Sound of JOSH scarpering, the front door flung wide as he escapes across the gravel path into the night.

BULLEN (*hurrying after, shouts after*). Run like the wind, Bullen's kid!

Barking all around.

Good doggies . . . Good doggies . . . Arhhhhhhh, gerrroffffff!!!! Geroooffffffffff!

Hounds woofing and jumping on BULLEN. They pull him down with a whump. He struggles, but they have him held between their growling jaws.

BULLEN (*pinned down, in resignation*). I always hated Rottenweileralsationdouberhounds.

OWNER OF HOUSE (*wandering in, toffee-nosed, yawns*). I say, what's all the bother? Oh, is this a burglar?

BULLEN (*in despair*). Yeah.

A Rottenweileralsationdouberhound woofs in the affirmative.

THROCKMORTON (*from lift, with Herb Alpert faintly muzaking*). So it was that Josh's burglarizing parent was caught in the act of burlgarizing and handed over to the police.

POLICEMAN. You are a very bad man, Mr Bullen, a very very bad man.

BULLEN (*in despair*). Yeah. I know.

THROCKMORTON. Josh, meanwhile, with a bagful of money, enough to buy all the chicken legs in the world, took the overnight coach to Gateshead, which is somewhere in the North of England, apparently.

Snowflakes danced in the air and sudden gusts of icy wind blew them into people's faces, smacking them like frozen custard pies. Josh found his Granny's house in a dark alleyway full of dustbins. A blind cat was singing the French National Anthem on the step . . .

A snatch of the cat's singing in background.
JOSH's knock on the door. The door opens.

GRANNY (*a frail old Geordie woman*). Not today thank-you.

JOSH. It's me.

GRANNY. No thank you. I'm 84.

JOSH. It's me! Josh!

GRANNY. Ooooh, Josh, pet. (*On her way back into the innards of the house.*) Haweey in . . . I've some nice whippet-and-leek soup on the boil.

JOSH steps in and steps on the cat.

JOSH. Ooops, sorry!

It desists its singing and yowls in pain. It yowls into the dustbins.

GRANNY. Mind you don't stand on the cat, it's French.

JOSH now reads a letter to his Dad. JOSH is a bad reader.
He jumps on a word at a time breathlessly . . .

JOSH. Dear Dad, Well here's your kid in this miserable rotten place. Granny's okay, except she throws coal at me if she sees me picking my nose . . . and she makes me eat this puky soup of hers with hair floating on the top and claws scratching on the bottom. She keeps saying that if I'm not good someone called Mickey Mookey

A duck quacks in the distance.

will come in the night and take me away. Social worker, I expect. But I ain't done much wrong so far, except I strangled a singing cat and threw it in a dustbin . . . but it came alive again anyway . . .

Cat singing in dustbin.

. . . I've gone through all the houses around here but there isn't nuffink worth burglarizing. I did get some medals from off an old geezer's mantelpiece but they're not worth much.

Briefly breaks off his letter writing to open the window and throw a boot at the cat. The boot clatters noisily on the dustbin. Silence from cat.

That Judge was a triple-stinking-pig, Dad, for sentencing you to five years. (*Becoming increasingly upset.*) Don't worry about me though, Dad. Granny's given me an okay bedroom with a dead tree outside. I can climb down it if the plods come. By the time you gets out I'll have done so many burglarizing jobs I'll be a millionaire, never mind wot we've got stashed away already. (*With a sad blankness.*) Yours faithfully, Bullen's kid.

DOREEN (*a nasty childish ingratiating whine*). Hello.

JOSH (*calling from a height, brusque*). Hello.

DOREEN. What you doing climbing up that drainpipe for?

JOSH *jumps down. His feet crunch on the gritty back street.*

JOSH. Wasn't climbing up. I was climbing down.

DOREEN. What you climbing down that drainpipe for, then?

JOSH. Practising for Mount Everest.

DOREEN. Oh, aye.

JOSH. Yeah. My Dad's going to take me up it when he gets out . . . when he gets back from his latest expedition in the Himmeylayerers, I mean.

DOREEN. Your Dad a mountain-climber-upper, is he?

JOSH. Yeah.

DOREEN. You the lad staying with Granny Dwindley in number 21?

JOSH (*suspiciously*). Yeah.

DOREEN (*a tongue-out taunt*). Your Dad's a burglar, so there! He's in clink!

JOSH. It's not true!

DOREEN. Is!

JOSH. Isn't! That's the other lad, the one I shares a room with. Not me.

DOREEN (*duped*). Oh, I see. (*A big sniff.*) Don't mind if I sniff, do you? I get in trouble if I pick it.

JOSH. Go ahead.

DOREEN (*after an enormous sniff, coquettishly*). I'm Doreen, by the way.

JOSH. Oh, yeah.

DOREEN. Here, what's all them things dangling on yer jacket?

JOSH. Medals, awarded to me after the Battle of Waterloo.

Tinkle of medals.

DOREEN. Never!

JOSH. Pinned on by Napoleon himself.

DOREEN. Wasn't he on the other side?

JOSH. What other side?

DOREEN. The other side from our side.

JOSH. Yeah, that's right. I played the first half on their side. Second half I played for our lot.

DOREEN. Wait on, I think my Grandad's got some medals like that. D'yer think he were at the Battle of Waterloo? He never said. (*Already on her way.*) I'll go and ask.

An angry door-knocking.
Door opens.

GRANNY. Not today, thankyou.

DOREEN'S GRANDAD (*a huge old Geordie, barks*). WHERE IS HE?

GRANNY. No thank you. I'm 84.

DOREEN'S GRANDAD. I beat Napoleon black-and-blue to get them medals and I want them back!

DOREEN (*explains calmly*). Your lad's nicked my Grandad's medals, Gran Dwindley.

GRANNY. He hasn't, has he?

DOREEN'S GRANDAD. AYE!!!! AND IF I DOESSENT GET THEM BACK THIS MINUTE I'LL BE OUT HERE AT TEA-TIME WITH ME BAZOOKA!!!!!

DOREEN. Don't fret, Grandad, you'll get them back.

DOREEN'S GRANDAD. BETTER HAD, IN ALL!!!!

JOSH. Dear Dad, I have a girlfriend. She's very ugly but she'll be good practice for when I get beautiful ones when I'm older . . .

From JOSH's *room we hear* GRANNY *stomping loudly up the stairs.*

GRANNY (*shouting angrily up the stairs*). Josh! Josh! Josh!

The door bursts open.

GRANNY. Where are they!?! Where've yer got them hid!?!

JOSH. What?

GRANNY. You know.

JOSH. No.

GRANNY. He's coming back with his bazooka.

JOSH. Who is?

GRANNY. Right! You've asked for it!

A worried 'meeeeow' from the cat.

JOSH. What you doing?

GRANNY. I'm going to hit you with the cat until you tell me where Mr Hudspith's medals are!

A whump. 'Ow!!' from JOSH. *'Meeowwww!!!' from the cat.*

JOSH. I never nicked nuffink, honest!!!!

A whump. 'Ow!!!' from JOSH. *A more painful 'Meeeooooow!!!' from the cat.*

JOSH. Wasn't me!!! Wasn't!!!

GRANNY (*while hitting*). Thief! Thief! Where are they!!!

Several more whumps, ows and meeeowwwws.

JOSH (*through the whumping*). All right! All right! Here they are!

Drawer opens, brief rifle in drawer, tinkle of medals as JOSH finds them and as GRANNY snatches them. The cat complains of a headache with a weak meeeow.

GRANNY. You've had it, bonny lad. Mickey Mookey'll come for yer now, for sure. Don't say I didn't warn yer!

JOSH (*defiantly*). Who's this Mickey Mookey, then?

GRANNY. You'll soon find out. With rotten apples like yer Dad it's the plods that comes. But for young lads like you . . . (*A sinister whisper.*) . . . It's Mickey Mookey.

A duck quacks. It quacks every time 'Mickey Mookey' is mentioned.

GRANNY (*calls in a slightly posher voice*). Mr Hudspith, it's quite all right, I've found your medals for you . . . it were all a mistake! (*On her way barks back into room.*) And no more whippet-and-leek soup for you, either!

Door slams.

JOSH (*shouts angrily after, sounding like his father*). I don't want none of yer filthy soup, you old witch! And I ain't frightened of no boogeyman, neither!

The cat begins singing.

JOSH (*a severe warning*). Sherrrrrrrrrtup . . .

THROCKMORTON (*very close, whispers hushed, portentously*). That night, very late, by a dim light, in a room full of slanting shadows, Josh was sitting on his bed sticking a knife into a piggy bank he'd stolen, trying to get the coins out.

We hear him doing this, muttering curses.
MICKEY MOOKEY *speaks with a voice like a razor shaving a pig. At the end of every second word he hisses like a drip of water hitting a hotplate.*

MICKEY MOOKEY. Josh . . . ua. Josh . . . ua.

JOSH. Is that you, you stupid French cat?

MICKEY MOOKEY (*after an evil chuckle*). I am the furthest thing from a cat, Joshua.

JOSHUA (*he has guessed who it is, a tremble in his voice*). Who is it, then?

MICKEY MOOKEY. You know who it is that I am. Everybody knows me when they see me.

JOSHUA (*bravely but scared-to-bits*). But I can't see you. You're hiding behind the wardrobe.

A creak as MOOKEY *steps out.*

MICKEY MOOKEY. Can you see me now?

JOSHUA. You're Mickey Mookey.

A duck quacks.

MICKEY MOOKEY. Mickkkkkkkkyyyy Mookeyyyyyyyyyyyyyy.

A duck quacks.

THROCKMORTON. Mickey Mookey

A duck quacks.

was seven-feet-three, a long bloodless man with no flesh at all, just dry skin stretched over bone and a smile like white knuckles. He wore a faded black suit and a tall black hat with tongues of flame on the top like the fire on a Christmas pudding. His eyebrows were cockroaches. Sometimes they crawled down his face and were a moustache instead.

MICKEY MOOKEY (*he chuckles evilly*). What's that you're playing with, Mookey's kid?

JOSH. Nuffink.

MICKEY MOOKEY. Where'd you klep it from, Mookey's kid?

JOSH. I didn't klep it, honest, and I'm not Mookey's Kid! I'm Bullen's Kid!

MICKEY MOOKEY (*chuckles evilly*). Let's go, Mookey's kid.

JOSH (*terrified*). Go where?

MICKEY MOOKEY. To my house. On the other side of things.

JOSH (MOOKEY *has his nose*). Owya! Owya!

A slow ghostly howl, over and over, fading during THROCKMORTON's *speech* . . .

THROCKMORTON. Mickey Mookey

A duck quacks.

grabbed Josh's nose between his bony fingers and led him into the slanting shadows. They seemed to walk straight through the wall and should have been in his Granny's room where the cat slept on her face to stop her snoring. But they weren't! They were on the other side of things, in Mickey Mookey's

A duck quacks.

house.

THROCKMORTON's *voice echoes, wings flap.*

Their footsteps clunk in the huge house. Things snuffle and squeak in the background, everything has a metallic echo.

JOSH (*through a blocked nose*). Owya! Owya!

MICKEY MOOKEY. Do you like my house? There's horrible things hiding everywhere, more and more getting born all the time, even horribler than last year's and they were horrible enough. (*Angrily, twisting* JOSH's *nose.*) How many rooms do you think I've got? How many?

JOSH (*through his blocked nose*). Owya! Dunno! Dunno!

MICKEY MOOKEY. HOW MANY???

JOSH. A billion-and-six!

MICKEY MOOKEY (*as pleasant as can be*). Wrong! A billion-and-fourteen! And every one's full of dead people, crying their heads off. And when their heads comes off, I kick them down the stairs.

JOSH (*a sudden determined snap into action*). Wot! Like this!

JOSH's kick makes a sound like someone kicking a skeleton. A crocodilish cry from MOOKEY. He falls down the stairs making a sound like the bag of bones he is.

After an instant's silence, some part of him slowly descending from step to step, bump, bump, bump.

THROCKMORTON. Josh ran as fast as he could, looking for a way out.

We hear JOSHUA panting, running on boards.

Horrible things bit his ankles.

We hear them squeak nastily.

Every time he opened a door Mickey Mookey

A duck's quack

was behind it and lots of miserable people crying their heads off.

A roomful of weeping people. Door slams. Weeping stops. JOSH runs along a corridor. Door opens. Weeping people again. Door slams. JOSH runs along a corridor. Door opens. Weeping starts again. JOSH out of breath.

MICKEY MOOKEY (*sings sinisterly the old music hall song*). Josh . . . ua . . . Josh . . . ua . . .

JOSH (*out of breath*). All right . . . okay . . . I give in. You got me.

MICKEY MOOKEY (*suddenly much more reasonable, almost human*). You really are very bad, you know.

JOSH. Yeah, I know.

MICKEY MOOKEY (*chuckles*). Worst boy I ever collected.

JOSH. What happens now? Do you lock me up in a room where I can cry my head off?

MICKEY MOOKEY. Badness me, no! I've other plans for you.

JOSH. O-oh!

MICKEY MOOKEY (*almost shy*). If you'd like, I mean, if you've the time, would you mind being my assistant? Some of these boys are very sticky, especially their noses. I don't like to touch them. I'll pay you.

JOSH. How much?

MICKEY MOOKEY. A cockroach a day and an invisible octopus every second Thursday. You'll not do better anywhere else.

JOSH (*increasingly delighted*). I can help you just like I helped my Dad. Yeah, sounds good, Mr Mookey. And after five years, when my Dad gets outa clink, I can go back to him, can I?

MICKEY MOOKEY. Thou canst.

JOSH. Right-ho, yerh on! Let's shake on it.

They shake hands. MOOKEY *chuckles happily and rattles like a bag of bones.*

MICKEY MOOKEY. Eurgh! You're all sticky!

JOSH. No I'm not!!!!

THROCKMORTON (*Herb Alpert faintly, a grandfather clock ticks*). And so Josh became Mickey Mookey's

A duck quacks.

helper. During the day he wandered around the boogeyman's house asking weeping people what they were crying about while stealing the loose change from their pockets. In the long boring evenings he squashed crabs on the landing, or taught a bony old parrot to swear. When it was late and dark an invisible octopus tapped him on the shoulder and he hurried to Mickey Mookey's

A duck quacks.

side . . . and they walked through the wall to collect a wicked youngster or two.

Snoring of a wicked boy.

JOSH. Here, Mickey?

MICKEY MOOKEY. Yes, Mookey's kid.

JOSH. How do you know who's been bad?

MICKEY MOOKEY (*slowly and sinister*). I feels it in my bones. (*A discreet rattle.*)

DENNIS, A BAD BOY (*snoring phutters out, he awakes*). Who's there?

JOSH (*whispers to* MOOKEY). Let me say it, go on!

MICKEY MOOKEY. I like to say it.

JOSH. Go on.

MICKEY MOOKEY. Say it properly then.

DENNIS, A BAD BOY. I know there's someone there. Who are you?

JOSH (*doing a* MOOKEY *voice*). You know who it is that I am.

BAD BOY (*utterly terrified*). You're . . . Mickey Mookey!

A duck quacks.

MOOKEY *and* JOSH *laugh sinisterly. The boy screams and wails.*

JOSH's voice has acquired a Mookeyish edge.

JOSH. Dear Dad, I'm enjoying working for Mickey Mookey

A duck quacks.

like mad. He hasn't had a night's sleep since Queen Victoria died, so he's taking tonight off and letting me go out by myself, in his black hat and everything. When we collect a rotten kid what we usually do is lock it in a room until it cries its head off, but all billion-and-fourteen rooms are full, so what we've been doing lately is take them to the library, a whopping-ginormous spidery room with water dripping from the ceiling into buckets full of piranha fish . . .

We hear the plink-plonk of water and the snap of piranhas.

. . . and we slots the bad kiddies into the books. (*Laughs with delight.*) We just slot them in! And there they stay, wandering through the book's story forever! I'm in the library now. Mr Snavelthomas, the librarian, is helping me choose a book to put tonight's rotters into. Can't wait for tonight! This job's even betterer than being a burglar!

JOSH, *who by now is more than a touch Mookeyish, is dragging two protesting victims into the library.*

JOSH. Two more for the treatment, Mr Snavelthomas!

CHESTER, AN INNOCENT BAD BOY. No! No! I'm innocent! I never did nowt never, honest!

JOSH. That's wot they all says!

MILLIE, A BAD GIRL. Gerroff me, you! Gerrofffff!

JOSH. Mr Snavelthomas! Get those books ready!

MR SNAVELTHOMAS. I have them!

Clunk of books, pages being turned.

CHESTER, AN INNOCENT BAD BOY. I'm innocent! I'm as pure as snow!

A scuffle, books knocked over, some into buckets of piranha-infested water.

JOSH. Mr Snavelthomas! Help me get him in!

MR SNAVELTHOMAS (*in a dither*). I've been dead for years! He might snap my fingers off and I'll not be able to turn the pages of my lovely books!

Muffled sound as the protesting boy is pushed into a book.

JOSH (*pushing hard*). I've got him! He's going in!

MILLIE, A BAD GIRL. If I help you shove him can I go into a book about horses?

JOSH. Yeah, okay. Give him a shove!

The grunts of JOSH *and* MILLIE *as they push. A sudden collapse of success! The muffled sound ceases. The book slams shut.*

MICKEY MOOKEY (*approaching with a huge yawn*). I haven't been to bed for ninety years and I still can't sleep. (*A smaller yawn.*) A good collection tonight, Joshua?

JOSH. Just pushed one into a book called . . . (*Picks it up to refer to the title.*) . . . *The Decline and Fall of the Roman Empire.* They'll chuck him to the lions, for sure.

MICKEY MOOKEY (*after a ho-hum yawn, with great distaste*). And what about this beastly child?

JOSH (*as polite as can be*). In here, miss.

MILLIE, A BAD GIRL. A book about horses, is it?

JOSH (*plainly lying*). Horses, sure. Kicking their heels in a meadow full of daisies.

MILLIE, A BAD GIRL (*getting in*). Oh, thankyou! Thankyou.

The book slams hard on her final thank you. JOSH *giggles wickedly*.

JOSH (*triumphant*). It's not about horses at all! It's called *Insects of the Amazonian Jungle*. They'll be all over her, beetles and ants and stingy-buzzy-crawly things in her hair forever . . . forever!

He laughs wickedly.

MICKEY MOOKEY (*yawns*). Very droll, I'm sure. (*Yawns a bigger yawn, while walking across thin, creaky floorboards*.) By the way, that boy in the Roman book, he was the wrong one, you went to the wrong address.

JOSH. Yeek, sorry! Shall I haul him out?

MICKEY MOOKEY (*going away*). Doesn't matter. No harm done.

THROCKMORTON. Every night for five years, 1,821 nights, Josh went out collecting wicked boys and wicked girls, dragging them by their noses into the other side of things. Sometimes Mickey Mookey

A duck quacks.

went with him, but mostly he did not. Mickey Mookey

A duck quacks.

became more and more lazy. He sat in the library playing whist with Mr Snavelthomas and every time he yawned a frog waved from the back of his throat.

A frog's croak.

JOSH *bringing a bad boy into the library*.

JOSH. Only one tonight, I'm afraid. The other one was strangled by his Headmaster this afternoon.

MICKEY MOOKEY. Tish-tosh.

JOSH. Thissun's a real stinker, though.

HUW (*a slow, stupid Welsh voice*). Hello, I'm Huw. I'm a real stinker. Horrible I am. I wee-wee in milk. Give me milk and I'll wee-wee in it and leave it on the table for somebody to drink. Nobody's died yet. But I eats spiders to make my wee-wee more poisonous.

MICKEY MOOKEY (*delighted*). Ooooh, isn't he horrible!

JOSH. The very last rotter on my very last night in the job, and easily the horriblest wot I ever collected.

HUW. I'm horrible, me. Horrible.

JOSH. Sorry about this, Huw. No hard feelings, eh?

HUW. Ooooh, no. I deserve everything I gets.

MR SNAVELTHOMAS (*fetching book*). I've found an exceedingly boring book to lose this monster in: *A Road Atlas of Great Britain and Ireland.* (*Chuckles.*)

MICKEY MOOKEY. Joshua, did you just say that this was your last night on the job?

JOSH (*shoving* HUW). Go on, you, get in!

HUW. Don't want to, thank you.

JOSH (*shoving* HUW). My last night, yeah. We agreed. Five years, remember. My Dad gets outa clink tomorrow. I've gotta get back to the real world.

MICKEY MOOKEY. Oooh, no. No, no, no. We can't allow that. Oh, no.

JOSH. But you said!

MICKEY MOOKEY *chuckles evilly*.

MICKEY MOOKEY. Huw.

HUW. Yes, sir.

MICKEY MOOKEY. Would you like to be my assistant?

HUW. Assistant?

MICKEY MOOKEY. A cockroach a day and an invisible octopus every second Thursday.

HUW. Sounds good to me.

MICKEY MOOKEY. Excellent! Your first job is to put Joshua there into yonder book.

JOSH. Me? No. No. (*He is already struggling with* HUW.) I'm going home. You promised!

HUW. Cum-cum, boyo. I'm a prop-forward. I'm much stronger than you.

JOSH's hands gripping and wobbling the tabletop. The 'Uerrrrrrrrrrrrr!!!!' effortful whine of his resistance. The pages turning in the wind. Beasts squeak. Water drips. A storm seems to rage in the library, more and more full of animal noises.

MICKEY MOOKEY (*calls above the racket*). Come here, Mr Snavelthomas . . . give us a hand shoving him in!

MR SNAVELTHOMAS. All right, then.

The storm rises. Camels bark. A duck goes mad. The wind gets worse.

HUW (*very calm and slow*). I'm much stronger, aren't I? Much stronger than anyone else in the world, I should think.

MR SNAVELTHOMAS. My fingers! (*Weepingly.*) My lovely fingers! All snapped off!

Effort sounds of JOSH resisting. Suddenly they stop. Abrupt silence . . .

MICKEY MOOKEY. Shut the book, Huw, there's a bad boy.

The book shuts quietly.

Exterior acoustic: a vast plain, silent as a shut book. JOSH speaks nervously with snuffles, having just pulled himself together after a blub. He is more himself now, the Mookeyishness is nearly gone.

JOSH. Dear Dad, I don't suppose you'll ever get this letter. But maybe you can see the writing in yerh glass eye, eh? Sorry I won't be there at the gates when you're released.

BULLEN (*from faraway*). I sees yerh Bullen's kid! I seees yerh in me oyy.

JOSH's footsteps on thick paper.

JOSH (*continues his letter*). I'm in a map of England. I'll never get out. It's just like the real England, same fields, same buildings and roads, only there's lettering wherever you look and everything's made of paper. But no people to speak of, just paper ones with no faces. And no sky, just another page, high up, all blurrily dark over yerh head like when you've gone asleep with a book over yerh face. I was in a blue bit to start with, the North Sea, but it wasn't the least bit wet. Then I was in a city. The letters were too big to see all at once. I thought it was West Hartlepool but now I think it was Wolverhampton. I've trudged down red roads, green roads, little white roads. A while ago I was in the middle of a field of white grass. I thought I saw a fox, a white fox running towards a glow of far-off green. I ran as fast as I could. I ran and ran.

JOSH (*in the atlas, running away from us*). Foxy! Foxy! I won't hurt you! I promise! I'm good! Good!

A cry. He falls over, going through the paper with a heavy tear.

JOSH (*in the letter*). I tripped on a tiny black letter F and fell right through the page, and the next page, and the next. I landed on the top of a black windowless church. It was just a ball with a cross on the top.

A bell tolls frantically.

It rolled and rolled, ringing like a bell. It rolled for miles, falling towards the edge of the page like a pinball down its hole. I jumped off just outside Peterborough

The bell tolling towards distance.

and ran after it towards the edge of the page. I thought it might crash a hole that I could escape through. But the book was tight shut. When I found the church it was a crumpled mess beside the dark, locked edge. A faceless paper congregation had poured out of it.
I'm walking along the M1 now.

His feet on the paper road.

It's so silent. I'm the only person in the whole of England!

The sudden, loud, zoom-past of a car.

JOSH. What the . . . ? A car! A car! (*Chasing.*) Hey! Hey! Stop! (*Running after.*) Please!

As THROCKMORTON *speaks we hear* JOSH *running, panting, resting and setting off again on the paper road.*

THROCKMORTON. Josh ran along the M1 for hours and hours. He was exhausted, dizzy. Little bits of paper floated around him like snow. Then at last there it was! The car! Parked in the car-park of a huge service station. Where could the driver be? Josh opened a stiff paper door and went into a paper cafeteria. All the tables and chairs were paper. The food on the counter was paper and served on paper plates.

JOSH. Good morning.

MAP MAKER (*startled*). EUGH!!!! (*Calming down, filling his mouth with food. The voice of a tedious civil servant.*) What a fright you gave me, Mickey.

JOSH. I'm not Mickey. I'm Josh.

MAP MAKER. You're Mickey Mookey.

A duck quacks.

JOSH. I just worked for him, that's all. Now I look like him. I expect it'll wear off. Who are you?

MAP MAKER (*enjoying his food*). I'm the man who drew this map.

JOSH. How did you get in here?

MAP MAKER. I was always getting lost in my work. This time I'm stuck for good. Go on, try a pork chop!

JOSH. But . . . it's paper.

MAP MAKER (*mouth fuller than ever, tearing of paper as he bites*). It's . . . mmmmm . . . delicious!

The sound of a man chewing paper.

JOSH. That's not ink you're drinking, is it?

MAP MAKER. Ink, yes. Very refreshing. It wasn't you I met in the index last Thursday, between 'Hambledon, Bucks' and 'Hambledon, Hants'?

JOSH. No.

MAP MAKER. Someone else, then.

JOSH (*excited*). We're not the only ones here?

MAP MAKER. Ooooh, no. There's dozens. All sorts. And the foxes, of course. Beautifully drawn, isn't it?

JOSH. Is there maybe a way out?

MAP MAKER. OUT! You don't want to go out, surely! It's lovely here. Quiet. No traffic jams. The food's excellent. (*Chewing again.*) Always something handy to blow your nose on. (*Blows it politely.*)

JOSH (*lying*). It's great here, yeah. But I've gotta meet my Dad tomorrow. He's arriving back from the Himmeylayerers, you know.

MAP MAKER. Getting out's easy. Have a sausage! All you do is go to your old house, your old room, where Mickey Mookey

A duck quacks.

took you from, go to sleep in your old bed and you'll wake up back in the real world. Works for everyone except me!

JOSH (*zooming off delighted*). Thanks, mister!

MAP MAKER (*calling after*). Try a rissole before you go. They're really . . .

JOSH has gone, the MAP MAKER's enthusiasm suddenly dies on his tongue, he says in deepest despair.

. . . quite horrible, actually.

A frantic tearing of paper, long noisy tears.

JOSH (*yelling above his paper-tearing*). DAD!!! DAD!!! Can you see me, Dad!

BULLEN (*faraway*). I sees yer!

JOSH. I'll not be long. I'm in the index. I've found the map reference for Gateshead: 2662 124. I'm tearing my way towards it! Won't be long now! I'll sleep in my bed in Granny's house tonight and in the tomorrow I'll be there when they let you out! Promise I will! And we're still rich! All the money wot we nicked is still stashed behind the wardrobe in Granny's!

BULLEN. Good boy!

JOSH (*breathless, the tearing stops*). 124. This is it!

THROCKMORTON (*suddenly, closer, Herb Alpert plays faintly*). Josh walked across the North Sea towards a dark lighthouse. Foxes sat watching him from the flat cliffs but ran away when he called to them.

JOSH. Hellooooo Foxieeeeessss!!!!!!!

THROCKMORTON. Up the River Tyne he hiked, then took a green road into a dark splodge called Gateshead. The paper houses were thick with black ink. Behind the drawn-on windows Josh could hear arguments . . .

Mumble of Geordie men and women arguing: they say 'Mickey Mookey' over and over.

. . . but couldn't make out the words. His Granny was a faceless paper cut-out in her paper backyard, hanging out paper washing.

JOSH. Granny? Gran? That you?

THROCKMORTON. Somewhere in the dark mumbling streets a vixen howled.

A vixen howls.

Josh climbed the stairs, pulling paper hats off his head. Every time he pulled one off there was another one there. He hadn't been to sleep for five years and when he saw his bed his eyes grew heavy and . . .

A huge clunking and whizz, snapping of springs. The sound of a lift coming alive. Its doors fizzing open. Herb Alpert muzak playing healthily.

THROCKMORTON (*speaks double-briskly on his way*). Ah, fixed at last. What time is it? Mind my saddle, madam.

MRS LIPPE. Ooooh! (*This is the same 'Ooooh!' she makes at the beginning.*)

THROCKMORTON (*leaving*). Good morning!

THROCKMORTON's *clipping footsteps in the store. Buzz of shoppers. Woman demonstrating a food-mixer.*

BINSLEY (*chasing after*). Here! Here, you! Colonel whatsyername! You haven't finished the story.

THROCKMORTON (*walking briskly*). What story?

BINSLEY. That you were just telling!

THROCKMORTON. Never seen you before in my life!

BINSLEY (*utterly confused*). But . . . in the lift . . . just now!

THROCKMORTON. Ah, Josh, my boy!

BINSLEY. Is this him? Him that was in the map, that Mickey Mookey

A duck quacks.

took.

JOSH (*very excited indeed*). Hiya, Uncle Diggers!

THROCKMORTON. Sorry I'm late. I've been stuck in a lift. What time do they let that dreadful father of yours out of jug?

JOSH (*in an excited rush*). Uncle Diggers! Your horse! Whopping Neddy! He's won the Grand National!

THROCKMORTON. He never has! And with that limp!

JOSH. I put all my money on him. Everything wot Dad and I nicked! We're rich. MILLIONAIRES!!!!!

THROCKMORTON. Buns all round I think!

Raise the sound of shoppers. Bring up slowly the ludicrous 1950s 'going shopping' music.

THROCKMORTON (*walking away from us, fading*). We'll stop at the betting-shop on our way.

As the end music rises it is interrupted by . . .

MICKEY MOOKEY (*announcing himself in his usual announcing himself manner*). Mickkkkkkkkkkyyyyyyy Moookeyyyyyyyyyyyyyyyyyyy.

A duck quacks.

Play out with ludicrous 1950s 'going shopping' music.

FIGURE WITH MEAT

by Craig Warner

for Micheline Steinberg, my great agent and friend,
for Andy Jordan, with whom I share this award,
and for Alan Drury, for his many valuable insights

Craig Warner had written eleven stage plays before being seduced by the radio. He participated in the First Young Playwrights Festival for Radio 4, and his most recent work was for the Globe Theatre Season. In addition to continued pursuits in radio, his new stage play, *Caledonian Road*, opened in London in September. This is his second Giles Cooper Award. This autumn he begins university at King's College London to study French and Philosophy.

Figure with Meat was first broadcast on BBC Radio 3, on 'Drama Now' on 20 August 1991. The cast was as follows:

GOSPEL SINGER/
  HAPPY CATS/
  SERVER TWO
	Craig Warner

OLDER WOMAN/ MOTHER	Judy Parfitt

EDNA PENFOLD
  (MISS)/
  ANNOUNCER
	Lynsey Baxter

POPE/GOD	Brett Usher
CARDINAL/ WORKMAN	Paul Cresswell
COLIN	Clive Merrison
MALCOLM	Alan David Marriott

MR ANALBY/
  FATHER/
  SOLOMON/
  SERVER ONE
	Alan Barker

PLATO/FLY/ NOAH	Ronald Herdman
GHOST/LESBIAN	Joanna Myers

Director: Andy Jordan
Running time, as broadcast: 55 mins

Musical director and composer of additional music:
  Stuart Gordon
Gospel pianist: Will Gregory

The play opens with piano chords, which are joined by a GOSPEL SINGER.

GOSPEL SINGER. You are such a big man, Johnny God
You have such a big hand, Johnny God
You just stroked your beard
And the whole wide world appeared
You have got a big fan, Johnny God.

You coughed up the skies, Johnny God
Cried the oceans from your eyes, Johnny God
You just did a sneeze
And gave us all the trees
You're a nice man for your size, Johnny G –

The song is cut off when the tape player is smashed with a sledgehammer. A crowd in a large hall applaud and cheer this. An OLDER WOMAN *speaks to them on a microphone.*

OLDER WOMAN. You're a nice man for your size, Johnny God?! What an appalling reduction of our Great Creator! God does not look like an old man with a white beard. He looks more like a pair of clouds with multicoloured light streaming between them. I'll tell you, the direction our country is taking is a downward spiral straight into Hell. This afternoon I attended an art auction entitled 'Images of God', and I could not have been more appalled. The wanton perversion! God's almighty name dragged through the mud! I had the exhibition closed of course (using the Blasphemy Act of 1689, which my research taught me was still on the books). But I've brought examples with me, so that the fullness of their obscenities may be revealed to you as well. Slides, please.

Slide click.

The first painting shows . . .

ANNOUNCER. . . . a religious man in a dank tiled room musked over with the smell of incense. He watches blood trickle down from two carcasses which hang on hooks at either side of his chair.

Barbra Streisand singing 'Dank Sei Dir, Herr' by Handel. After a bit, the needle is torn from the record, scratching violently across the grooves.

POPE. Cardinal!

CARDINAL. Holiness . . .

POPE. What was that music?

CARDINAL. Georg Friedrich Handel, Holiness.

POPE. Not one of ours, I take it?

CARDINAL. No.

POPE. And the singer?

CARDINAL. One Miss Barbra Joan Streisland. Very popular amongst the Jews and homosexuals.

POPE. Oh?

CARDINAL. In fact Jewish homosexuals, when the combination arises, are said to faint at the very mention of her name.

POPE. From America, no doubt.

CARDINAL. Malibu, Holiness. The very Babylon of colonial libertinism.

POPE. Decadeı

CARDINAL. Oı. yes: naked footraces, dog shaving parties, vodka enemas passed round in a circle . . .

POPE. Burn it to the ground.

CARDINAL. Yes Holiness.

POPE. And as for Miss Streisland, have her stripped, washed, and brought before us. We will question her before passing judgement.

CARDINAL. What am I to accuse her of?

POPE. Blasphemy, Jewry, and taking breaths in all the wrong places!

CARDINAL. Yes Holiness.

POPE. And you, my Brothers, look: look upon the carcasses of sinners, and see their filthy blood puddling on the floor. On my left –

Cut into auction acoustic for COLIN/MALCOLM *scene, with the* POPE's *echoey voice imposing itself and drowning out all other sounds when he speaks.*

COLIN. – is a female.

MALCOLM (*American accent*). Pardon?

COLIN. The one on his left.

POPE. She was guilty of adultery.

MALCOLM. How can you be sure about that?

COLIN. I'm an art dealer.

MALCOLM. Oh.

COLIN. And the one on his right –

POPE. – was a man. He was guilty of the even more odious sin of buggery, and was unable to plead any . . . mitigating circumstances . . .

MALCOLM. But they're just carcasses. How can you tell what sex they are?

COLIN. I know everything about this painting.

MALCOLM. Do you?

COLIN. Ya. I've come to bid for it.

MALCOLM. Oh.

COLIN. I'd lay down everything I own to have it.

MALCOLM. Why is that?

COLIN. Because it perfectly describes the evil of beauty . . . and the beauty of evil.

POPE. The adulteress was hardened to the street. She would wait for her husband to arrive home drunk and she would slink out of the house, practically naked, slide lankily, lustily into the dark mist between buildings, her black soul comfortably camouflaged there. At the hotel she'd take the stairs three at a time, her thighs slapping one against the other, give the secret knock, and collapse in his strong arms, drooling in anticipation of the carnal pleasure to come. She would flap against the bed like a fish and squeak at the end, then throw her dress over her head and ooze home silent, dreaming and satisfied.

COLIN. I do believe I'd bid my gallery away for it.

MALCOLM. Wow.

COLIN. Will you be bidding against me?

MALCOLM. Oh no, not at all. I was abandoned by my friends who went to see a matinée of Chekhov.

COLIN. Can't stomach Chekhov?

MALCOLM. No. There's nothing you can come out humming.

COLIN. But thought you'd stay for a drink.

MALCOLM. Yeah.

COLIN. Glad you did. I'm Colin Fitzroy Langham-Brown.

MALCOLM. Malcolm Reingewertz.

COLIN. How do you do.

MALCOLM. How do *you* do . . .

POPE. The sodomite was fond of men. He loved them with an abandon so great he threw spirituality to the wind, touching the knees of those bathing nearest, no doubt flicking his tongue, lizard-like, at their ears; and every time he firmed up down below at the sight of a leg with hair on it, the smell of bodily perfume unique to our gender, the touch of a hand rippling with masculine veins, the firmed-up part formed a banner waving up to the firmament, crying out in its muted purple voice: 'I sin! I sin!' in an exultation of betrayal, wantonness, and frank, godless lust! (*He composes himself.*) And it is our view that this is not to be tolerated. Yes, that is our view; no, it is not to be tolerated.

MALCOLM. I didn't think there was any beauty in evil.

COLIN. Oh yes. It has a wicked charm.

MALCOLM. And evil in beauty?

COLIN. Without an element of evil, beauty loses complexity and ceases to be beauty.

MALCOLM. So what does it become?

COLIN. A doily.

POPE. So I had their clothes removed. They were in the same room when this was done, no doubt it titillated the sinners both. It didn't titillate me. It didn't titillate me. They were chained on tables and sliced from their throats down to their sullied parts, neatly, shallowly, and slowly. Once their skin was hanging off the edges of the tables, I had their legs spread by monks until we heard the cracking of the joints – I made a wish – and the legs, now bound to the bodies by nothing but skin, were severed from the torsos with what amounted to little more than the fingernail of an archbishop. Finally, we twisted their heads until the flesh had no slack and was forced to tear, and ripped the remaining skin off their backs to reveal them as you see them now. Quite naked, wouldn't you say, Brothers?

POPE *laughs*.

COLIN. If this painting doesn't frighten or thrill you, you must not have a Catholic bone in your body.

MALCOLM. No, not one. I'm Jewish.

COLIN (*frisson*). Oh, 'Jewish' are you?

MALCOLM. I have some Jewish blood. What about you?

COLIN. No, no, no 'Jewish' blood.

MALCOLM. Catholic blood?

COLIN. I wouldn't say 'blood'. I'm converted.

MALCOLM. Why did you convert?

COLIN. Well, Catholicism has such rich imagery, such a grand sense of theatre . . . By comparison the English church is dull, tacky and . . . well, just a bit North of the Park.

MALCOLM. Which park is that?

COLIN. There's only one park.

The OLDER WOMAN, *surrounded by murmuring crowd and the odd popping flash, approaches.*

OLDER WOMAN. Excuse me gentlemen.

She speaks on a megaphone.

And this one here – it's appalling! Although more superficially ecclesiastical and closer to what we might loosely define as an 'Image of God', it's all the more dangerous because it associates violence with the church – the church, which has really always been a sleeping lamb of love and kindness.

Popping flashes.

COLIN. I don't know if I'll be bidding after all. Not if she has her way.

MALCOLM. Who is she?

COLIN. One of those lunatic women on a moral rampage. She'd have us shut for a bum in a Rubens.

OLDER WOMAN. Subjects like this are not fit to bear the name of 'Art', nor are, I might add, works exposing any of the three B's: buttocks, breasts and (ahem) bibbity-bobs. Art should be pretty and decorative, its proper subjects being things like flowers and bowls of fruit. Everything but daisies should be burned!

Crowd applauds. Flashes pop. Crowd moves on.

MALCOLM. I don't understand what this is all about, but then I don't know much about art or . . . religion or . . . well anything, really.

COLIN. What is it you do?

MALCOLM. I'm a chorus boy.

COLIN. A chorus boy?

MALCOLM. In shows. Musicals.

COLIN. I thought perhaps you may have been a model.

MALCOLM. They tell me I coulda made money on my face, but I'd rather make it on my legs. I guess I have the gypsy in my blood.

COLIN. The gypsy blood can keep the Jewish blood company. Ha ha ha.

MALCOLM. At least I don't have to confess every little sin I do.

COLIN. It's just like going to the lavatory really. Only you don't have to wipe.

MALCOLM. But isn't it embarrassing to say it all out loud?

COLIN. There's nothing they haven't heard before. Most of them are woofters anyway.

MALCOLM. I like that word 'woofter'.

COLIN. Do you?

MALCOLM. But then I don't have to be a good boy, like you.

COLIN. One doesn't have to *avoid* sinning. Confession is absolution. That's why Christ died. Two thousand years before I was even born it was predetermined that I could commit any sin I liked and still get into Heaven, as long as I was willing to accept Christ as my saviour and make a confession on my deathbed. It's terribly convenient.

POPE *laughs. Fly buzzes.*

COLIN. But then . . . I have heard that people like *you* can be quite good-looking.

MALCOLM. What do you mean 'like' me?

COLIN. Well . . . Jewish.

MALCOLM. We're just like normal people. There's nothing 'different' about us.

COLIN. No.

MALCOLM. Except for the . . .

COLIN. Ya.

MALCOLM. Little difference down below.

COLIN. That doesn't bother me. I'm widely travelled.

MALCOLM. Actually only my father was Jewish, so I was never bar mitzvah'd or anything.

COLIN. I see.

MALCOLM. It's just the blood.

COLIN. Yes well, it's got to come from somewhere.

MALCOLM. Apparently the Reingewertzes were a warring
tribe in Bavaria in the ten hundreds.

COLIN. Were they?

MALCOLM. Yeah, so if I'm argumentative maybe it's just
in my nature. Ha ha ha ha!

COLIN. Yes well, by now surely something would have
diluted the blood.

MALCOLM. All that raping.

COLIN. Quite. So where is Mister Reingewertz pitching his
spear tonight?

MALCOLM. I'm staying in Belgravia.

COLIN. Must be a bit quiet compared to New York.

MALCOLM. Yeah. New York's an interesting place. It's full
of weirdos. That's the scary part, but it's also what makes
it exciting. If you're the average person going there to be
normal you probably won't like it, but if you're a bit of a
weirdo yourself, there's plenty of people to be . . . weird
with.

COLIN. Can I ask you something, without fear of . . .

MALCOLM. Sure.

COLIN. Would you like to be weird with me tonight?

MALCOLM. Why not?

POPE. You can't get away with anything, members of the
church – not really, not ultimately. So remember to think
before you act. And now, time for some real music.

Puts on record: 'Ridin' High' sung by Ethel Merman.

ETHEL. Life's great, life's grand
Future's all planned
No more clouds in the sky
How'm I ridin'? I'm ridin' high!

Song fades, leaving us in BEDROOM.

MALCOLM (*post-coital*). What a great . . . collection of . . .
books you've got . . .

COLIN. Yes well, they fill up the stool.

MALCOLM. And all the right ones . . . Melville, Flaubert, Brontë . . .

COLIN. Brontë's my favourite woman writer.

MALCOLM. She is?

COLIN. Can I let you in on a little secret?

MALCOLM. Sure.

COLIN. Sometimes I pretend I'm one of the Brontë sisters. The fourth one. I sit before the mirror and act how she would act.

MALCOLM. And how would she . . . act?

COLIN. Well she'd . . . purse her lips, like this . . . Her back would be straight, bust out, like this . . . She'd lower her forehead and look up at herself, like this . . . and wink.

MALCOLM (*nervous laugh*). Oh.

COLIN. It's just a little game I play. Do you think it's silly?

MALCOLM. No, I think it's very . . . healthy.

COLIN. Do you really?

MALCOLM. Listen, I've got to get back to Belgravia now, but don't get dressed. I'll call a cab.

COLIN. I said I'd drive you. Taxis can be difficult this time of night. (*Pause.*) Well I must say the day has been nice . . . in parts. Ha ha. Shame about that blasted hag.

MALCOLM. Who?

COLIN. The one who had the auction closed. Twisted old thing. I would have loved to have that painting.

POPE *laughs, distant.*
Fly buzzes. Buzzing is cut off by slamming of two car doors. Engine is started, car moves, long pause. Car radio is switched on, stations tried, settles on song from 'The Pajama Game'.

RADIO. When will old man Hassler break down and come up with that seven-and-a-half-cent raise?
How in hell can I buy me a swell new second-hand car on that salary he pays?
What do you think of the new superintendent?

He's cute!
He'll never last!
He's kinda fresh for a new superintendent!
I like a man with spunk!
You like a man . . . period!

Radio switched off. Pause.

MALCOLM (*clears throat*). I was in that show you know.

COLIN. What?

MALCOLM. *The Pajama Game*. I had to learn the unicycle.

COLIN. Did you?

MALCOLM. Yeah.

Pause.

COLIN. Do you think you might like to . . .

MALCOLM. What?

COLIN. . . . get together again sometime?

MALCOLM. No I – my stay is short, I –

COLIN. Sure.

MALCOLM. Have to get back to America.

COLIN. Uh huh.

MALCOLM. And there's –

COLIN. Right.

MALCOLM. The other things.

Substantial pause.

COLIN. What other things?

MALCOLM. Oh you know, finding my passport, packing . . .

COLIN. When are you going back?

MALCOLM. In five weeks.

Pause. A car passes going the other way. Sound of a fly buzzing inside the car.

There's a fly in here.

Pause with fly buzzing louder.

I said, there's a fly in here.

COLIN. Open your window. He'll be sucked out.

Window opening. Frantic fly sound.

MALCOLM. He's still in here.

COLIN. Well lure him to the left.

MALCOLM. With what?

COLIN. Some excrement or a beam of light.

MALCOLM. I don't have those things.

COLIN. Catch him then.

MALCOLM. How?

COLIN. With your hand.

MALCOLM. Then he'll squoosh inside.

COLIN. So?

MALCOLM. So I don't want fly juice all over me!

COLIN. Do *some*thing, he's distracting my driving!

MALCOLM. Be careful, here comes a truck!

COLIN. He's crawling in my ear!

MALCOLM. Shake him out!

COLIN. I'm shaking! I'm shaking!

MALCOLM. You're swerving!

COLIN. He's crawling in my brain!

MALCOLM. Look out, you're going straight for it!

A lorry horn blast. Crash. Glass breaking, metal crumpling, hubcap swirling on the pavement. Silence.

Fade up on this telephone conversation.

MISS PENFOLD. I know. Every time he bends down . . .
But people have little quirks like that, it's an indication of
how they're constructed . . . Well, that's true, he does have
hairy earholes . . . Uh huh . . .

Footsteps.

(*Louder.*) Uh: yes, that's right, three lots of A4 paper and a box of jumbo paper clips . . . By tomorrow? That's right. Thank you. Goodbye!

Hangs up.

That was the stationery department confirming our order. It wasn't a personal phone call.

MR ANALBY. You know, they've come out with machines that will record all the numbers dialled from each extension and tally the costs as well.

MISS PENFOLD (*nervous*). Oh really?

MR ANALBY. We're getting one next week. I just thought I'd let you know.

MISS PENFOLD. That's very interesting, Mr Analby, though for me its purely academic.

MR ANALBY. Can I see the work you've done this morning?

MISS PENFOLD. What work?

MR ANALBY. Any of it.

MISS PENFOLD. Well the problem with the kind of work I did this morning is that it doesn't exactly . . . *show* . . .

MR ANALBY. I think perhaps you'd better see to the gentlemen in reception.

MISS PENFOLD. Gentlemen? Oh, *those* gentlemen, the gentlemen in *reception*. I was just going to see to them now.

MR ANALBY. Time is virtue, Miss Penfold.

MISS PENFOLD. And I'm a virtuous woman.

Door opened.

All my men have said that.

Door shut.

MISS PENFOLD. Hello, gentlemen. I'm Edna Penfold (Miss).

COLIN. It's about time somebody deigned to appear. Could you kindly inform us what's going on?

MALCOLM. We don't know what we're doing here.

COLIN. And where is 'here'?

MISS PENFOLD. All right, let's work this out together, calmly calmly.

COLIN. Look, I don't know what this is or who you are, but I've got some important clients coming to my gallery in the morning and I don't intend to be late.

MISS PENFOLD. Well, let's discover the truth together step by step, then, shall we?

COLIN. No! I have a meeting! Can't you understand that? I can't keep them waiting! It's the Al-Fayeds! I'M TOO BUSY TO DIE!

MISS PENFOLD. Now Colin, do you think it would be fair if I gave you special treatment when everyone else waits patiently? Look at Malcolm, quiet, sitting up straight . . .

MALCOLM. I won Mr Goody Two-Shoes at school.

COLIN. I am not Malcolm. I am Colin Fitzroy Langham-Browne, and I would ask you to kindly expedite this process or I can guarantee a fuss will be made!

MISS PENFOLD. Colin . . .

COLIN. Mr Fitzroy Langham-Browne . . .

MISS PENFOLD. Colin, there's none of 'that' anymore, let's get rid of that habit, shall we, there's a good lad.

COLIN. Don't you 'there's a good lad' me, I'll have your job!

Harp strum.

MISS PENFOLD. You now have my job.

Telephones ringing, office machines whirring.

MR ANALBY. Colin, what have you been doing all morning? Make me a cup of tea! Is that a personal phone call? You were three minutes late back from lunch, I'll have you docked!

COLIN. I – I –

MR ANALBY. Quiet! No talking during work hours! Make me a cup of coffee! Frank this post! Take a letter!

What is this mess? WHO PHOTOCOPIED THEIR ARSE?!

MISS PENFOLD. Colin . . .

COLIN. Help!

MISS PENFOLD. Do you still want my job?

COLIN. No, please, take me back!

Buzzer sounds. Office machines stop.

MISS PENFOLD. There now . . . Shall we proceed to the introduction or would you like to make any more clever comments?

COLIN. Can I ask you something?

MISS PENFOLD. Yes.

COLIN. Who or what are you?

MISS PENFOLD. I'm just a blond girl doing a job, okay? Now before we begin, do you have any requests?

COLIN. I'd like to get my hands on that blasted fly.

Harp strum.

MISS PENFOLD. And here he is.

FLY (*singing out of tune*).
Buzz buzz buzz
I got in your ear
Now you both are here
What a life it was . . .

MISS PENFOLD. Thank you fly.

FLY. Buzz buzz buzz
Little things like me
Can make you cease to be
Oh what a life it was . . .

MISS PENFOLD. I said, thank you fly.

FLY. I also do the splits.

MISS PENFOLD. Right. We'll call you.

FLY blows party whistle. Buzzer sounds.

COLIN. Just answer one question.

MISS PENFOLD. One question.

COLIN. Where are we? Are we here for Eternity?

MALCOLM. Yeah!

COLIN. What's going to happen to us? Is this Heaven or Hell? Are we dead or in some sort of ante-chamber of our corporeal life?

MALCOLM. Yeah!

COLIN. And are we NORTH OF THE PARK?!

MALCOLM. Yeah! (*To* COLIN.) Which park is that?

COLIN. There's only one park!

MISS PENFOLD (*thinks*). The answer is: No. There. That's the answer to one question. You said *one question*! (*Laughs.*)

COLIN. Well which question is that the answer to?

MISS PENFOLD. Ooooh, that's another question! (*Laughs harder.*)

MALCOLM. You're playing with us.

MISS PENFOLD. I know, isn't it FUN? A little bit of power for a petty bureaucrat like me, it just makes me wanna DANCE!

COLIN. You're off your trolley!

MISS PENFOLD. Ooooh, watch what you say, there could be trouble, couldn't there, *wheeeee*! (*Laughter stops abruptly.*) There. That was fun. Now, where do you think would be the best place to start?

MALCOLM. At the beginning?

MISS PENFOLD. Right, Malcolm, two bonus points.

COLIN. What is the answer then?

MISS PENFOLD. The answer is that you are dead. That's point A.

MALCOLM. What's point B?

MISS PENFOLD. That there is no 'truth' about what happens after death.

COLIN. No truth?

MISS PENFOLD. After death, you find what you expected to find.

MALCOLM. How do you mean?

MISS PENFOLD. If you believed in reincarnation, you will be reincarnated. If you believed in the attainment of spiritual perfection, you will attain spiritual perfection.

COLIN. You mean there's no objective truth?

MISS PENFOLD. None. It's entirely subjective.

COLIN. But Plato said that if a vase is beautiful, it would still be beautiful if no one were there to perceive it as beautiful.

MISS PENFOLD. He's just spent the last twenty years here with Einstein. I think you'll find him a changed man.

Harp strum.

PLATO. Hello. I'm Plato.

MALCOLM. Hi, Plato!

PLATO. And I've changed my mind about objective truth.

COLIN. But you were an idealist!

PLATO. So, I've had time to think. Everything turns out to be relative. Take a glass of water.

MALCOLM. Thank you.

PLATO. I mean theoretically. Why does the glass hold liquid? Why does the liquid not go through the glass?

MALCOLM. Because the glass isn't broken?

COLIN. Shut up Malcolm. Because the atoms of the liquid are farther apart than the atoms of the glass.

PLATO. Exactly. But if the glass were perceived by an entity that was smaller than its atoms, it would look like a lot of soccer balls and cricket balls floating around and bumping into each other.

MALCOLM. I understood that.

PLATO. So if everything is relative, everything is subjective. And if everything is subjective, what better answer to your life after death than a subjective reflection of your own beliefs? I only wish I'd realised this during my life.

MISS PENFOLD. We all progress in our thinking.

PLATO. Yes but now I'm dead and students are reading what I no longer believe.

MISS PENFOLD. Why would that matter? If truth is subjective then your current views bear no more relationship to an absolute truth than your early ones did.

PLATO. True – but then why do I bother to go on thinking at all?

MISS PENFOLD. Because that's your hell – to think incessantly, passionately, searchingly, and never to arrive at anything. But that's another story, and I don't want to confuse them. Thank you, Plato.

Buzzer.

COLIN. All right – whatever you believed would happen, will happen. But what if someone had some completely naff belief, like death meant sitting on an old man's lap and being given sweets?

MALCOLM. Hey, don't knock it!

MISS PENFOLD. We don't assess people's beliefs based on aesthetics or originality. If we did we'd be editors, not the Almighty.

COLIN. But what if someone had . . . neurotic or . . . fetishist perspectives? What if they believed irresponsibly?

MISS PENFOLD. We don't interfere. We simply comply. To clarify things, let's take a trip to the gallery, where I'll show you some portraits of the dead.

Harp strum, giving way to blues piano.

MISS PENFOLD. This first portrait is of a woman who believed in ghosts, so in death she became one. She now haunts the old booze hall where she once sang. Her story is as bleak as any ever told by the blues. And now she sings her song forever. Look at her: her hair has the hint of smoke always lingering around it. Her eyes are giant drunken tears reflecting ashtrays, her lips cracked from the acid taste of booze.

GHOST (*singing*).
If I'd had all the right juices
I might have been a star

If I'd had all the right juices
I might have been a star
Maybe my chemistry was imbalanced
But happiness was always just an inch too far . . .

COLIN. She sounds dreadfully unhappy.

GHOST. I'm so unhappy you can see right through me. I'm a shadow. A wisp of smoke.

MALCOLM. Some ghosts must be happy . . .

MISS PENFOLD. But what is a ghost to her?

GHOST. It's when you're there . . . and not there. When you look at your own hand and think it might belong to somebody else.

MISS PENFOLD. Some people have no control over their own happiness.

COLIN. Rubbish. One has only to keep one's faith and heed one's parents and prosperity unfolds like a map.

MALCOLM. Maybe her parents didn't give such good advice.

GHOST. My parents' advice was shit.

MOTHER. Always brush your hair a hundred times before going to bed.

FATHER. To get bubble gum out of your hair, use peanut butter.

MOTHER. If you use no expression in your face you won't get wrinkles.

FATHER. If you dry between your toes you won't get athlete's foot.

MOTHER. To avoid pregnancy, jump up and down before, after, and during sex.

FATHER. To avoid hysterical pregnancy, slap yourself across the face.

GHOST. I had so many abortions the foetuses started their own rugby team. Sometimes I'd have three or four men a night. I'd slug back whiskey over their shoulders. They brought me a bottle of Thunderbird, that was good for twice. Sex got to bore me so much if I burped it meant I

was finished. The toilet seat was always up . . . and I was
always down.

COLIN. That kind of experience is pathetic.

MISS PENFOLD. But what's made her this way?

GHOST. I don't know. When you're young you have all the
advantages of a clean outlook. The world is full of
possibilities, which you shed one by one as the years go
by. I think I shed more than most. In the end, in the
drunken early hours of the morning, I'd catch a glimpse of
my face in the bar room mirror and I found . . . I believed
in ghosts.

MISS PENFOLD. And then?

GHOST. And then I became one. My eternal life now is the
same as my life on earth. I walk through walls. I carry
chains. I cry out in the night. I fade. I disappear.

COLIN. How very bleak.

GHOST (*singing*).
Once I had some big plans
But now all the doors are closed
Once I had some big plans
But now all the doors are closed
I dug my grave, now I'm lying in it
Oh well, I guess that's just the way it goes . . .

Her last note echoes and fades.

MALCOLM. Is the whole introduction going to be this
depressing?

MISS PENFOLD. It's an education. Education is never
pleasant.

COLIN. Tell me this: if you comply with any vision of
death, what happens to atheists?

MISS PENFOLD. Nothing. They simply cease to exist.

MALCOLM. What happens to animals?

MISS PENFOLD. Well, few animals have an awareness of
their own imminent death, so most of them die, they rot,
eternal repose, nothing to write home about.

MALCOLM. But some do believe in something?

MISS PENFOLD. Yes, you get the odd animal with talent, a 'bright' animal who somehow manages to form concepts in the abstract region of his language-less brain. We had three cats here just last week who believed that when they died they'd be able to fly. Here's their portrait.

Harp strum.

MALCOLM. Wow! All they wanted was to be free!

MISS PENFOLD. Now they are. And let me tell you these are three happy cats. Hit it boys!

CATS (*singing*).
We are happy cats, we are happy cats
We are happy cats, we are happy cats
No one has the right to say we don't know where it's at
'Cause now we're things with wings that sings
And there ain't nothing wrong with that

We fly like arrows through the sky
We'll climb a mile, we have no fear
We chase the sparrows way up high
Wearing a smile from ear to ear

We are happy cats, we are happy cats
We are happy cats, we are happy cats
Down below we're bored of chasing string and getting fat
But we're not bored above, the Lord above
Has kindly seen to that.

Gospel interlude.

Yeah . . .
We're so moved, we're so moved, *etc.*

TOM CAT (*spoken*). Oh my brothers, we were not always the chirpy little things you see before you now, uh uh! We were suffering from Feline Melancholia, you ever heard of it?! Our faces were so long you could launch a B-52 off them! There was no end to the hot tin roofs it seemed that life could bring! But we had a little thing called Faith, my brothers . . .

CATS (*singing*). And now we fly and sing!

Operatic trio bridge.

Ohhh . . .

Can-can bit.

We are happy cats, we are happy cats
We are happy cats, we are happy cats
We like flying low so baby hold onto your hat
'Cause we're adoring our soaring
Our engine's always roaring
We are choric, euphoric
Our mirth is categoric
We're ecstatic, elated
'Cause we're emancipated
and we're HAPPY CATS!

MALCOLM. What a strange and wondrous land this is.

COLIN. Cats that fly!

MISS PENFOLD. They believed it, they created it themselves.

COLIN. But one could believe anything!

MALCOLM. Anything!

COLIN. This is beginning to frighten me.

MISS PENFOLD *laughs grandly*.

COLIN. Why are you laughing? Where did you come from? Did you ever have a life and lose it?

MISS PENFOLD. Where I come from is none of your business.

MALCOLM. Look at this! Here we are, *dead*, and we've got some *bitch* being *rude* to us!

MISS PENFOLD. What did you call me?

MALCOLM (*retracting*). I'm just angry, that's all.

MISS PENFOLD. No, no, what did you say I was?

MALCOLM. Nothing, honest, I'm just –

MISS PENFOLD. Say it!

MALCOLM (*sotto*). Well I called you a 'bitch'.

Harp strum.

MISS PENFOLD. You now have the body of an armadillo.

MALCOLM. I have the body of an armadillo!

MISS PENFOLD (*laughing*). See? Isn't it fun what we can

do here? Aw, it's hard having the body of an armadillo, isn't it, especially for someone who used to be a paragon of male pulchritude. But never fear. Say I'm pretty and you'll be returned to normal.

MALCOLM. You're pretty.

MISS PENFOLD (*sing-song*). I don't believe you . . .

MALCOLM. You're pretty, you're very pretty!

MISS PENFOLD. Well . . .

MALCOLM. Honest!

MISS PENFOLD. All right you're not an armadillo.

Buzzer.

But you're on probation.

COLIN (*admiration*). You're so decadent.

MISS PENFOLD. Yes I know but who cares? I'm having FUN! And it's eternity, you know, what's the risk? Hit me if you like, you'll go right through me! I'M A HAPPY WOMAN! I'M YOUNG! I'M VIBRANT! I'M ALIVE!

BOTH MEN. You're alive?!

COLIN. If you're alive then there's no excuse for your behaviour.

MALCOLM. Or your position!

COLIN. To laugh at the misfortunes of others!

MALCOLM. To turn me into an armadillo!

COLIN. To take pleasure in our pain!

MISS PENFOLD (*tearful*). All right, you want the truth? I'm dead! Dead! DEAD! (*Breaks down crying.*)

MALCOLM. If she's dead, that means she was once alive.

MISS PENFOLD (*bitter, sniffing*). You got it in one, pretty boy. I was alive. All right, now you're gonna hear the whole story, the story of my rotten, stinking life. (*Hard.*) You wanna know why I'm such a 'bitch', don't you? Give me a cigarette.

Match lighted, she exhales.

I was a secretary. I typed forty words a minute. Oh I did a little shorthand . . . but not much. I was a good timekeeper, too, God was I good. I was up there with the best of 'em. But the job didn't provide many challenges for a girl with unseen . . . talents. At least, not at first.

My boss, Mr Lidskin, used to make me bend over to find things in the drawer marked 'Z'. He became a veritable collector of clients with names like Zimmerman . . . Zanzibar . . . and Zebra Crossings plc. One day I bent down to open the drawer, as usual, and I felt a giant blob of his spit splash on my buttock. I turned and said, 'What is it you want from me?' 'Miss Penfold,' he said . . . 'tonight you will sleep in my bed. You will perform any act I require . . . or in the morning you'll find yourself out of a job.' What could I do? I needed that job, much as I hated it . . . much as I hated *him* . . . So I bit my lip, brushed aside a tear . . . and I followed him home.

It was the most disgusting night of my life. He made me do things I've never even read about. Upside-down. Wearing ornaments. His bedroom was decorated like a mock version of my reception area, and for a full hour I had to type, naked, while he squeezed the pimples on his own buttocks, drooling and chanting:

Demonstrates primal chant (which, by the way, is 'We are Happy Cats' backwards).

There was a dictaphone by the typewriter. I turned it on, and from that moment I had him.

At the next office party, as the Beaujolais Nouveau was flowing, I played that tape over the paging system. Everyone listened in stunned horror. Mr Lidskin turned purple and backed away, cursing me to hell, and fell onto a fax machine, which began to whirr. He screamed, and the director tried to pull him free . . . but it was too late. Within seconds the machine had faxed him to Brussels.

You see? It was my vengeance that killed him. Though he was an evil man . . . it was my black hand that reached out and plucked that life away from him. And what is my eternity for this? What is my hell? An office job, 9 to 5, Monday through Friday, forever. Sure, I get four weeks holiday each year. Yes, there's a subsidised canteen. But is there any of that lovely oblivion I've so longed for since birth? Not for Edna Penfold (Miss). She's bound forever to an Amstrad 9512 with a letter-quality printer.

MALCOLM. That's the saddest story I ever heard.

MISS PENFOLD. Thanks for the sympathy.

MALCOLM. I don't suppose there's anything we can do.

MISS PENFOLD. There might be something . . . *you* can do, Malcolm . . .

MALCOLM. What's that?

MISS PENFOLD. Well it's just that it's . . . so quiet here . . . It gets so lonely.

MALCOLM. I bet it does.

MISS PENFOLD. And I realise that you're not . . . a *whole* man . . . but if you could take pity on a wretched blonde like me, just for an hour, I know it would ease the pain.

COLIN. Enough of all this! You've drawn your lot, the die is cast, but for us there's nothing but a big black QUESTION MARK! Now *I'm* ready to find out the truth! The introduction is clear! I understand the rules of the game, now LET ME PLAY!

MISS PENFOLD. Colin I don't like you. You cause trouble. But a job is a job, so we'll proceed. Malcolm, is there anything you'd like to ask before you go?

MALCOLM. No. I'm not afraid. I believed what my mother told me. I believed if I'd been basically good until I died then I'd go to Heaven.

Drumroll begins.

MISS PENFOLD. Yes, Malcolm, you believed it would be like an enormous drinks party on a cloud where you'd meet Noah and Isaac, Solomon and Moses, and where there would always be enough good food to eat and delcious wines to drink, and where you'd never feel pain or misgiving about anything ever again for eternity!

MALCOLM. That's it, that's exactly what I believed!

MISS PENFOLD. Voilà, Malcolm – here is the portrait of your afterlife!

MALCOLM. It's the cast of the Bible!

MISS PENFOLD. So it is! Enjoy your eternity!

End drumroll with cymbal crash.

A cocktail lounge piano version of 'Dancing Cheek to Cheek' is played in the background.

SERVER ONE. Champagne sir?

MALCOLM. Oh yes please.

SERVER TWO. Canapé?

MALCOLM. Thanks.

NOAH (*American accent*). Hello Malcolm. Welcome to Heaven. I'm Noah, and these are my animals.

All animal sounds at once.

May I introduce Solomon?

SOLOMON (*Brooklyn*). How do you do.

MALCOLM. How do *you* do!

NOAH. Do meet God.

GOD. Hello, Malcolm. Welcome. I love you. I am all warmth and goodness and I'm here to take you into my soothing arms for eternity.

MALCOLM. Oh, God! It's all true! Take me then, God! Take me for all eternity! Bless me and thrust me into bliss!

Piano swells, then fades.

MISS PENFOLD. Well, Colin . . . it seems your friend has done well for himself.

COLIN. I knew these other people's fates were perversions! I knew there would be something wonderful in store!

MISS PENFOLD. Prepare, then!

COLIN. I'm prepared! I'm ready for grace! I'm ready for harmony! I'm ready for all that wonderful imagery promised by Michelangelo!

MISS PENFOLD. Is that what you believed in?

COLIN. Yes!

MISS PENFOLD. Did you believe you deserved it?

COLIN. Yes!

MISS PENFOLD. All right then, let me just look in your file. (*Looking.*) Oh dear . . .

COLIN. What?!

MISS PENFOLD. Oh dear . . .

COLIN. What does it say?!

MISS PENFOLD. It says here you believed confession was absolution.

COLIN. I did!

MISS PENFOLD. But unfortunately you died having been with a man, which is forbidden by the faith you'd chosen, and you never confessed. You died in a state of mortal sin!

COLIN. I'll confess now!

MISS PENFOLD. I'm afraid it doesn't work that way.

COLIN. But there must be some room for negotiation!

MISS PENFOLD. You set your own rules.

COLIN. If I set them, let me change them!

MISS PENFOLD. You can't change them now. You set them during life. So here it is, Colin, the portrait of your afterlife as you've painted it.

Harp strum.

COLIN. No! Not him! It's . . . the painting I wanted to buy the day I died!

MISS PENFOLD. Well you've bought it now, baby! Have fun!

A long, mirthful, echoey laugh from Miss Penfold. The slam of an iron door with reverberating finality.

POPE. Hello Colin.

COLIN. God, I really don't know what to say.

POPE. You've been naughty, haven't you.

COLIN. God –

POPE. Nasty. Dirty. Do you think I like to see that?

COLIN. No, I'm sure God that you don't.

POPE. It makes me angry. Angry and disgusted.

COLIN. Yes I have no doubt about that. But –

POPE. Let's start at the beginning, shall we?

COLIN. Oh dear . . .

POPE. When you were four years old you went between the houses with that little girl Betty from next door and took off your clothes, didn't you. You showed her your willy.

COLIN. We were children, we didn't know what we were doing!

POPE. But you knew there was something wrong with what you did. That's what made you do it.

COLIN. I didn't mean to sin, I . . . well one . . . doesn't ever really mean to sin . . .

POPE. Doesn't one?

COLIN. Are we going to go over everything?

POPE. We've only got eternity! Oh, we won't go over it all at once. We'll go over a few things, then I'll mete out some punishments, and once you've served you'll come back and we'll move on to the next few items on the list.

COLIN. What kind of tortures will there be?

POPE. Horrid things, things you've never dreamed of. Having to put your face in a toilet that's been used, and ants eating out your stomach and laying eggs in your brain, and ugly people licking your face and sweating and drooling and making noises . . .

COLIN. What, just for showing Betty my thing?

POPE. You showed her your 'peepee'. Now we're going to burn it off.

COLIN. Please . . .

POPE. Or perhaps you'd prefer the vice clamp!

COLIN. No, please!

POPE. Perhaps you'd like us to make you eat a live rat!

COLIN. Oh God no!

POPE. Well! Look who's finally coming round! What a pity it's too late! Oh well! Should've thought of that before, shouldn't we?

COLIN. Yes God!

POPE. Here – catch!

COLIN. AHHHHH!

POPE. You act as though you've never seen an Amazonian Facebug before!

COLIN. Get it off me!

POPE. All right! I'll get it off with this!

COLIN. AHHHHHHH!

POPE. Amazonian Facebugs are the principal diet of the New Guinea Eight-Lipped Jellyfish! But they can be sloppy eaters.

COLIN. Please get them off me!

POPE. All right – I'll just use this blowtorch!

Blowtorch.

COLIN. AHHHHHHHHHHHH!

Blowtorch off. Beginning of Pergolesi Stabat Mater.

God, please! I'm so sorry! I'll do anything! Anything at all!

POPE. There's nothing you can do!

COLIN. There must be! I believed I died in a state of mortal sin, it's true – and I did believe that that meant Hell! But there's another side to it! I believed my God to have compassion! I believed Him to be firm, but capable of the greatest love! I did not worship a monster!

POPE. What do you expect me to do now?

COLIN. I'm begging you to let me go back to earth! Let me spend a hundred years doing good deeds! I'll be a paragon of virtue! I'll read to the blind! I'll wash lepers! I'LL MARRY A WOMAN!

POPE. Do you really think you can do this?

COLIN. Oh, YES, God, YES, I know I can!

POPE. Do you believe you could live a life without sin?

COLIN. No question at all!

POPE. All right then – I'll send you back. I'll let you live out your days until you die a natural death. But the instant you commit a single sin, if you so much as stretch the truth, you will be back here instantly and you will spend eternity in the sin bin.

COLIN. Oh, thank you God, I worship you! I prostrate myself before you!

POPE. Grrmph.

COLIN. But how do I get back?

POPE. You've had the power all along!

COLIN. I have?!

POPE. Just click your heels together three times and say 'There's no place like home'.

COLIN. There's no place like home.

Three clicks.

There's no place like home.

Three clicks.

There's no place like home.

Three clicks.

But I'm not home yet!

POPE. Of course you're not! That's just one of the many fun pranks we'll be playing on you for eternity! Here – CATCH!

COLIN *screams*, POPE *laughs*.

Pergolesi swells, then fades to leave us in acoustic of large, crowded hall.

OLDER WOMAN. I think it's appalling! Just look at it! The Pope himself with two carcasses hanging – oh, I seem to have remembered wrongly, I now see there are three.

The Pope himself with three carcasses dripping by his sides
and a face of unspeakable malice! I'm sure you all see why
I found this auction hellish and wicked, and why I'm
pleased to have closed it down.

LESBIAN (*shouting from the crowd*). You are the true
pervert, and I kill you now on behalf of all sister poets
from Hackney Vegans for Greenpeace!

Gun is fired.

OLDER WOMAN. Oh! I've been shot . . . just left . . . of
centre . . .

She falls. Murmur of crowd, dreamily in distance.

(*Dying.*) But I've won now, haven't I, God? I've lived up
to my end . . . now you live up to yours. I believed if I
worked hard during my life to inhibit sexual and moral
freedoms, that after death I'd be reincarnated as Madonna!
I've earned it! I've waited so long! And now, now, forever
there will be fishnets! Ha Ha! Slippery things! Ha! Come
and get me! Rub me and poke me and lather and take me
to Heaven forever and ever amen! Hurry! Come, death
and love! COME, DEATH AND LIFE!

*She dies with a croak. Ambulance siren approaches, which
echoes and fades into gallery acoustic.*

Workman's footsteps approach.

WORKMAN. Where do you want it?

MISS PENFOLD. Just there. And hang it straight. Dead
straight.

*Madonna singing 'Like a Virgin'. After a verse or two, this
fades.*